Romantic Days and Nights®
IN DALLAS/FORT WORTH

HELP US KEEP THIS GUIDE UP TO DATE

Every effort has been made by the authors and editors to make this guide as accurate and useful as possible. However, many things can change after a guide is published—establishments close, phone numbers change, facilities come under new management, etc. We would love to hear from you concerning your experiences with this guide and how you feel it could be made better and be kept up to date. While we may not be able to respond to all comments and suggestions, we'll take them to heart and we'll make certain to share them with the authors. Please send your comments and suggestions to the following address:

The Globe Pequot Press
Reader Response/Editorial Department
P.O. Box 480
Guilford, CT 06437

Or you may e-mail us at:
editorial@globe-pequot.com
Thanks for your input,
and happy travels!

ROMANTIC DAYS AND NIGHTS® SERIES

Romantic Days and Nights®

IN DALLAS/FORT WORTH

Romantic Diversions
In and Around the Metroplex

by June Naylor Rodriguez

The Globe Pequot Press

GUILFORD, CONNECTICUT

Cover photo: ©Wes Thompson/The Stock Market
Text design and illustrations by M.A. Dube
Map design by Mary Ballachino
Spot Art: www.arttoday.com
Romantic Days and Nights is a registered trademark of The Globe Pequot Press.

Library of Congress Cataloging-in-Publication Data
Rodriguez, June Naylor.
        Romantic days and nights in Dallas/Fort Worth : romantic diver-
sions in and around the metroplex / by June Naylor Rodriguez. — 1st ed.
        p.   cm. — (Romantic days and nights series)
        Includes index.
        ISBN 0-7627-0411-X
        1. Dallas Region (Tex.) Guidebooks.   2. Fort Worth Region
(Tex.) Guidebooks   I. Title.   II. Series.
    F394.D213R635   1999
    917.64'28120463—dc21
                                                      99-15496
                                                      CIP

Manufactured in the United States of America
First Edition/First Printing

For Anna Claire—
may your life be forever filled with love

Contents

Introduction 1

The Best of Dallas/
Fort Worth 5

URBAN AFFAIRS

1. To the Heart of Big D:
   Downtown Dallas 10
2. Two-Stepping with Your
   Pardner: *Downtown
   Cowtown* 16
3. Dazzling Your Darling:
   *Fort Worth's Cultural
   Crown Jewels* 23
4. Artistic Passion in Dallas 30
5. Arm in Arm: *Taking in
   Fort Worth Theater* 39

NIGHT AND DAY

6. From Alternative to Zydeco:
   The Dallas Club Scene 48
7. Boot-Scootin' and Singin'
   the Blues: *Fort Worth's
   Nightlife* 52
8. Pleasure for the Palate:
   *Wining and Dining in
   Dallas–Fort Worth* 57

9. Acquisitions: *A Twosomes
   Guide to Collecting and
   Decorating* 63
10. Wheeling and Dealing:
    *Treasure Hunting in the
    Metroplex* 70

ACTIVE AMOUR

11. Getting to First Base:
    Baseball in Arlington 76
12. Playing Games:
    *Major-League Fun at
    Reunion Stadium* 81
13. Retreat at the Four
    Seasons: *An Interlude
    in Irving* 86
14. Resorting to Romance at
    Possum Kingdom Lake 92
15. Dude Ranch Dalliance 97

THE NATURE OF LOVE

16. Return to Eden:
    *The Natural Wonders
    of Dallas* 102
17. Wild Things: *A Wilderness
    Escape in Fort Worth* 108

18. Tracking Together
Through Time:
*Dinosaur Hunting
in Glen Rose*   116

RENDEZVOUS WITH HISTORY

19. The Fall of Camelot
and Other Historic
Happenings   124

20. Courting Adventure
at the Stockyards
Historic District   131

21. Flirting on the
Frontier: *A Weatherford
Getaway*   138

22. Pioneer Passion:
Historic Denton   144

COZY COUNTRYSIDE B&B GETAWAYS

23. Cuddling in Collin County:
A McKinney Respite   152

24. East Texas Escapade:
Comforts in Athens   158

25. Granbury and Hood
County Victoriana   164

26. Gingerbread Bliss in
Waxahachie   169

27. Love that Crazy Water:
*Rejuvenating in
Mineral Wells*   174

Appendix of Events   181

Special Indexes

Romantic Lodging   186

Romantic Restaurants   186

Evening Diversions   189

Museums and Galleries   190

Shopping   191

Outdoor Activities   192

Historic Sites/Buildings   193

Speciality Tours   193

Geographic Index   194

General Index   202

*The prices and rates listed in this guidebook
were confirmed at press time. We recommend, however,
that you call establishments before traveling to obtain
current information.*

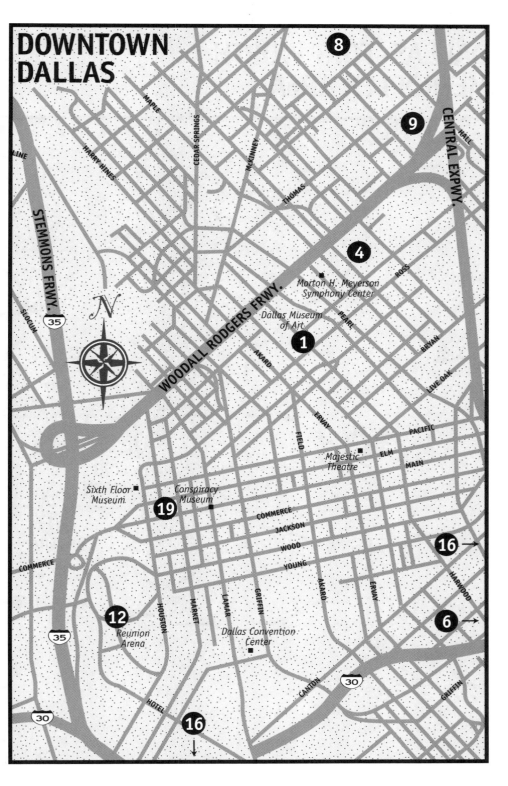

DOWNTOWN DALLAS

DALLAS–FORT WORTH METROPLEX AREA

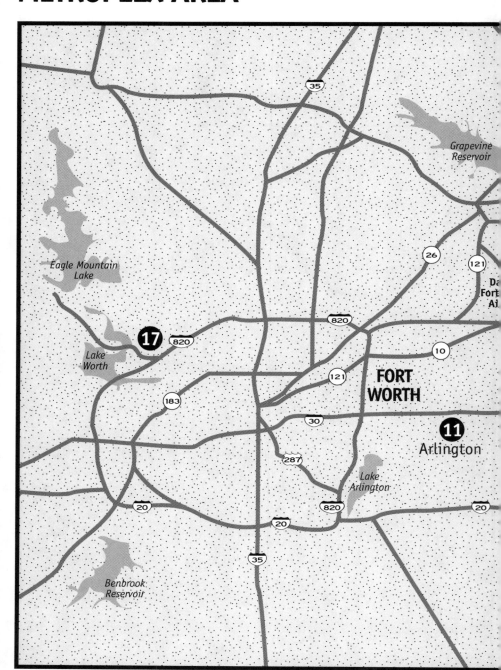

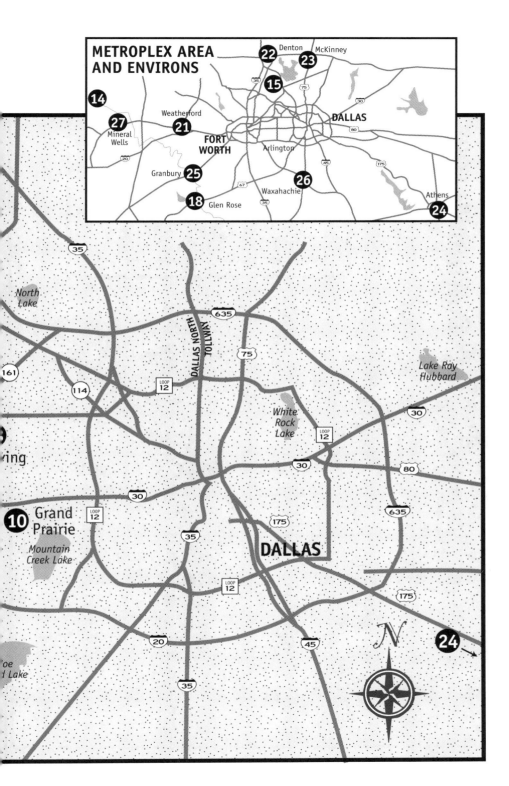

METROPLEX AREA AND ENVIRONS

Denton

McKinney

22

23

15

35

75

14

Weatherford

DALLAS

30

27

21

80

Mineral
Wells

FORT
WORTH

Arlington

20

25

45

175

Granbury

26

67

18

Glen Rose

Waxahachie

Athens

35

24

35

North
Lake

635

DALLAS NORTH TOLLWAY

75

Lake Ray
Hubbard

161

114

LOOP
12

White
Rock
Lake

30

30

LOOP
12

ing

30

80

635

10

Grand
Prairie

LOOP
12

175

Mountain
Creek Lake

35

DALLAS

LOOP
12

175

oe
l Lake

20

45

N

24

35

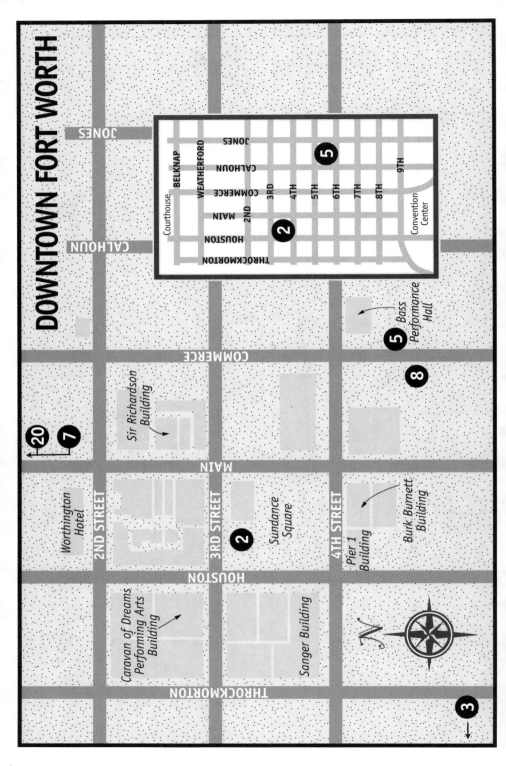

DOWNTOWN FORT WORTH

Acknowledgments

THIS BOOK MIGHT NOT HAVE BEEN POSSIBLE if not for the assistance of my friends at Historic Accommodations of Texas and Bed & Breakfast Texas Style, and I have great appreciation for the valuable help that flows from the Texas Department of Transportation and from Texas Parks and Wildlife. And I don't know what I would have done without the careful, good-natured help of my longtime friend, Sarah Williams. Finally, I must thank my sweet, tireless companion in travel and romance, Mike Dooley.

Introduction

FOR THE RIGHT TWO PEOPLE, anyplace in the world is a romantic spot. But because the two of you want to revel in your time together in the Dallas/Fort Worth area, this book will help make the most of the days and nights you will share in this compelling, energizing region. Having grown up and lived all my life in Dallas and in Fort Worth, I've done my share of falling in and enjoying love right in the places you'll find in these pages.

The Metroplex, as the area is dubbed, is home to a combined population of more than four million people, which means that there's an amazing host of activities for you to explore. Fine arts choices range from the Dallas Opera performances at the marvelously art deco Fair Park Music Hall and the Dallas Symphony Orchestra at the multimillion-dollar Meyerson Symphony Center in Dallas, to the touring productions of *Rent* and *Stomp* at the spectacular new Bass Performance Hall in Fort Worth, which is home also to the renowned Fort Worth Dallas Ballet.

Downtown Dallas boasts two outstanding museums, the Dallas Museum of Art and the Sixth Floor Museum, the latter a brilliant exhibit in the old Texas School Book Depository Building exploring the life and death of President John F. Kennedy.

Fort Worth, however, has the lion's share of museums in the Metroplex. Gathered in the Cultural District and in easy walking distance of one another, four excellent museums include the internationally famed Kimbell Art Museum, where touring exhibits have included works of Michelangelo and of Monet, Picasso, and Matisse. The Amon Carter Museum offers artwork from the early nineteenth century to the present; the Museum of Science and History includes the domed Omni Theater; and the Modern Art Museum features contemporary works from around the world.

The cities know how to show you a rollicking good time as well. Fort Worth claims Billy Bob's Texas as the world's largest honky-tonk, while Dallas has the sensational neighborhood of Deep Ellum, where a legion of live music venues offer everything from blues and jazz to alternative country and zydeco. Dining out is a primary event in both cities, with a depth of choices in cuisines from Caribbean and Central American to Mexican and Southwestern to Moroccan and Vietnamese.

When it's time to play games, Dallas offers professional football action with the Cowboys, basketball with the Mavericks, and hockey with the Stars. Arlington, Fort Worth's sister with Six Flags and Wet 'n Wild entertainment parks, is home to major league baseball's Texas Rangers.

THE ITINERARIES

This book consists of twenty-seven itineraries, designed to help you explore the Metroplex with ease—and with a plan.

There are several itineraries that show you around the downtown areas, with particular interests including museums, theaters, historic sites, art galleries, and important stores. For those who love the great outdoors, there are pastoral adventures in the parks, gardens, and nature preserves, as well as hikes and wildlife watching away from town.

For pairs of sports nuts, I've included some golf, tennis, and spa retreats, as well as days and nights built around watching professional football, baseball, basketball, and hockey. And if the two of you long for simpler times, there are several itineraries that provide you with bed-and-breakfast escapes in charming, endearing towns within driving times of a half hour to two hours from Dallas/Fort Worth.

For lovers of wines and ethnic foods, explorations are supplied. If your curiosities lean toward the live music scene, that's covered, too. And should you wish to peruse the piles of goods at flea markets, your wishes are granted.

USING THIS BOOK

Keep in mind that the itineraries are intended as suggestions, and that you may well find your own variations for plans as your desires demand. As you put the book to work, however, remember that things change between the date the book was written and the day you're reading this. Prices may go up, restaurants may change chefs, and shops may move to entirely new locations. And at this writing, the telephone area codes for Dallas/Fort Worth included 214, 817, 972, 940, and 254—but there could be more codes by the time you're ready to visit

In general, restaurant prices here are described as inexpensive when a meal for two (including drinks but excluding tip) costs between $10 and $25; moderate when two dine for $26 to $50; and expensive for a $51-$100 meal for two. There are a few places cited as very expensive, where the bill will exceed $100. Hotel rates quoted in this book are often the standard prices, called rack rates. When calling hotels and bed-and-breakfast lodgings, ask for special package or corporate rates; these can save you money and may be particularly reasonable during off-peak periods.

GETTING HERE AND GETTING AROUND

Dallas Fort Worth International Airport sits between Dallas and Fort Worth; travel time to each downtown is about twenty-five minutes, provided there are no traffic tangles. It's the second busiest airport in the nation, with nonstop service to more than 200 cities worldwide and more than 2,500 flights daily.

The top ground transportation outfit is Super Shuttle, reached by calling (817) 329-2001, and there are dozens of taxi companies represented at the airport. Note that you'll need a car to get around the Dallas/Fort Worth area; all major car rental companies are represented here as well

If you're visiting Dallas only, it might be wise to inquire about flights into Dallas Love Field for the sake of convenience.

If you didn't arrive in the Dallas/Fort Worth area by car, by all means rent one. Taxi services are widely available, but a car is still most convenient. All major rental companies are represented at both airports.

If your activities will be in downtown Dallas only, you can get around by Dallas Area Rapid Transit (DART) shuttle buses in a system called the Rail Runner, operating from 6:00 A.M. to 7:30 P.M. Monday through Friday. The fare is 50 cents.

You might consider using the new DART Light Rail system, which operates safe, clean, air-conditioned, electric trains in a north-south path through the middle of Dallas. The train fares are 50 cents to $1.00. For details, call (214) 979–1111.

And if your Dallas plans are limited to the revitalized area called Uptown (immediately north of downtown's Arts District), you can use the McKinney Avenue Trolley. The system consists of four restored streetcars as old as one hundred years, as are some of the tracks that are embedded in the original brick stretches of historic McKinney Avenue. The trolley, which costs $1.50 for a round-trip ride or $3.00 for a full-day pass, operates from 10:00 A.M. to 10:00 P.M. Sunday through Thursday and 10:00 A.M. to midnight Friday and Saturday. Correct change is required. Call (214) 855–0006 for details.

Fort Worth's public transportation system—city buses—is called The T. It offers service from downtown to the Cultural District. For schedules and information call (817) 215–8600. You should, however, be able to walk downtown Fort Worth as it is small.

FOR MORE INFORMATION

Find detailed information about Dallas by calling the Dallas Convention & Visitors Bureau at (214) 746–6677 or the twenty-four-hour hotline number at (214) 746–6679. Visit the Web site at www.cityview.com/dallas.

For Fort Worth information call the Fort Worth Convention & Visitors Bureau at (817) 336–8791 or (800) 433–5747. The events line is (817) 332–2000, and the Web site is www.fortworth.com.

A wealth of good, free information is available, too, from the state highway department. Call (800) 452–9292 to get a complimentary copy of the colorful *Texas State Travel Guide,* plus an accommodations guide and a new highway map.

The Best of Dallas/Fort Worth

BEST PLACES TO BE ALONE TOGETHER

Carriage rides, Sundance Square, Fort Worth
Greenwood Cemetery, Weatherford
John F. Kennedy Memorial, Dallas
Little Chapel in the Woods, Denton
Mineral Wells State Park
Tarantula Train, Fort Worth

BEST PLACES FOR DRINKS BY CANDLELIGHT

Angeluna, Fort Worth
The Grape Escape, Fort Worth
Mediterraneo, Dallas
Sambuca, Dallas
Tarantino's, Dallas

BEST PEACEFUL WALKS

Dallas Nature Center
Fort Worth Nature Center
Hummingbird Lodge, Glen Rose
Old City Park, Dallas
Rails-to-Trails, Mineral Wells–Weatherford
River Legacy Park, Arlington

BEST PLACES TO WATCH THE SUN SET

Fort Worth Nature Center
Fossil Rim Wildlife Center, Glen Rose
Mineral Wells State Park
Reata, Fort Worth
Reunion Tower, Dallas

BEST CULTURAL SETTINGS

African American Museum, Dallas
Bass Performance Hall, Fort Worth
Dallas Museum of Art
Kalita Humphreys Theater at Dallas Theater Center
Kimbell Art Museum, Fort Worth
Longhorn Gallery, Denton
Webb Gallery, Waxahachie

TEN MOST ROMANTIC LODGINGS

Adolphus Hotel, Dallas
Angel's Nest Bed and Breakfast, Weatherford
The Carriage House, Athens
Courtyard on the Trail, Dallas
Etta's Place, Fort Worth
Four Seasons Resort at Las Colinas, Irving
Iron Horse Inn, Granbury
The Lodge at Fossil Rim, Glen Rose
The Mansion on Turtle Creek, Dallas
Hotel St. Germain, Dallas

BEST-KEPT SECRETS

Antiquarian of Dallas
Black Beauty Ranch, Athens
The Cliffs, Possum Kingdom Lake
Heard Museum and Wildlife Sanctuary, McKinney
Meadows Museum of Art, Dallas
Recycled Books, Records and CDs, Denton
Sid Richardson Collection of Western Art, Fort Worth
Texas Exotic Feline Foundation, Boyd

BEST ROMANTIC PICNIC SPOTS

The Dallas Arboretum
Botanic Garden, Fort Worth
Dinosaur Valley State Park, Glen Rose
Trinity Park, Fort Worth

TEN MOST ROMANTIC RESTAURANTS

Beau Nash, Dallas
Café Istanbul, Dallas
Fish, Dallas
The Grape, Dallas
The Green Room, Dallas
Mediterraneo, Dallas
Morton's of Chicago, Dallas
Randall's, Fort Worth
Reflections, Fort Worth
Saint-Emilion, Fort Worth

Urban Affairs

To the Heart of Big D
DOWNTOWN DALLAS

HE BOLD, BRASH BACKDROP OF DOWNTOWN DALLAS may be the ideal place to fall in love for the first time, or all over again. The center of the city embodies both the raw power and pioneer spirit that led founders to build something important here some 160 years ago, and that energy today makes even casual observers like yourselves want to take chances.

Whether you're strolling along vintage brick streets or beneath gleaming towers, touring great collections of art or admiring classic art deco structures, you're bound to be caught up in the rejuvenating mood that has overcome downtown in its renaissance.

DAY ONE: *Morning*

The most romantic of Dallas's more intimate lodgings is easily the **Hotel St. Germain** (2516 Maple Avenue; 214–871–2516; $200 and up). The exquisite Victorian home, built in 1906, has been renovated into a European-style luxury hotel and is ideal for pure escapism. Inside the three-story house are seven exceptional suites, adorned with lush fabrics and antiques befitting a French chateau. Tucked into the fabulously revitalized Uptown area immediately adjacent to the Dallas Arts District and facing the Hotel Crescent Court, the St. Germain has a concierge, free valet parking, and elegant, prix fixe dinners on Thursday, Friday, and Saturday evenings. Chances are that once you're inside you won't want to leave. Check-in isn't until

4:00 P.M., so you may just want to drop your bags early and go exploring.

If less-expensive lodging is in order, the **Stoneleigh Hotel** (2927 Maple Avenue; 214–871–7111; $150 and up) is a gracious, older hotel in the same lovely neighborhood. There also is a **Hampton Inn** in downtown Dallas (10105 Elm Street; 800–426–7866; $109 and up). It's convenient to the Art District.

Head just across the expressway, about 3 blocks south of the St. Germain, to the **Dallas Museum of Art** (1717 North Harwood Street; 214–922–1200). Founded in 1903 and moved into its current residence—designed by Edward Larrabee Barnes—in 1983, the museum is internationally recognized as a major center for collections of African, Asian, contemporary, and Indonesian art. The museum also houses significant photographic works, pre-Columbian artifacts, American Colonial–era antiques, and Impressionist and post-Impressionist European works. Among the latter are a number by Renoir, Van Gogh, Cézanne, and Degas, housed in a gallery reminiscent of a French villa.

The DMA is also a good place for the two of you to catch major traveling exhibits; in the recent past these have included the jewels of Lalique as well as works by Claude Monet and Robert Rauschenberg.

The DMA's hours are 11:00 A.M. to 4:00 P.M. Tuesday, Wednesday, and Friday; 11:00 A.M. to 9:00 P.M. Thursday; and 11:00 A.M. to 5:00 P.M. Saturday and Sunday. General admission is free, but some special exhibits require an admission fee.

DAY ONE: *Afternoon*

LUNCH

You'll need a Texas-size appetite to do justice to a meal at **Y.O. Ranch** (702 Ross Avenue; 214–744–3287;

Romance
AT A GLANCE

◆ Check into the **Hotel St. Germain** (2516 Maple Avenue; 214–871–2516) or the **Stoneleigh Hotel** (2927 Maple Avenue; 214–871–7111), and then while away time together at the **Dallas Museum of Art** (1717 North Harwood Street; 214–922–1200).

◆ Lunch at the **Y.O. Ranch** (702 Ross Avenue; 214–744–3287) or book tea time at **Lady Primrose** (Hotel Crescent Court; 214–871–8334) or the **Adolphus Hotel** (1321 Commerce Street; 214–742–8200).

◆ Have sunset drinks at **Reunion Tower** (300 Reunion Boulevard; 214–712–7145) and watch the city's lights come on. Dinner is the ultimate in romantic experiences at **Mediterraneo** in the Quadrangle (2800 Routh Street; 214–979–0002).

moderate), named for one of the great ranches in the Texas Hill Country. The food here is trademark fare from Matt Martinez, who helped make Austin notorious for Mexican food. At the Y.O., however, he's added cowboy foods to his usual repertoire of chilies rellenos. Feast on the excellent chicken-fried steak or grilled quail, but don't miss the seafood corn cakes.

The Art of Love

An especially romantic element of the Dallas Museum of Art is the Wendy and Emery Reves Collection, representing a love of beauty and art that lasted throughout the lifetimes of a husband and wife. While the pair lived at Villa La Pausa on the Riviera, they amassed an exquisite collection of art, which was enjoyed by many distinguished visitors, including Winston Churchill, Albert Einstein, the Duke and Duchess of Windsor, Aristotle Onassis, and Noel Coward. Upon Emery's death in 1983, Wendy donated the couple's works—including richly vibrant paintings by such artists as Edouard Manet, Pierre-Auguste Renoir, Paul Cézanne, Camille Pissarro, Paul Gauguin, Vincent van Gogh, and Claude Monet—to be displayed in a setting resembling the Reves's villa, to be enjoyed by lovers of art for all time.

At the Y.O. you're already in what's called the West End Historic District. While away the afternoon by touring the renovated Victorian-era collection of warehouse buildings and poking around shops in the **West End Marketplace** (603 Munger Avenue; 214-748-4801). Within the 33-block West End area, you'll find this four-level shopping center with fifty specialty stores selling jewelry, local art, souvenirs, clothing, and antiques. The two of you could have some laughs by experiencing virtual reality games at Tilt.

If you feel like having a drink, pop into Planet Hollywood, in the West End Marketplace (214-749-7827) where among myriad movie memorabilia there's Paul Newman's costume from *HUD*. Nobody ever played a sexier Texan.

On the other hand, taking afternoon tea is always a relaxing way to review the day, spend some quiet time together, and take a moment to consider plans for the evening and the next day. Two charming places that are handy for downtown denizens are **Lady Primrose** (Hotel Crescent Court; 214-871-8334; Monday through Saturday, 3:00 to 5:00 P.M.) and in the lobby of the **Adolphus Hotel** (1321 Commerce Street; 214–742–8200; Wednesday through Saturday, 3:00 to 4:45 P.M). Both include sandwiches and pastries and require reservations.

DAY ONE: *Evening*

For Dallas's most breathtaking view—at its most magical after the sun goes down—head about 4 blocks south of the West End district to the Hyatt Reunion and **Reunion Tower.** Since opening in 1978 the geodesic sphere poised fifty stories in the sky above downtown offers a 360-degree survey of the land. The observation floor is called the Lookout (open Sunday through Thursday from 10:00 A.M. to 10:00 P.M. and Friday and Saturday from 9:00 A.M. to midnight; $2.00 admission fee), but you might enjoy having a cocktail the next level up at the Dome, a cocktail lounge making one revolution per hour.

DINNER

For something stylish and impressive, book dinner at **Mediterraneo** at the Quadrangle (2800 Routh Street; 214–979–0002; moderate to expensive). With a romantic theme of the Riviera, this elegant restaurant with low lighting, stucco walls, and paintings of Mediterranean seaside towns does beautiful things with sea bass, duck, lamb, pork, and veal, incorporating couscous, port wine, foie gras, or fresh herbs.

Mediterraneo is only a few blocks from the St. Germain, but even more convenient is **Palomino,** across the street in the Crescent Court (214–999–1222; moderate). The mood in this contemporary room, splashed in reds, is a little more spirited than at the Mediterraneo. Signature dishes are spit-roasted garlic chicken and elegant pizzas from wood-fired ovens.

Palomino is also a good place to end the evening with a cappuccino or a cognac. Afterward you can stroll past the gorgeous shop windows of Stanley Korshak and Lady Primrose in the Crescent Court.

DAY TWO: *Morning*

Continental breakfast is included with your stay at Hotel St. Germain, but why not just make do with coffee before heading off for a breakfast or brunch to fill you for the day? Both are quite good at **Beau Nash** (Hotel Crescent Court; 214–871–3240; moderate) and are done in traditional buffet form with New American touches. Specialties include red snapper and house-made sausage, in addition to egg creations.

Or for a sumptuous, country-style breakfast in a no-frills setting, head to **Brownie's** (5519 East Grand Avenue; 214–824–2996; inexpensive). You'll reach it by heading east on Interstate 30 a short drive, then taking the Grand exit and turning north a couple of blocks. Known for more than a half century for good, solid home cooking, you can't go wrong with the amazing biscuits, omelettes, and pancakes.

Brownie's puts you right in the neighborhood to explore **Fair Park** (3809 Grand Avenue; 214–670–8400), a 227-acre assemblage of buildings representing one of the nation's largest collections of art deco structures. A National Historic Landmark, the park and its buildings were erected in 1936 by the Works Progress Administration (WPA) for the state's centennial celebration of independence from Mexico. Fair Park is the site of Starplex, where touring musical attractions range from Janet Jackson to James Taylor; the Cotton Bowl, where college football is played; and the State Fair of Texas, the largest such event in the nation, held for three weeks in October.

The newest of Fair Park's buildings is the impressive **African American Museum** (3536 Grand Avenue; 214–565–9026; free), which represents another city rejuvenation effort. A $6-million, cross-shaped building crafted of ivory stone showcasing a wonderful assortment of black culture, arts, and history collections, the museum is known for the Billy R. Allen Folk Art Collection, one of the nation's largest such collections. Among traveling exhibits has been a collection of photographs of blues musicians. The museum is open Tuesday through Friday from noon to 5:00 P.M.; Saturday from 10:00 A.M. to 5:00 P.M. and Sunday from 1:00 to 5:00 P.M.

For a contrast in tone, the two of you could take a long stroll across Fair Park to the **Hall of State** (3939 Grand Avenue; 214–421–4500; free), the centerpiece building for the 1936 Texas Centennial and a stunning model in art deco style. You'll enter through bronze doors adorned with various Texas symbols and find yourself greeted in the Hall of Heroes by the enormous bronze statues of Stephen F. Austin, Sam Houston, Mirabeau B. Lamar, Thomas J. Rusk, James Walker

Fannin, and William Barret Travis, the six heroes of the Republic of Texas. In other sections of the building are murals and exhibits pertaining to Texas's regions and history.

The Hall of State is open Tuesday through Saturday from 9:00 A.M. to 5:00 P.M. and Sunday from 1:00 to 5:00 P.M.

If the two of you are lovers of nature or young of heart, the **Dallas Museum of Natural History** (3535 Grand Avenue; 214–421–3466; $4.00) is another Fair Park option. Also built for the 1936 Texas Centennial, the museum has permanent exhibits of rare and extinct animals, big-game mounts, fossils, bugs, and dioramas. You may have the most fun in the Hall of Prehistoric Texas, which includes a reconstructed Texas Tenontosaur, the nation's largest prehistoric sea turtle. Among visiting exhibits to the museum has been the Ramses the Great Egyptian collection, pulling in more than one million visitors.

If time allows for more touring, head a few blocks north of Fair Park to the neighborhood of Deep Ellum, a magically renovated district filled with shops, galleries, and restaurants.

Two-Stepping with Your Pardner

DOWNTOWN COWTOWN

THE HEART OF FORT WORTH'S DOWNTOWN is a 16-block area named Sundance Square, so named for the city's attachment to the days of Chisholm Trail cattle drives and gunfights of the nineteenth century. The drives came right through what's now downtown, and the related lore pertains to the outlaws who visited during the period—specifically, Butch Cassidy, the Sundance Kid, and the Hole in the Wall Gang. What's remarkable today about this district is the wonderful restoration of the lovely, turn-of-the-century storefronts and brick streets of this landscaped downtown, filled with shops, galleries, and restaurants to keep the two of you amused and charmed for a weekend. Injecting a carnival atmosphere during evening hours is an assortment of street performers. Strolling musicians, mimes, clowns, jugglers, and caricature artists are on nearly every corner.

PRACTICAL NOTE: If you visit on the third weekend of April, be aware that the Main Street Arts Festival is a massive event that draws thousands of revelers to Sundance for four days.

DAY ONE: *Morning*

You have three excellent lodging choices, depending on your style. The **Worthington Hotel** (200 Main Street; 817–870–1000; $155 and up) is a 504-room luxury hotel accorded four stars by most national ratings. Inside are three restaurants—including Reflections, a gourmet restaurant open only for dinner; the Star of Texas Grill, serving three meals daily; and the Bridge, a lunch-only spot with salad, pasta, and sandwich buffets. The hotel also has a charming Lobby Bar, with good choices in better Scotches and tequila, as well as a full athletic club. The Worthington's convenience and service make it the first choice for travelers to Fort Worth.

The choice for greater intimacy is **Etta's Place** (200 West Third Street; 817–654–0267; $125 and up), a boutique hotel that functions as a bed-and-breakfast. Each room is named after a member of the infamous Hole in the Wall Gang, thus the name—Etta Place was the legendary girlfriend of the Sundance Kid. Furnished with Texas antiques, each room has its own private bath. The four-story B&B also has a library, lofted music room, garden patios, and a dining area.

An enjoyable budget choice in downtown lodging is a 203-room **Courtyard by Marriott** (601 Main Street; 800–321–2211; $89–$114). Recently renovated in 1999, the Blackstone Hotel was established in 1929 by oilman Christopher Augustus O'Keefe as Fort Worth's distinctive hotel—the illustrious, art deco masterpiece was visited by guests such as Eleanor Roosevelt, Lyndon B. Johnson, Richard Nixon, Elvis Presley, and Bob Hope.

Whether the two of you are new to Fort Worth or longtime residents, you should visit *150 Years of Fort Worth History*, a permanent exhibit inside historic **Fire Station No. 1** (Second and Commerce Streets; 817–255–9310; free).

Romance

AT A GLANCE

◆ Settle into the **Worthington Hotel** (200 Main Street; 817–870–1000), **Etta's Place** (200 West Third Street; 817–654–0267) or the **Courtyard by Marriott** (601 Main Street; 800–321–2211), and then wander over to see the paintings and sculpture at **Sid Richardson Collection of Western Art** (309 Main Street, 817–332–6554).

◆ Lunch is enjoyed at **Mi Cocina** (509 Main Street; 817–877–3600), a great place for Tex-Mex.

◆ Have a lavish dinner while viewing a spectacular sunset at **Reata**, high atop the Bank One building (500 Throckmorton Street; 817–336–1009).

◆ Wind the evening up by listening to music and sipping cocktails at **8.0** (111 Third Street; 817–336–0880) or taking a **horse-drawn carriage ride** from the Worthington.

The Love Call

Within the Sid Richardson Collection of fifty-six paintings by Western legends Remington and Russell is Remington's poignant, romantic oil, The Love Call. Painted in 1909, this lesser-known work of a lone Indian playing his flute by moonlight is radically different from the images usually associated with the artist. Whereas Remington typically offered dramatic and often tragic depictions of warriors and hunters, this peaceful, blue-toned painting offers a dreamlike quality that captures a marked variation on this master's romantic fascination with the West.

Tracing Fort Worth's development from its beginning as a frontier outpost, the exhibit takes you through its rowdy youth as a cattle town into the present day. Graphics, historical artifacts, photographs and documents, reproduced paintings, and original posters help illustrate the people and events that shaped the city. The old fire station itself is a place to enjoy, built in 1907 and once the original city hall. The exhibit is open daily from 9:00 A.M. to 7:00 P.M.

Fans of Western art or not, you're both bound to enjoy a trip 1 block from the Worthington to see the **Sid Richardson Collection of Western Art** (309 Main Street, 817–332–6554; free). Housed in a replica of an 1895 building, this museum opened in 1982 to exhibit fifty-six paintings of the revered artists Frederic Remington and Charles M. Russell. The famous works are the legacy of Fort Worth philanthropist Sid Williams Richardson, who treasured the ideals of the Old West and collected these paintings from 1942 until he died in 1959. The collection is open Tuesday and Wednesday from 10:00 A.M. to 5:00 P.M., Thursday and Friday from 10:00 A.M. to 8:00 P.M., Saturday from 11:00 A.M. to 8:00 P.M., and Sunday from 1:00 to 5:00 P.M.

Art of a different but still significantly romantic nature is found right across the street at **Thomas Kinkade at the Main Street Gallery** (302 Main Street; 817–335–2060). The small space features the work of California artist Thomas Kinkade, whose paintings feature dreamy street scenes and landscapes, from California seasides to Parisian markets in the rain—all of which display his knack for capturing light. The gallery is open Monday, Wednesday, and Thursday from 11:00

A.M. to 6:00 P.M., Friday and Saturday from 11:00 A.M. to 9:00 P.M., and Sunday from 1:00 P.M. to 5:00 P.M.

DAY ONE: *Afternoon*

LUNCH

Get ready for the city's most stylish Tex-Mex restaurant, **Mi Cocina** (509 Main Street; 817–877–3600; inexpensive/moderate). Decorated in a contemporary but colorful style, this extremely popular restaurant is loved for its selection of salsas—some of which are pretty spicy—and gratifying dishes, from shrimp enchiladas and fajitas to *queso con hongos* (thick, melted cheese with mushrooms). If you're game, try the Mambo Taxi, a drink blending frozen ribbons of margarita and sangria.

Head south a couple of blocks to The **National Cowgirl Museum & Hall of Fame** (111 West Fourth Street; 817–336–4475; free). The entire collection won't be on display until a new, $15-million museum is built (probably in 2003 or 2004), but the excellent gift shop provides an idea of the honor paid to women who have distinguished themselves as rodeo stars, artists, philanthropists, and civil servants while exemplifying the pioneer spirit of the American West. Established in 1975, the museum honors painter Georgia O'Keeffe; Laura Ingalls Wilder, author of the *Little House on the Prairie* books; and Wilma Mankiller, the first woman to serve as the Cherokee Nation's Principal Chief. The shop is open Monday through Friday from 9:00 A.M. to 5:00 P.M.

Two can easily while away a few hours browsing at **Barnes & Noble Booksellers** (401 Commerce Street; 817–332–7178), one of the chain's largest stores. Inside this two-story superstore with more than 180,000 book titles, you'll be able to find plenty of love poems, as well as books on Western art and the Old West. There are plenty of sitting areas for reading, as well as an on-site Starbucks cafe to have a couple of cappuccinos to sip while you browse.

As you head back to your hotel, two stops are worth noting. Because chocolate is said to reproduce feelings similar to love, why not indulge yourselves at a store called **Pangburn's** (400 Main Street; 817–882–9781)? Here's where you buy the Texas-born Millionaires chocolates and a truckload of other goodies, and there's a soda fountain, too, where the two of you can split a hot-fudge sundae. Note the backside of the building, where Sundance's famous Chisholm Trail mural has a 3-D appearance that makes the stampeding cattle look as though they're moving toward you.

And then there's **Haltom's Jewelers** (317 Main Street; 817–336–4051), a lovely and expensive store for exquisite jewelry and gifts. If you're in the market for a diamond or a silver locket, a piece of crystal or porcelain, this is your spot.

DAY ONE: *Evening*

DINNER

For the finest view in all Fort Worth and a dining experience long remembered, head to **Reata** at the top of the Bank One building (500 Throckmorton Street; 817–336–1009; moderate). Named for the Rock Hudson–Liz Taylor ranch in the movie *Giant*, this popular spot serves what's termed "cowboy cuisine." It's the place for smoked prime rib, steak with enchiladas, chili relleno stuffed with smoked chicken, grilled vegetables, chicken-fried steak the size of a placemat, and elaborate desserts. Ask for a window table for two, and be sure to walk around to see all sorts of memorabilia from *Giant*.

Several enticing postdinner options for couples await you in Sundance Square. Sip coffee and Kahlua in one of Reata's two bars, or head 2 blocks over to **Caravan of Dreams** (312 Houston Street; 817–429–4000), a nightclub with an assortment of interests. On the top level is the Grotto Bar, an open-air spot with a cactus garden shielded by a neon-lined dome. On the lower floors is a cabaret space that books nationally known jazz and blues acts, and a theater center with periodic shows.

The **8.0** (111 Third Street; 817–336–0880) is a restaurant and bar with a great patio. If the weather's cooperative, this is a nice place to sit outside and listen to music; if you dare, try one of the house specialty drinks called the Blue Thing, a frozen concoction that is more sweet than strong.

From Wednesday through Saturday evening, you can see Sundance under the stars on a **horse-drawn carriage ride** through downtown. These are taken from in front of the Worthington, after 7:30 P.M. Wednesday through Saturday or by appointment (817–336–0400). Rate is $25 for up to four people.

DAY TWO: *Morning*

The most astounding Sunday champagne brunch in all of Texas is likely found at the Worthington, which may be the hotel where you are staying. In what's called the **Bridge** at the hotel, you'll find a moderately priced spread of incomparable proportions, including sushi, smoked salmon, salads, pastas, fresh fish, carved prime rib, omelettes and waffles, vegetables, and desserts.

If it isn't Sunday, head across the street from the Worthington to **La Madeleine** (corner of Main and Second Streets; 817–332–3639; inexpensive). This French-style bakery and cafe does a wonderful variety of omelettes, egg-stuffed croissants, potato cakes, pastries, and fruit dishes.

The two of you still haven't seen all of the Sundance Square bounty. You might want to find new champagne glasses, sofa cushions, armoires, dried flowers, aromatic candles, and bath goodies at **Pier 1 Imports** (501 Houston Street; 817–878–7845). The Fort Worth–based chain has its flagship store here, with goods from forty-four countries.

A half block away you could buy silver trinkets or wine racks for each other at **Earth Bones** (108 Fourth Street; 817–332–2662). Then discover just the right love seat at **Legacy Trading Company** (500 Main Street; 817–870–0160), a store filled with fashionable home furnishings.

The pair of you might enjoy seeing what additional renovations to vintage Sundance buildings have wrought. If so, don't miss a visit to the **Modern at Sundance Square,** in the historic Sanger Building (Houston at Fourth Streets; 817–335–9215; free), a 4,650-square-foot exhibit space and shop. Inside are permanent and small-scale traveling exhibits, as well as a fabulous place to buy books, handmade jewelry, lamps, educational toys, and artful stationery and cards. It's open daily.

DAY TWO: *Afternoon*

LUNCH

If you didn't fill up at breakfast, have a Cajun feast at **Razzoo's** (318 Main Street; 817–429–7009), a rollicking, friendly place with Louisiana-style specialties, such as seafood gumbo, jambalaya, blackened fish and chicken, as well as filling appetizers like fried alligator tail and rat toes, which are crawfish-stuffed jalapeños.

Why not spend the afternoon snuggled up together, watching a romance or a Western? Chances are good for either one, as there are twenty movie theater choices in Sundance Square. The **AMC Palace 9** (220 Third Street; 817–870–1111) offers first-run flicks, stadium seating with overstuffed, high seat backs, and a sophisticated high-impact sound system. The **AMC Sundance 11** (304 Houston Street; 817–870–1111) has 1,850 seats, midnight movies on Friday and Saturday, and Gourmet Cinema, a theater set aside for independent, foreign, and repertory films.

Dazzling Your Darling
FORT WORTH'S CULTURAL CROWN JEWELS

A SCANT 2 MILES FROM DOWNTOWN FORT WORTH lies the third-largest arts district in the nation, surpassed in size only by those in New York City and Washington, D.C. Here you'll find one of the richest privately endowed art museums in the world, the Kimbell, as well as the Amon Carter and Modern Art museums. The fourth museum in the district is the Fort Worth Museum of Science and History, home of the Omni Theater. What's remarkable about this neighborhood is not just the depth of museum offerings, but its natural beauty. It's a great place for wandering arm in arm under ancient live oaks and juniper trees, playing Frisbee, or just lying in the grass to talk or read.

PRACTICAL NOTE: During the last two weeks of January and the first week of February, this area is jammed with visitors to the annual Southwestern Livestock Show and Rodeo, held at the district's Will Rogers complex. It's fun but often frantic.

DAY ONE: *Morning*

Drop your bags at the **Texas White House** (1417 Eighth Avenue; 817–923–3597; $105), a charming bed-and-breakfast just south of downtown. The 1910 Colonial Revival home, which bears a historic landmark from the city, doubles as a place for weddings and business meetings. Three guest rooms, each of which has period decor, a private bath, and—on request—feather beds, are named Land of Contrast, Lone Star, and Tejas.

Prepare yourselves now to enjoy what's called one of the finest small art museums in America. Drive just a few minutes west to the **Kimbell Art Museum** (3333 Camp Bowie Boulevard; 817–332–8451; free), lauded for its spectacular art holdings and for its classic modern building, which was designed by the late great American architect Louis I. Kahn. Kahn—who died just two years after the museum's 1972 opening—made innovative use of natural light, space, and materials. The cool but infinitely soothing Kimbell, as a result, has been awarded the highest prize of the American Institute of Architects, as well as top national honors for lighting and construction. Said Kahn himself of the museum: "The building feels—and it's a good feeling—that I had nothing to do with it . . . that some other hand did it."

The museum's very existence is credited to a man named Kay Kimbell—a wealthy Fort Worth entrepreneur in the agriculture, real estate, and petroleum businesses—who established the Kimbell Art Foundation with his wife, Velma, and her relatives in the 1930s. Velma died before Kay. Upon Kay's death in 1964, the Kimbells' considerable art collection and personal wealth passed to the foundation with instructions to give Fort Worth one of the finest art museums in the nation.

Today the museum's holdings include masterpieces by Fra Angelico, Holbein, El Greco, Caravaggio, La Tour, Velazquez, Rembrandt, Houdon, Goya, Delacroix, Cézanne, Picasso, Matisse, and Mondrian. It's also one of the only institutions in the Southwest with a sizable collection of Asian arts, and with impressive, small groupings of Mesoamerican, African,

Romance AT A GLANCE

◆ Take a room near downtown at the **Texas White House** (1417 Eighth Avenue; 817–923–3597) bed-and-breakfast before driving a few minutes west to the Cultural District and the phenomenal **Kimbell Art Museum** (3333 Camp Bowie Boulevard; 817–332–8451), with centuries of art from around the world, and the **Amon Carter Museum** (3501 Camp Bowie Boulevard; 817–738–1933), famous for its collections of American artwork.

◆ Ease into the evening over martinis and appetizers at **Ancho Chile Bar** (3413 West Seventh Street; 817–877–3413), and then dine in utter elegance on country French cuisine at **Saint-Emilion** (3617 West Seventh Street; 817–737–2781).

and Mediterranean pieces and antiques. The Kimbell is typically a first-choice stop in the United States for prized visiting exhibits.

The museum, which has a top-notch gift shop, is open Tuesday through Thursday and Saturday from 10:00 A.M. to 5:00 P.M., Friday from noon to 8:00 P.M., and Sunday from noon to 5:00 P.M. Admission is charged only for special exhibitions.

DAY ONE: *Afternoon*

LUNCH

You don't have to leave the Kimbell to enjoy one of the better lunches in Fort Worth; the **Buffet** (inexpensive) is at the north end of the building and offers a sun-filled setting as intimate and lovely for dining as any around. Each week there's a new blackboard menu, featuring selections of excellent soups, salads, sandwiches, and inspired desserts. Lots of creativity and flavor go into every dish.

In the very next block—less than a two-minute walk from the Kimbell—you'll find another great Fort Worth treasure, the **Amon Carter Museum** (3501 Camp Bowie Boulevard; 817–738–1933; free). The museum was established in 1961 because philanthropist and *Fort Worth Star-Telegram* publisher Amon G. Carter, Sr., wanted a great place to house his collection of paintings and sculpture by Frederic Remington and Charles M. Russell, as well as a museum that would collect, preserve, and exhibit the finest examples of American art. He felt a great museum for American art belonged in the city that he said was "where the West begins."

He didn't live to see the final product, but those who knew him said he would have been hugely pleased by the creation of New York architect Philip Johnson. Johnson, whom Carter never met, wrought a "a simple, elegant design that combined the warmth and richness of bronze with the creamy, intricately patterned surface of native Texas shellstone," according to Carter Johnson Martin, author of *150 Years of American Art: Amon Carter Museum Collection*. A terraced plaza in front of the museum features a Henry Moore, *Upright Motives;* from this perspective the two of you can enjoy a picturesque view of the Cultural District and park areas, as well as downtown immediately east.

Two entire galleries are devoted to paintings by Remington and Russell, and there are other Western scenes by John Mix Stanley, Albert Bierstadt, and Georgia O'Keeffe. The collection of works on paper is amazing, from more than 600 watercolors and drawings by early nineteenth-century artist-explorers and twentieth-century abstractions to more than 5,700 prints, and from lithographs of the Mexican War to complete sets of prints by George Bellows and Stuart Davis. The photography collection spans the history of the medium and includes more than 6,000 actively used exhibition prints by nearly 400 different photographers. Important American photographers featured include Eliot Porter, Laura Gilpin, and Nell Dorr.

Having outgrown itself, the Carter museum will undergo an almost complete reconstruction project in the next few years. Be sure to visit the museum's excellent store. The museum is open Tuesday through Saturday from 10:00 A.M. to 5:00 P.M. and Sunday from noon to 5:00 P.M.

A cozy spot to repair after this art immersion is at the **Ancho Chile Bar** (3413 West Seventh Street; 817–877–3413). Share some quiet time over one of the house martinis or an excellent glass of Pinot Noir, and perhaps have an appetizer pizza topped with smoked chicken. In cool weather a fire will be crackling on the hearth.

DAY ONE: *Evening*

How do the two of you feel about this evening? Ready for something sumptuous and intimate, or does an informal, loud place hold appeal?

DINNER

For a luxurious dinner done in utmost style, book a table for two at **Saint-Emilion** (3000 South Hulen Street; 817–737–2781; expensive). The city's premier restaurant serving country French cuisine is also one of the most romantic hideouts anywhere. A converted small brick house, Saint-Emilion does a superb job with rack of lamb, grilled fresh fish, and desserts. There's an ample permanent menu, as well as an intriguing menu of daily specials, and the wine list is sensational. Everything's prix fixe, and reservations are a good idea.

Young at Heart

*One of Fort Worth's most delightful diversions is also its most simple one. Before, between, or after visits to the Kimbell, Carter, or Modern museums, take an hour just to be kids again. The enormous open lawn sitting on the west side of the Kimbell, beyond a serene reflecting pool, is lined with rows of giant trees, where the young at heart can almost always be seen throwing Frisbees or just sitting together in the cool grass to unwind. For a treat, the **Back Porch** (3400 Camp Bowie Boulevard; 817–332–1422)—directly facing this lawn—offers ice cream cones (banana pudding is a house favorite) and frozen lemonade, perfect for enjoying on a fine day in the sun.*

But if jeans and tennis shoes are your desired attire, head over to the **Railhead Smokehouse** (2900 Montgomery Street; 817–738–9808). The favorite among all barbecue spots in town, the Railhead offers a casual decor of old railroad photos and beer signs. (You'll also see a sign reflecting the Fort Worth–Dallas rivalry that says, LIFE'S TOO SHORT TO LIVE IN DALLAS.) Not only will the two of you find some exceptional, hickory-smoked beef brisket, meaty pork ribs, tender chicken and turkey breast, and spicy sausage, but you also will encounter one of the most enthusiastic crowds in all Tarrant County. The beer's frosty, the diners are friendly, and the patio is a treat in mild weather.

If you'd like to dance the night away, there are plenty of good places for country, jazz, or pop music. See Itinerary 7 on Fort Worth's nightlife.

DAY TWO: *Morning*

Have breakfast at your B&B, or you may want to try **Jubilee Café** (2736 West Seventh Street; 817–332–4568; inexpensive). Sitting about 5 blocks east of the Cultural District, this no-nonsense, simple diner does a bang-up job of home cooking. Best breakfast bets are enormous breakfast tacos, stuffed with eggs, black beans, cheese, potatoes, and bacon; giant buckwheat pancakes; and homemade biscuits with gravy. Jubilee does a great lunch, too.

Thus fortified you're both ready to take on the oldest art museum in Texas, the **Modern Art Museum of Fort Worth** (1309 Montgomery Street; 817–738–9215; free). The museum is dedicated to collecting, presenting, and interpreting international developments in post–World War II art in all media. Established in 1892 as the Fort Worth Public Library and Art Gallery Association, it opened to the public in 1901, purchased its first painting—*Approaching Storm*, by George Innes, 1875—in 1904, and offered its first exhibition in 1909. Between 1910 and 1987 the name changed a few times, the museum moved to different sites—settling at the corner of West Lancaster and Montgomery Streets—and the museum continued to grow.

In 1987 its name became the Modern Art Museum of Fort Worth, and in 1996 the museum announced plans to build a new, hugely expanded home a few steps from the Kimbell Museum. Six architects were invited to submit proposals, and the museum board chose that of Japan's Tadao Ando. The new museum should be finished in 2002.

Inside the museum are major twentieth-century American and European paintings, sculptures, and works on paper by such artists as Picasso, Pollock, Rothko, and Warhol. If you'd like to take a free docent-led tour of current exhibitions, be at the museum at 2:00 P.M. on a Saturday. The museum is open Tuesday through Friday from 10:00 A.M. to 5:00 P.M., Saturday from 11:00 A.M. to 5:00 P.M., and Sunday from noon to 5:00 P.M.

DAY TWO: *Afternoon*

LUNCH

For a really great burger, head over to **Tommy's** (3431 West Seventh Street; 817–332–1922; inexpensive), a tiny cafe with exceptional sandwiches and fries. If you're there on a Sunday (when Tommy's is closed), try **La Familia** (2720 West Seventh Street; 817–870–2002; inexpensive), a wonderfully friendly family business in a remodeled McDonald's serving fresh, solid Mexican fare. The beef fajitas, chicken enchiladas, chicken *chalupa*, and cheese chili relleno are all great.

A visit to the **Omni Theater** is a perfect way to wind up your Cultural District wanderings. Part of the **Fort Worth Museum of Science and History** (1501 Montgomery Street; 817–255–9300), the

Omni incorporates the most advanced super 70mm, multi-image projection and sound systems in the world and offers a domed screen, 80 feet in diameter, tilted at a thirty-degree angle to the horizon. You truly are enveloped by sight and sound; seventy-two gigantic speakers in ten clusters are strategically placed behind the screen to allow six-track sound to "move" across the theater in synchronization with the action on the screen. A delightful place to relax and be thrilled at the same time, the Omni has presented features on Hawaiian volcanoes, outer space, the African savannah, oceans of the world, and Mount Everest. Shows are offered throughout the day, every day. Tickets cost $6.00 per person.

Adjacent to the Omni is **Noble Planetarium**, the first in the world named for a woman, Miss Charlie Mary Noble. A treat for stargazers is the Noble's Spitz A3P star projector, which allows the two of you to imagine all sorts of journeys together through space and time. Several shows are offered on Saturday and Sunday; tickets cost $3.00 per person.

For MORE ROMANCE

If the weather is welcoming, take a stroll together through nearby Fort Worth Botanic Garden, its Conservatory, its Japanese Garden or all three. See Itinerary 17 for details.

Artistic Passion
IN DALLAS

THE DALLAS STAGE, LIKE THAT IN ALL MAJOR CITIES, has evolved over the decades from one or two solid theaters to a diversity of venues to meet every taste. Your evenings together can be filled with classical music or avant-garde plays, opera or ballet, Latin dance or touring Broadway musicals; whatever suits your passion. During the day, the two of you might opt to do a bit of low-key artistic exploring—if you're not taking in a matinee performance—to conserve your nighttime energies.

PRACTICAL NOTE: Before planning this itinerary, check with individual theaters to find out schedules and ticket availability. Two good Internet sources to check are the local newspapers' entertainment Web sites. These are the *Dallas Morning News* at www.guidelive.com and the *Fort Worth Star-Telegram* at www.just-go.com.

DAY ONE: *Morning*

If you can, treat yourselves to one of the world's great plea-sures, a stay at **the Mansion on Turtle Creek** (2821 Turtle Creek Boulevard; 214–559–2100; $200 and up). A masterpiece in style, the Mansion features an internationally acclaimed hotel and restaurant, nestled in a gorgeous setting that spreads over almost five acres near old Highland Park. Within the

10,000-square-foot Sheppard King Mansion, built seventy years ago by a local cotton magnate, are the restaurant and bar at the Mansion. A fireplace at each end of the main dining area and a collection of art and antiques, together with the original wood paneling, carved ceilings, and lead glass windows, keep a warm, residential feeling intact.

Executive Chef Dean Fearing, named by *Food and Wine* magazine as one of "America's top 10 young chefs," has placed the Mansion at the head of national lists of best restaurants. A noted pioneer of American Southwestern cuisine, Fearing continues to update his imaginative, innovative approach to food—specialties include tortilla soup, warm lobster tacos, and roasted pheasant—and he frequently hosts food and cooking events with famous visiting chefs such as Wolfgang Puck and Julia Child.

The Bar at the Mansion is a lovely setting for casual lunch and supper. It displays hunting trophies and eighteenth-century hunting theme paintings and lithographs hung on forest-green fabric walls.

The hotel's 141 guest rooms, including 15 suites, are known for antiques, fine fabrics, and original works of art. Typical amenities include flowers in the room, imported bottled water, 100-percent cotton oversize bed and bath linens, deluxe terry bathrobes, three telephones, in-room safe, minibar, and videos. Limousine service arrangements are available through the concierge, and sedans and limousines are also available for airport pickup and return at special rates.

Romance AT A GLANCE

◆ Get your bearing either at the **Mansion on Turtle Creek** (2821 Turtle Creek Boulevard; 214–559–2100) or the less expensive **Melrose Hotel** (3015 Oak Lawn Avenue; 214–521–5151) or **Southern House** (in Uptown; 972–298–8586) before heading out to see the exceptional collection of Spanish artworks at **Meadows Museum of Art** on the Southern Methodist University campus (Owens Fine Arts Center, Bishop Boulevard at Binkley Avenue; 214–768–2516).

◆ Eat lunch at the Mediterranean delight called **Bistro A** (6815 Snider Plaza; 214–373–9911).

◆ In the evening, slake your thirst for theater at the **Arts District Theater** (2401 Flora Street; 214–522–8499), **Kalita Humphreys Theater** (3636 Turtle Creek Boulevard; 214–522–8499), **Theatre Three** (2800 Routh Street; 214–871–3300) in the Quadrangle shopping center, or **Teatro Dallas** (2204 Commerce Street; 214–741–6833).

◆ Wind up the evening with drinks in the bar at the **Mansion,** where **Henry Muñoz** is the featured pianist and singer.

If the Mansion exceeds your budget, another good choice nearby is the **Melrose Hotel** (3015 Oak Lawn Avenue; 214–521–5151; $175 and up). A graceful, restored old hotel, it has a wonderful bar called the Library.

Less expensive and more personal than the Mansion is a new bed-and-breakfast choice called the **Southern House,** booked through Bed & Breakfast Texas Style (972–298–8586). Located in the State-Thomas Historic District in Uptown, this new home was built to requirements of the historic area, yet incorporates contemporary style. There are two guest rooms, both with queen beds, one with a private bath. The $150 nightly rate includes exceptional breakfasts, which might be a Texas-style eggs Benedict on polenta or a Mexican eggs migas with potatoes or grits.

A budget choice in the area is **La Quinta City Place** (4440 North Central Expressway; 800–687–6667; $69). This chain serves families as well as couples.

A Tradition of Culture

Your appreciation of Dallas's fine arts scene might not be possible were it not for the cultural commitment and perseverance of the city's early elite. Even before the railroad came to town, Dallasites built an opera house that hosted such stage luminaries as Edwin Boothe, Lily Langtry, and Sarah Bernhardt. The Dallas Shakespeare Club was founded in 1886 and was guided by May Dickson Exall, who also pioneered adult education for women in the city. When the two of you visit the Majestic Theater, imagine vaudeville acts there in 1905. As you enjoy opera at the Fair Park Music Hall, remember that Dallas ancestors first enjoyed the same in 1912.

Perhaps the two of you could spend the morning boosting your combined fine arts quotient with a visit to the **Meadows Museum of Art** on the Southern Methodist University campus (Owens Fine Arts Center, Bishop Boulevard at Binkley Avenue; 214–768–2516; $3.00 donation suggested). Begun in 1962, the small but exceptional museum is home to a collection of Spanish art amassed and donated by Texas oil magnate Algur H. Meadows. Thanks to his generosity, SMU is home to what's considered among the finest and most complete collections of Spanish art outside of Spain and the finest in the United States. The permanent collection's 670 pieces include major works by Velazquez, Rivera, Zurbaran, Murillo, Goya, Miró, and Picasso.

In addition you'll find Renaissance altarpieces, stupendous baroque canvases, rococo oil sketches, modernist abstracts, and much more. Exceptional traveling exhibits, such as a retrospective of abstract artist Gerardo Rueda, are scheduled throughout the year. The Meadows is open Monday, Tuesday, Friday, and Saturday from 10:00 A.M. to 5:00 P.M.; Thursday from 10:00 A.M. to 8:00 P.M.; and Sunday from 1:00 to 5:00 P.M.

DAY ONE: *Afternoon*

LUNCH

Just a few blocks from the Meadows Museum of Art and SMU is a delightful restaurant called **Bistro A** (6815 Snider Plaza; 214–373–9911; moderate), which is tucked into a lovely, old restored shopping center that bears a marked Spanish architectural design. The restaurant walls are splashed in shades of mustard, and a Mediterranean decor theme is carried out in rustic wood furniture and gorgeous imported pottery. All of that will become secondary to your interests once you've tasted the food. Best bets are baked oysters with applewood-smoked bacon and spinach, grilled lamb chops with feta, and cool appetizer plates with hummus, eggplant dip, and fancy olives.

Your chances of catching a matinee theater performance are pretty good on Saturday and Sunday, when the **Dallas Summer Musicals** events at **Fair Park Music Hall** or at the **Majestic Theater** often have such schedules. Sunday matinees are typical for performances at **Meyerson Symphony Center**, for ballet and Dallas Symphony Orchestra events, as well as specially featured vocalists on tour. All of these venues are described in greater detail later in this itinerary.

If the two of you would rather just relax, you could just have a long bath and rest at your hotel. Your evening's likely to be busy.

DAY ONE: *Evening*

DINNER

For a low-key but lovely dinner before heading to the theater, take a table for two at **Javier's Gourmet Mexicano** (4912 Cole Avenue; 214–521–4211; moderate to expensive), a villa-esque place offering the best of Mexico City cuisine. Salsas—both green and red—are served pleasantly warmed, and margaritas are absolutely authentic. Try the cheese-stuffed file mignon, which is wonderfully rich.

But if you're dressing up for the evening, make reservations in advance for an early dinner at **Al Biernat's** (4217 Oak Lawn Avenue; 214–219–2201; very expensive). Named for the owner, who was a twenty-year veteran of the venerable Palm restaurant downtown, this palace of fine food and service created a sensation when opened in mid-1998. It's a hot spot for local celebs and well-dressed others with money to burn or a need to impress somebody. The menu offers contemporary twists on favorites such as rack of lamb with goat-cheese potatoes and potato-crusted calamari. Everything's expensive and worth it. Make sure you allow plenty of time to enjoy it.

Your choices for the evening's entertainment depend on what tickets you've been able to secure. The Dallas Theater Center consists of two venues, the **Arts District Theater** (2401 Flora Street; 214–522–8499), where recent presentations have included *Tartuffe*, Moliere's zinger of a satire; and the **Kalita Humphreys Theater** (3636 Turtle Creek Boulevard; 214–522–8499), the only theater designed by famed architect Frank Lloyd Wright, where Paula Vogel's play *How I Learned to Drive*—winner of the 1998 Pulitzer Prize for Drama—was a hit.

Another, delightfully intimate option is petite **Theatre Three** (2800 Routh Street; 214–871–3300) in the stylish Quadrangle shopping center. Contemporary and classic theater works have included *The Threepenny Opera*, the Brecht-Weill musical about Mack the Knife; and *We Won't Pay! We Won't Pay!*, a political farce by Dario Fo; winner of the 1997 Nobel Prize for literature.

At **Teatro Dallas** (2204 Commerce Street; 214–741–6833), *Howling at the Moon* was a presentation of four short plays by Alfredo

Cardona Pena, Elena Garro, and Michelle de Ghelderode, all written for a Day of the Dead celebration. Dallas's deep Hispanic heritage is honored here in classical and contemporary plays by Latin American and Hispanic American playwrights.

After the show and before retiring, do have a drink in the bar at the Mansion. Henry Muñoz is the featured pianist and singer, and there's a trio on weekends.

DAY TWO: *Morning*

BREAKFAST

Have a lovely spread at the Mansion if that's where you're staying, or head over to **Breadwinners** (3301 McKinney Avenue; 214–754–4940; inexpensive), a hip bakery and cafe in a vintage brick building that held a pharmacy in the decades-ago day when streetcars were the main mode of transportation on the street in front. It's quite nice for couples who enjoy lingering over coffee and newspapers.

Walk just 2 blocks down to **McKinney Avenue Contemporary** (3120 McKinney Avenue; 214–953–1622). Also called the MAC, it is a contemporary arts center presenting new work in visual arts, theater, performance, dance, music, film and video, and the literary arts. Opened in October 1994, the MAC was the first North Texas venue where all forms of contemporary art were offered under one roof. In addition to various exhibits, you'll find a great book and gift store, library, and the Cyber Café, whose offerings include computer work-stations, snacks, cappuccino, and bottled waters. Hours at the MAC are 11:00 A.M. to 10:00 P.M. Wednesday through Saturday and 1:00 to 5:00 P.M. Sunday.

DAY TWO: *Afternoon*

LUNCH

To see what an opera would look like if it were food, head over to **EatZi's** (3403 Oak Lawn Avenue; 214–526–1515; inexpensive to moderate), a heavenly—if often crowded—market of dream cuisine. Opera music accompanies shoppers through an assortment of walls, counters, and bins overflowing with extraordinary ready-to-eat dishes, breads, produce, cheeses, and more. Pick out a bakery item, some sushi, seafood salad with fresh scallops, smoked salmon, stuffed chicken breast, and marinated, grilled vegetables. Or skip over to the sandwich bar, where chefs will create your hearts' desires from a selection of meats, cheeses, grilled veggies, and condiments on your choice of freshly baked breads. Or just grab one of the 2-inch-thick pieces of focaccia, topped with herbs and cheeses. Wines, beers, and soft drinks are sold, too. There are a few tables inside and out on the sidewalk, or you can pack your goodies up to eat together on a grassy spot beside Turtle Creek, about 4 blocks east.

After you've stuffed yourselves, this might be the time to head off to a matinee—or just to read love poems beside Turtle Creek, or in your hotel room.

DAY TWO: *Evening*

DINNER

Close to downtown—and the Meyerson, if your evening consists of seeing a performance there—is **Star Canyon** (3102 Oak Lawn Avenue; 214–520–7827; very expensive), where reservations are required well in advance. Among the state's more famous restaurants, this upbeat, stylized ranch setting offers the ultimate in New Texas Cuisine, created by celebrity chef Stephan Pyles. Renowned dishes include moonfish with hibiscus couscous, spit-roasted *cabrito* (baby goat) quesadillas, and ribeye steak piled with onion rings.

Something far less pricey is the delightful **Tin Star** (2626 Howell Street; 214–999–0059; inexpensive). Self-described as a place for "salsa, smoke, and sizzle," this quick, casual diner adorned with earth tones and wall decor cut-outs shaped like a sheriff's badge, offers flavorful, Southwestern cuisine without any fuss. Specialties include thickly battered chicken-fried steak with jalapeño-cream gravy, grilled vegetable tacos, and fried chicken tenders with sautéed mushrooms in a smoky chipotle chile sauce.

Now the two of you are off again, perhaps to the **Meyerson Symphony Center** (2301 Flora Street; 214-692-0203) to see the Dallas Symphony Orchestra (DSO). The center was designed by lauded architect I. M. Pei and has been hailed internationally for its architectural brilliance and acoustical excellence. A recent Super Pops series featured Arturo Sandoval, international jazz trumpet virtuoso; the Boys Choir of Harlem; and Debbie Reynolds and Johnny Mathis. The DSO classical season, which begins in September and continues through May, features Andrew Litton conducting and such guests as violinist Anne Akiko Meyers; pianist Jon Nakamatsu, the 1997 Van Cliburn winner; and violinist Nigel Kennedy, now modestly known as KENNEDY.

The fall also brings the Turtle Creek Chorale, a 225-member men's chorale, to the Meyerson.

But if you're opera buffs—is there anything more romantic than Verdi?—your destination will be the **Fair Park Music Hall** (First and Parry Streets; 214-565-2226) for a night of Dallas Opera (214-443-1000).

After seeing a production at the Music Hall, have an after-dinner cognac or glass of wine at **Tarantino's** (3611 Parry Avenue; 214-821-2224). A dark, trendy spot, this renovated bar offers Mediterranean tapas dishes, too.

DAY THREE: *Morning*

BREAKFAST

Sleep late, then have coffee sent up by room service. After you've checked out, wander over to **Dream Café** (2800 Routh Street; 214-954-0486; inexpensive), a cheery place in the Quadrangle for cosmic Tex-Mex or vegetarian brunch; the black bean enchiladas are outstanding. If it's a nice day, sit on the patio, enjoy the fresh air, and start planning your next romantic getaway.

FOR MORE ROMANCE

If your lust for theater demands more ideas, consider **Dallas Summer Musicals at the Fair Park Music Hall** (First at Parry Streets;

214–373–8000), offering national touring shows of such productions as *Phantom of the Opera, Oklahoma, Showboat, Les Miserables,* and *Riverdance* in summer and fall. Another choice is **the Majestic Theater** (1925 Elm Street; 214–647–5700). Built in the Renaissance Revival style in the 1920s, the Majestic is the last of the city's Theater Row structures. Touring productions stopping here have included a version of *Deathtrap* starring Elliott Gould and Mariette Hartley.

$\mathcal{A}$rm in $\mathcal{A}$rm
TAKING IN FORT WORTH THEATER

UCH AS IS THE CASE IN DALLAS, Fort Worth has enjoyed a burst of creativity and growth in the performing and visual arts since the 1970s. The city forsakes its "Cowtown" reputation with a depth of theater, music, and dance. The two of you will find plenty to see on stage during the evening in Fort Worth, while you can spend your daylight hours in a fascinating living history museum or take in some matinees.

PRACTICAL NOTE: Of course, you'll want to call theaters well in advance to inquire about schedules and tickets. Check the local newspaper's Web site at www.justgo.com to read up.

DAY ONE: *Morning*

Stay downtown at either the Worthington or Etta's Place (see Itinerary 2) or go the bed-and-breakfast route at **Azalea Plantation** (1400 Robinwood Drive; 817–838–5882; $98 and up), a plantation-style home tucked into a quiet, oak-shaded residential neighborhood about five minutes northeast of downtown. The acre-and-a-half grounds are filled with trees and graced with rock terracing, gazebo, and fountain. Inside the 1947 home are four guest rooms, furnished with antiques and accompanied by private baths. Ask about the Magnolia Cottage, a romantic suite with a whirlpool tub for two and a cozy parlor area. Weekend stays include a lavish breakfast, while continental is the deal on weekdays. The weekend breakfast buffet typically includes French toast, ham or sausage, muffins, fresh fruit, juice, and coffee.

In keeping with your escape to fine arts, you could spend the day visiting one of Fort Worth's famous art museums (see Itinerary 4). But for something rather offbeat, you could stroll hand in hand around the charming little hideout near the Cultural District called **Log Cabin Village** (University Drive at Colonial Parkway; 817–926–5881). Seven restored pioneer cabins—moved here from other sites—are contained within this living history museum, illustrating life in the early and mid-1800s with period furniture and tools.

Romance
AT A GLANCE

◆ *Drop your things at* ***Azalea Plantation*** *(1400 Robinwood Drive; 817–838–5882), then take a little tour through seven restored pioneer cabins at* ***Log Cabin Village*** *(University Drive at Colonial Parkway; 817–926–5881).*

◆ *Lunch on steaks and chicken at* ***Hoffbrau*** *(1712 South University Drive; 817–870–1952), then catch a matinee downtown at* ***Jubilee Theatre*** *(506 Main Street; 817–338–4411),* ***Circle Theater*** *(230 West Fourth Street; 817–877–3040), or* ***Casa on the Square*** *(109 East Third Street; 817–332–2272).*

◆ *Have a romantic feast at* ***Randall's*** *(907 Houston Street; 817–336–2253) before walking down the street to see a musical or concert at the widely acclaimed new* ***Nancy Lee and Perry R. Bass Performance Hall*** *(555 Commerce Street; 817–212–4200).*

Inside each cabin you'll find villagers, or interpreters wearing authentic frontier clothing styles, who will tell you how pioneers lived. They'll also demonstrate various pioneer skills, such as spinning wool and making candles. History buffs will appreciate one cabin in particular, the one that belonged to Isaac Parker, uncle of Cynthia Ann Parker, who was abducted as a young girl by the Comanches. She married Chief Nocona and mothered Quanah Parker, the famous Comanche chief who was instrumental in establishing peace between the settlers and Native Americans of North Texas.

Log Cabin Village is open Tuesday through Friday from 9:00 A.M. to 5:00 P.M., Saturday from 10:00 A.M. to 5:00 P.M., and Sunday from 1:00 to 5:00 P.M. Admission costs $1.50 per person.

DAY ONE: *Afternoon*

LUNCH

Just a few blocks north of Log Cabin Village, you'll find **Hoffbrau** (1712 South University Drive; 817–870–1952; inexpensive/moderate), a rowdy little Texas steakhouse and saloon that happens to have great deck seating during nice weather. If the two of you are eating light, there are good salads, topped with grilled chicken or shrimp, as well as marinated chicken sandwiches. But the burgers and chicken-fried steak are great, too, as are the house special, brau chips—thickly sliced potatoes that are fried to a crisp and eaten dunked in ranch dressing.

After lunch, you might be in luck on Saturday or Sunday for a matinee at **Bass Performance Hall** or at one of the regional theaters, all of which are described in greater detail later in this itinerary. Otherwise, take a leisurely driving tour through **Elizabeth Boulevard Historical District**, south of downtown and north of Berry Street (along Elizabeth Boulevard between Eighth and College Avenues). This exceptional street—listed on the National Register of Historic Places—was the central thoroughfare lined with grand homes built by cattlemen and oil barons between 1910 and 1930. The building boom ended with the Great Depression, but you'll see the phenomenal beauty of the age in many of the restored (but private) homes. Many bear historical markers.

DAY ONE: *Evening*

DINNER

Before heading off to the theater, have an intimate dinner at **Randall's** (907 Houston Street; 817–336–2253; moderate), a seductive room that feels far more like San Francisco or Soho than Texas. Specialties include tuna and smoked shrimp in a portobello cream sauce, artichoke soup, beef medallions in a red wine bordelaise sauce, and unforgettable cheesecakes. The wine list is winning, too.

Evening entertainment options are plentiful—but plan ahead. Downtown choices include **Jubilee Theatre** (506 Main Street; 817–338–4411), a leading venue for African-American theater in Texas. Consistently good reviews go to productions here, which have included such delights as the hilarious play *One Monkey Don't Stop No Show*.

There's also **Circle Theater** (230 West Fourth Street; 817–877–3040), whose professional troupe presents six productions each year. Recent offerings have included an unusual, entertaining adaptation of Henry James's *Turn of the Screw*, as well as special children's productions.

Casa on the Square (109 East Third Street; 817–332–2272) is a terrific, small (130-seat) theater on the upper level of the marvelous Knights of Pythias building. Touring shows are offered here; a satire that drew rave reviews was *Complete History of America {abridged}*, a celebration of the oddities of American culture and history.

For a nightcap after the show, try **Blue Mesa** (1600 South University Drive; 817–332–6372) just south of Interstate 30 (convenient to Stage West), or downtown spots such as **Reata** (500 Throckmorton Street; 817–336–1009), at the top of the bank building at Throckmorton and Fifth Streets, or the **Lobby Bar** at the Worthington (200 Main Street; 817–870–1000).

DAY TWO: *Morning*

BREAKFAST

Enjoy a leisurely breakfast at your hotel or B&B, or dive into a Texas feast at **Cactus Flower Café** (509 University Drive; 817–332–9552). The biscuits are divine, the cinnamon rolls are devastating, the pancakes are fluffy. If you want to imitate the cowboys in the diner, have eggs with chicken-fried steak.

You're right in the neighborhood anyway, so if you two haven't explored three of the finest art museums in the Southwest—or as many experts in such matters would argue, the nation—plan to share your morning poking around either the **Kimbell Art Museum**, the **Amon Carter Museum**, or the **Modern Art Museum of Fort Worth**. The Kimbell features art from all cultures spanning a period of more than 3,000 years; the Carter offers a permanent collection of nineteenth- and early twentieth-century American art, with a remarkable photography collection; and the Modern is known for major twentieth-century European and American works. All three are about 6 blocks from the Cactus Flower in the **Cultural District**. For complete details, see Itinerary 4.

DAY TWO: *Afternoon*

LUNCH

If you managed not to stuff yourselves silly at breakfast, head west from the Cultural District along the main, bricked boulevard to **Uncle Julio's** (5301 Camp Bowie Boulevard; 817–377–2777; inexpensive/moderate). The atmosphere and decor here project the feeling of a fiesta in progress in a village someplace along the Texas-Mexico border, with pastel-painted stucco walls, cement floors, a tortilla-making machine at the entrance, and the sort of constant flurry of activity you'd expect in a Mexican marketplace.

You'll both like the food a lot, too, which ranges from quesadillas stuffed with gooey jack cheese and mushrooms, shrimp fajitas, and chicken enchiladas to lighter fare, such a tortilla soup and spinach salad topped with jicama and bacon. If you've found yourselves in a jubilant mood, have a couple of Swirls, the house drink of frozen ribbons of margarita and sangria in an icy mug.

After lunch, head to the north end of town to tour the **Vintage Flying Museum** (Hangar 33 South, Meacham Airport, 505 Northwest 38th Street; 817–624–1935). Even if you're not necessarily airplane buffs, the two of you can't help but be intrigued by this wonderful nonprofit, antique aircraft restoration place that restores or rebuilds flying museums. The pride of this collection—which includes numerous vintage planes, land vehicles, and support equipment from World War II and the Korean and Vietnam Wars—is Chuckie, a B-17 plane that was built in 1944 and served as a pathfinder, leading bomber squadrons to targets during World War II. Other displays range from a BT-15 World War II primary trainer to a Korean War-era F-86 Starfire and a T-33 jet trainer.

The museum is open from 10:00 A.M. until 5:00 P.M. Saturday and from noon to 5:00 P.M. Sunday, but you can usually call ahead on weekdays for a tour appointment. Admission is by donation, the recommended amount being $3.00 per person.

Now head back to your B&B or hotel and freshen up for the evening.

DAY TWO: *Evening*

DINNER

If you're looking for something elegant, head to **Reflections** (in the Worthington Hotel; 817–882–1660), the city's finest site for continental dining. Beef tenderloin, veal chops, grilled salmon, and the like are given imaginative treatments that can vary from Southwestern to French to Asian. Tableside preparations are especially pleasing. Be sure to book ahead.

The place for "global cuisine" is **Angeluna** (215 East Fourth Street; 817–334–0080), a see-and-be-seen spot with exceptional food, a cloud-painted ceiling, and hundreds of paintings of angels on the walls. Fort Worth's first foray into fusion food brings together Thai, Mexican, Caribbean, and other influences into ambitious dishes involving anything from pasta and beef to pizza and salads. The bar scene is lively, thanks to great martinis.

Directly across the street from Angeluna is the spectacular **Nancy Lee and Perry R. Bass Performance Hall** (555 Commerce Street; 817–212–4200), built in 1998 and hailed as "the last great hall built in the twentieth century." The $65-million world-class facility is home to the Van Cliburn International Piano Competition, the Cliburn Concert series, the Fort Worth Symphony, the Fort Worth Dallas Ballet, the

Heavenly Guardians

If the two of you are fortunate enough to catch a presentation of some variety at Bass Performance Hall, you are certain to fall in love with the pair of 48-foot-tall, cream-colored angels framing the entrance of this extraordinary building. Since the hall's inception, observers have been utterly smitten by these sculptures, gigantic images of grace and perfection,. The two angels were crafted over a three-year period by Hungarian artist Marton Varo, who calls them "the embodiment of human creative impulses, and humanity's guardians." Varo, whose sculptures are found in Greece, Amsterdam, and Hungary, among many other places, dreams that these angels will help bring people together for good.

Fort Worth Opera, and special productions of Casa Mañana musicals. You can't miss it, what with gigantic angels towering above the street with their massive trumpets.

The Fort Worth Symphony Orchestra's season lasts from September through May. Featured concerts have included works by Strauss, Canteloube, Ravel, Bernstein, Debussy, and more, with guest appearances by mezzo-soprano Frederica von Stade, clarinetist Richard Stoltzman, violinist Cho-Liang Lin, pianist Barry Douglas, and violinist Jose-Luis Garcia. The inaugural season also featured the Saint Paul Chamber Orchestra, conducted by Bobby McFerrin, and the Superstar Pops Series, which brought Marvin Hamlisch, Dionne Warwick, and others to town.

Hundreds of other attractions at the Bass Performance Hall have included Ballet Folklorio de Mexico, James Galway, the St. Petersburg Philharmonic Orchestra, Maynard Ferguson and His Big Bop Nouveau Band, and the touring production of *Phantom of the Opera*.

To see what's playing, check with the *Fort Worth Star-Telegram* Web site at www.justgo.com.

After the show enjoy a rooftop drink together under the stars at **Caravan of Dreams** (312 Houston Street; 817–877–3000). The open-air grotto bar has a cactus garden and a superb view of downtown.

DAY THREE: *Morning*

BREAKFAST

Enjoy the morning offerings at your hotel or B&B. If you're still a bit full from last night's indulgences, just have coffee and a pastry in the **Starbucks** inside the Barnes & Noble bookstore on Commerce Street. Maybe you'll want to buy a book on pioneer life, art, or vintage aricraft as a reminder of your trip together. Then head for home.

FOR MORE ROMANCE

About ten minutes west of downtown, facing Texas Christian University, is **Stage West** (3055 South University Drive; 817–784–9378). This professional regional theater puts on about ten productions each year; a monster hit in 1998 was *Proposals*, Neil Simon's newest play.

If it's summertime, catch a musical at **Casa Manana** (3101 West Lancaster Avenue at University Drive; 817–332–2272). Begun in the 1930s as a creation by infamous showman Billy Rose, this 1,800-seat domed theater brings such productions as *The Unsinkable Molly Brown, Carousel,* and *42nd Street* to town.

Night and Day

ᶠrom ᴬlternative to ᶻydeco

The Dallas Club Scene

THANKS TO THE BLAZING MUSIC SCENE farther south in Austin, Dallas's trove of live music venues has exploded in the past decade or so. More than a few Texas bands and solo acts—such as Lyle Lovett, Robert Earl Keen, Edie Brickell, and Shaun Colvin—began their work in these two cities, cementing the reputation of several Dallas bars and night spots.

And if you like dancing, there are plenty of places to cut a rug. This itinerary, which is loaded with options to accommodate whatever whims the two of you have, will give you a start to a memorable evening on the town.

PRACTICAL NOTE: Dress casually for the nightclub scene, but don't go as far as shorts and tennis shoes. Black is the most fashionable color here, as in all large cities. Many places have valet parking, which is sometimes free but can be as much as $5.00. There are parking lots in the Deep Ellum area, but these typically cost $5.00, so you might be better off taking valet parking and walking around.

DAY ONE: *Afternoon*

Check into **Amelia's Place** (1775 Young Street; 214–651–1775 or 888–651–1775; $95–$115), a bed-and-breakfast newcomer to downtown. The warehouse loft building, which was erected in 1910 and remodeled in

1997, offers six rooms on two levels, all with private baths. Included with room rates are enormous gourmet breakfasts that are guaranteed to fill you for most of the day.

Get settled, and then it's off into the night with the two of you.

DAY ONE: *Evening*

Feeling kind of bluesy? Or perhaps some progressive country moves you? How about some jazz? Of course, it could be that alternative rock/pop strikes your combined fancy. Whichever the case, your destination tonight is Deep Ellum, the edgy, renovated warehouse district on the far east end of downtown Dallas. Here you'll find a hefty selection of nightspots with sensational local and touring acts.

DINNER

There are a number of distinct routes to go on the Deep Ellum dining front. High-end fare is done impressively at the **Green Room** (2715 Elm Street; 214–748–7666; expensive) by the fiercely creative chef, Marc Cassel. Braised pork chilaquiles, frog legs cilantro, horseradish-crusted sea bass, and black mussels in champagne-ginger sauce just scratch the surface at this house of hip-haute cuisine.

Sol's Taco Lounge (2626 Commerce Street; 214–651–7657; inexpensive), a futuristic looking café, offers a simpler menu. Tex-Mex dishes and after-hours breakfasts are specialties.

A romantic choice for dinner is the **Grape** (2808 Greenville Avenue; 214–828–1981; expensive), a lovely wine bistro featuring innovative New American dishes, such as chilled cilantro-avocado soup, tandoori barbecued pork, and black bean cake.

Always appealing, **Nuevo Leon** (2013 Greenville Avenue;

Romance
AT A GLANCE

◆ Get settled into **Amelia's Place** (1775 Young Street; 214–651–1775 or 888–651–1775), bed-and-breakfast, resting up for a big dinner at the **Green Room** (2715 Elm Street; 214–748–7666), a simple Tex-Mex plate at **Sol's Taco Lounge** (2626 Commerce Street; 214–651–7657) or Mediterranean fare with cool jazz at **Sambuca** (2618 Elm Street; 214–744–0820).

◆ You can listen to some blues at **Blue Cat Blues** (2617 Commerce Street; 214–744–2293) or folksy swing at **Sons of Hermann Hall** (3414 Elm Street; 214–747–4422).

◆ On a Thursday you can dance the night away at the **Red Jacket** (3606 Greenville Avenue; 214–823–4747).

214–887–8148; moderate) offers an authentic menu from Mexico's interior and a soothing stucco setting. Best bets are *cabrito* (roasted baby goat) or steaks in fiery chili sauces.

Feeling jazzed about this date? Want to eat some fabulous Mediterranean fare while listening to cool jazz? Head to **Sambuca** (2618 Elm Street; 214–744–0820; no cover), Deep Ellum's sexiest restaurant and nightspot. Dressy and bathed in candlelight, this is a very special place for two. The salmon is divine, as is any pasta with feta cheese. Be sure to have a flaming coffee with dessert.

Steppin' Out with Your Baby

In case you haven't noticed, ballroom dancing is making a mighty comeback—and not with your grandparents. Still one of the most romantic ways to communicate, dancing is also a great calorie-burning activity. If you're looking for just the right dance floor, or if your waltz and fox trot could use some help, here are great places in Dallas to find your fix:

◆ *Dancemasters Ballroom,* 10675 East Northwest Highway; 214–553–5188

◆ *Four Seasons Ballroom,* 4930 Military Parkway; 972–278–3939

◆ *Top Rail Ballroom,* 2110 West Northwest Highway; 214–556–9099.

Does the blues stir your souls? The neighborhood's only full-time blues joint is **Blue Cat Blues** (2617 Commerce Street; 214–744–2293; $6.00–$7.00 cover). Just inside the main entrance is a small beer garden. Through another entrance is a raised stage showcasing acts from Dallas's Andy Timmons and Smokin' Joe Kubek to national names, such as Bobby Patterson, Omar and the Howlers, and Savoy Brown. BCB is usually open Wednesday through Sunday and typically features live music Thursday through Saturday.

Alternative country groups with often folksy sounds, such as the Old 97s and Kelly Willis, are often seen at the Deep Ellum club called **Sons of Hermann Hall** (3414 Elm Street; 214–747–4422; cover $5.00 and up). This place is both saloon and dance hall in a historic building bearing photos of Hank Williams Sr. and other genre founders. Live music is heard Thursday through Saturday, and swing dance lessons are given on Wednesday night.

Deep Ellum's **Gypsy Tea Room** (2548 Elm Street;

214-744-9779) has become one of the area's most popular alter-native-country clubs. Colorful and comfortable and without too much attitude, this venue hosts everything from Dough Sahm & the Last Real Texas Blues Band to the washboard–squeeze box favorites, the Zydeco Kings. Cover charges range from $5.00 to $15.00.

If you like eclectic, you'll be ecstatic at **Club Clearview** (2806 Elm Street; 214-283-5358; covers in the $5.00-$8.00 range). This venue has four clubs under one roof and might present anything from rock-abilly to swing, pop, and rock on a given night. Music groups tend to be young and local. Live music is offered Thursday through Saturday. On Wednesday night it's a retro-disco spoof group called Le Freak.

If you long for the Frank and Dino kinds of tunes and a swanky place to swing your beloved on the dance floor, head over to Greenville Avenue on a Thursday night. That's when Johnny Reno and the Lounge Kings play the **Red Jacket** (3606 Greenville Avenue; 214-823-4747; $5.00 cover), a 60s-style spot featuring martinis, Manhattans, and cigars.

DAY TWO: *Morning*

BRUNCH

You'll probably be sleeping in this morning after the big night you had last night. Then you'll be ready for a hearty brunch at Amelia's. Enjoy a leisurely brunch prepared by Amelia herself, who sounds convincing when she says she is the best cook in three Louisiana parishes. Her enormous feasts are influenced by Cajun and Creole cuisine as seen in biscuits with tomato gravy, fried eggs and fried catfish, and sausage-grits. Amelia always includes fresh fruit, juices, and coffee.

Before heading home, check out the current exhibit at **Deep Ellum Center for the Arts** (2808 Commerce Street; 214-744-2787). One of the more contemporary spaces in town, it has featured such exhibits as "Searching for Form: 4 Artists Using Glass," by members of a group called Hickory Street Hot Glass Factory. The center is open from 10:00 am. to 6:00 P.M. Tuesday through Saturday.

Boot-Scootin' and Singin' the Blues

FORT WORTH'S NIGHTLIFE

OR TWO DECADES FORT WORTH HAS LAID CLAIM to the "world's largest honky tonk," that mammoth dance hall known as Billy Bob's Texas. Anchoring one corner of the Stockyards National Historic District, Billy Bob's is just one nightspot that helps keep Fort Worth high on the list of stops for touring country, rhythm and blues, jazz, and alternative music performers.

But that's not to say that Cowtown is mostly about cowboy music. There are several solid stages around town hosting performers of every musical persuasion. This itinerary is designed to help the two of you map out the evening that's perfect for your tastes.

PRACTICAL NOTES: The places in the Stockyards are all within walking distance of each other. For other destinations, you'll need to drive. All night spots are casual, meaning jeans are OK.

DAY ONE: *Afternoon*

Check into **Miss Molly's** (109½ West Exchange Avenue; 817–626–1522; $75–$170), a turn-of-the-century hotel that once operated as a bordello. Decorated in period style the charming spot has seven rooms that share baths and a suite with its own bathroom. A full breakfast and parking are included in the room rates.

Another lodging option is the **Stockyards Hotel** (109 East Exchange Avenue; 817–625–6427; $120–$350), a 52-room inn occupying the historic Thannisch Block Building, built in 1907. Rooms are decorated in varying period motifs and include suites with Jacuzzis. On the ground floor there's a rollicking bar and a steak restaurant.

DAY TWO: *Evening*

DINNER

A dining-and-dancing night in the Stockyards would likely begin with dinner at **H3 Ranch**, (105 East Exchange Avenue; 817–624–1246; moderate). Attached to the Stockyards Hotel, it is a cozy, comfortable steak joint with excellent smoked pork ribs as well as flame-broiled sirloin and rainbow trout.

The other must-go spot in the Stockyards is the **White Elephant Saloon** (106 East Exchange Avenue; 817–624–1887; cover $3.00 and up). You immediately appreciate the long, wooden bar with a brass foot rail, and the old-fashioned painting behind the bar of a reclining woman—er, elephant. The White Elephant— which *Esquire* magazine once named one of the nation's best 100 bars—has live local music every night, pool tables, dartboards, and a small dance floor. From April through October, an adjacent beer garden is open. Performers are typically regionally known folks such as Brian Gallagher, Michael Cote, Bret Graham, George Norris, and the Desert Outlaw Band.

Then it's around the corner to **Billy Bob's Texas** (2520 Rodeo Plaza; 817–624–7117; cover $5.00 and up), where headliners might include

Romance
AT A GLANCE

◆ Leave your bags at **Miss Molly's** (109 ½ West Exchange Avenue; 817–626–1522), and then head over to **H3 Ranch** (105 East Exchange Avenue; 817–624–1246) for a steak dinner.

◆ Dance the night away at the **White Elephant Saloon** (106 East Exchange Avenue; 817–624–1887) or **Billy Bob's Texas** (2520 Rodeo Plaza; 817–624–7117).

◆ Downtown options include tacos and margaritas at **Cabo Mix-Mex Grill** (115 West Second Street; 817–336–8646), followed by jazz and blues at **Caravan of Dreams** (312 Houston Street; 817–877–3000).

Willie Nelson, LeAnn Rimes, Trisha Yearwood, Robert Earl Keen, Jerry Jeff Walker, Gary Stewart, Mark Chestnut, Charlie Daniels, Merle Haggard, David Alan Coe, Roomful of Blues, or others. There's live music nightly.

Bailamos
—Let's Dance!

Possibly the sexiest dancing around is that done to a Latino beat. Fortunately for the two of you, El Paraiso Latin Club (1363 West Euless Boulevard in Euless; 817–267–3434) is an inviting Caribbean-flavored nightspot with salsa and merengue music and free dance lessons on Friday and Sunday evenings. Check on the frequent salsa dance contests, usually held on Saturday nights. Reach this club by driving west from Fort Worth via Highway 183 and exiting Euless Main Street. Go south to West Euless Boulevard.

Whether you know the headliner's work, you'll both get a kick out of the place. In addition to forty bars and a Texas-size dance floor, there's live bull riding every Friday and Saturday night, a general store selling all sorts of gifts, and one of the Skoal Bandit NASCAR cars on display. Don't know how to two-step? Free dance lessons are offered on Thursday night.

In downtown Fort Worth the nightclub of choice is **Caravan of Dreams** (312 Houston Street; 817–877–3000; cover $10–$20 and up). This avant garde venue hosts everyone from Wynton Marsalis and Danny Wright to John Mayall and the Old 97s—which is to say, it's a stage of many styles with a soothing, romantic setting.

Also downtown is **Flying Saucer Draught Emporium** (111 East Fourth Street; 817–336–7468), a cozy brew pub housed inside one of the city's oldest and most charming brick buildings. Every evening guitarists play on the patio, where picnic tables provide seating. There's no cover charge.

Nearby nibbling for Caravan-goers includes **Cabo Mix-Mex Grill** (115 West Second Street; 817–336–8646; inexpensive), a high-tech taco bar with excellent shrimp quesadillas, grilled yellowfin tuna sandwiches, and premium margaritas made with Grand Marnier.

Just west of downtown are two more worthwhile venues for live music lovers. First, there's **J&J Blues Bar** (937 Woodward Street; 817–870–2337; cover $4.00-$10.00), a longtime favorite for blues, jazz, and the like. The no-frills setting is little more than a warehouse, but the music will get your toes tapping. Look for performers such as Bugs Henderson, Ezra Charles, the Keller Brothers, Oreo Blue, and the Shadowcasters.

For something in a cozier setting, head to **Sardine's** (3410 Camp Bowie Boulevard; 817–332–9937), a dark little Italian bistro in the Cultural District where good jazz is served up nightly. A trio plays Tuesday through Saturday, and a pianist does a solo stint on Sunday and Monday nights after 8:00 P.M. There's no cover charge.

If the two of you are interested in the newest local alternative rock acts and like hanging out with a beer-guzzling college crowd, head right down to the **Wreck Room** (3208 West Seventh Street; 817–870–4900; $5.00 cover). Somebody's living room furniture is there for lounging in the front, pool tables are in back, and there's a freaky CD jukebox to survey when bands aren't playing. Acts here include Slow Roosevelt, Fixture, and Jibe.

If you want a late-night snack in the vicinity of J&J Blues Bar or the Wreck Room, try the **J&J Oyster Bar** (612 University Drive; 817–335–2756; inexpensive), a direct relation to the aforementioned bar. This ultracasual spot in a converted Taco Bell offers sensational fried oysters, shrimp, and scallops, as well as excellent oysters on the half shell, and you-peel-'em jumbo shrimp.

Another delicious option for munchies in the area is **Loredo's** (601 North Side Drive; 817–624–3915; inexpensive). This is more authentic Mexican than Tex-Mex, with sumptuous dishes including *carne asada* (steak simmered in red chile sauce) and *queso flameado* (flash-grilled cheese loaded with Mexican sausage).

DAY THREE: *Morning*

BREAKFAST

Sleep in, and then enjoy a leisurely breakfast. If you're staying at Miss Molly's and it's the weekend, your buffet will include an egg casserole that incorporates either sausage or green chiles, French toast, sausage patties, and biscuits. The weekday buffet offers homemade specialty breads, coffee cake, muffins, and fresh seasonal fruits.

Before heading home, rummage through the goodies at **Half-Price Books, Records and Magazines** (6912 Ridgmar Meadow Road;

817-732-4111). From downtown drive west on I-30, exit at Green Oaks Boulevard, and turn right (north). Watch for Ridgmar Meadow on your left.

W*i*n*i*ng a*n*d D*i*n*i*ng

PLEASURE FOR THE PALATE IN DALLAS/FORT WORTH

ERTAINLY A LATE BLOOMER AMONG AMERICA'S trend-setting urban areas, the Dallas–Fort Worth Metroplex is fast becoming a wonderfully diverse cuisine center. Thanks to a wealth of ethnic groups expanding here, diners with adventurous palates are finding their globe-trotting options multiplying almost daily.

And as Texas has risen to third place in the nation's wine production—behind California and New York—the Dallas–Fort Worth area has grown to be a place where wine is treasured.

This itinerary maps out two ways to spend a palate-pampering day, first in Dallas and then in and around Fort Worth. Do these on consecutive days only if you think your stomach and taste buds can handle it.

Dine on Middle Eastern delicacies at **Hedary's** (3308 Fairfield Avenue; 817–731–6961) or original Mexican seafood treasures at **La Playa Maya** (3200 Hemphill Street; 817–924–0698).

DAY ONE: *Afternoon*

Before heading to lunch, check into the **Adam's Mark Hotel** (400 North Olive Street; 214–922–8000; $89–$169), a large (505 rooms) and luxurious hotel that opened in 1998 in the historic Southland Center.

If the two of you would like to tour around in style, and not have to worry about drinking, then leave the driving to someone experienced. One limousine service to consider is **ExecuCar Sedan Service** (817–329–2002), a company that provides a Lincoln Town Car and driver for $38 per hour, with a two-hour minimum. For sheer extravagance and indulgence, call **First Limousine Service** (214–559–4733), a stretch-limo outfit that charges $65 per hour, with a four-hour minimum.

Romance
AT A GLANCE

◆ *In Dallas, check in at the* **Adam's Mark Hotel** *(400 North Olive Street; 214–922–8000) and pick up the limousine that will take the two of you touring.*

◆ *Feast on Salvadoran specialties for lunch at* **Gloria's** *(600 West Davis Street; 214–948–3672), taste excellent wines at* **Marty's** *(3316 Oak Lawn Avenue; 214–526–4070), and for dinner go for Moroccan fare at* **Marrakesh** *(5027 Lovers Lane; 214–357–4101; moderate), Ethiopian cuisine at* **Queen of Sheba** *(3527 McKinney Avenue; 214–521–0491), Japanese delights at* **Tei Tei Robata Bar** *(2906 Henderson Avenue; 214–828–2400) or tapas at* **Café Madrid** *(4501 Travis Avenue; 214–528–1731).*

◆ *In Fort Worth, sample the wines at the* **Grape Escape** *(500 Commerce Street; 817–336–9463); in Dallas,* **Marty's** *(3316 Oak Lawn Avenue; 214–526–4070).*

◆ *Dine on Middle Eastern delicacies at* **Hedary's** *(3308 Fairfield Avenue 817–731–6961) or original Mexican seafood treasures at* **La Playa Maya** *(3200 Hemphill Street; 817–924–0698).*

LUNCH

For some of the best Latin American fare ever, head to **Gloria's** (600 West Davis Street; 214–948–3672; inexpensive). For years, this favorite in the Oak Cliff neighborhood has brought happiness to tummies with Salvadoran specialties. Be sure to have the creamy black beans, cheesy *pupusas* (like cheese-filled corn pancakes), thick, steamy tamals, and sweet, fried plantains (like banana slices) all delivered by the cheerful waitstaff. Lots of neighborhood regulars swear by the hangover-busting bloody Marys here.

WINE TASTING

Whether you're wine novices or afficionados, the place for tasting in Dallas is **Marty's** (3316 Oak Lawn Avenue; 214–526–4070). For many years this exclusive Oak Lawn liquor store was known for spirits and a few gourmet food items. Now it's repositioned itself with an extensive gourmet take-out shop and a sensational wine shop. You can sample several wines in tiny servings to figure out which you'd most like to take with you. Pick a couple of favorites and head back to the hotel to do some further sampling in private.

DAY ONE: *Evening*

When the two of you are ready to venture out again, try something a little more exotic than regular meat and potatoes for dinner. Two of your choices are appropriately located on Lovers Lane.

DINNER

If Middle Eastern cuisine holds appeal for you two tonight, try **Marrakesh** (5027 Lovers Lane, 214–357–4101; moderate), a dark, vibrant room with closely placed tables. Devoted fans enjoy hearty, gutsy Moroccan dishes that feature couscous, lamb, salmon, and shrimp. Mint tea is a delight, too, as is the belly dancing. Open for dinner only.

Another intimate option is **Café Istanbul** (5450 West Lovers Lane; 214–902–0919), a serene spot with a warm interior of stucco and woods where excellent Middle Eastern dishes include grilled beef and fish, hummus, eggplant dip, and lemony salads. Open for dinner only.

If you've never tried Ethiopian cuisine, **Queen of Sheba** (3527 McKinney Avenue; 214–521–0491; moderate) will surely impress. Get a sampler platter that offers small portions of numerous spicy beef, lamb, chicken, and fresh vegetable dishes. What's fun is that you don't use utensils; instead, pinch bits of food with the traditional Ethiopian steamed flat bread called *injera*. Open for lunch and dinner.

Also, winners of the annual Dallas Wine Competition are sampled around the area at seminars and dinners in late April and early May. For details, call 214–887–9915.

A sumptuous Japanese dining experience is found at **Tei Tei Robata Bar** (2906 Henderson Avenue; 214–828–2400; expensive), which feels and looks much more like Vancouver than Dallas. A sleek, nouveau-Asian room washed in warm woods offers a lengthy menu of cool sashimi, served in bowls of crushed ice, while delightful grilled fish and $100 Kobe steaks are cooked over oak fires. Both the sake and the service are excellent as well. Open for dinner only.

For sushi, sashimi, yakitori, and gyoza presented in an especially stylish and intimate setting, head to **Teppo** (2014 Greenville Avenue; 214–826–8989; expensive). Contemporary surroundings feature decor combining brushed chrome, stone, and wood; choose between counter seating—where you'll watch sushi chefs and grill chefs at work—or tables for quiet talk over dinner. Open for dinner only.

Delicious food, reasonably priced wines, and chummy atmosphere are the reasons for a decade of popularity at **Café Madrid** (4501 Travis Avenue; 214–528–1731; moderate), Dallas's first tapas restaurant. Potato omelettes, calamari, manchega cheese, grilled steak, and marinated red bell peppers are our favorite tapas.

DAY TWO: *Morning*

BREAKFAST

Sleep in and then have a leisurely breakfast at your hotel. Over a final cup of coffee, decide whether your stomachs are ready for another day of epicurean delights.

If you're ready for a second day of wining and dining, head on into Fort Worth.

LUNCH

Until you've experienced a therapeutic bowl of *pho* at **Phuong** (4045 East Belknap Street in Haltom City; 817–831–2010; inexpensive), you can't possibly relate to those who love it with a passion. This Vietnamese specialty is typically made with rice noodles, chicken or beef, and any number of Asian vegetables, such as crunchy sprouts, cilantro stems and leaves, green onion, and fresh jalapeno or serrano chiles. (Haltom City is on Fort Worth's northeast corner; find it by traveling north on Beach Street from Highway 183.)

Another interesting lunch venue is **Filipiniana Bakeshop and Café** (209 Bedford Road in Bedford; 817–282–0655; inexpensive), a Filipino diner in Northeast Tarrant County. Among satisfying, soothing dishes are fish nuggets in hot-sour soup, puffy rolls filled with barbecued pork or tropical shrimp, and stir-fry dishes with chicken or

More Wining and Dining

On Saturdays in spring and fall, you and your beloved can take instruction from the most noted and popular chefs in the Dallas–Fort Worth area. Thanks to the Dallas chapter of the American Institute of Wine and Food, cooking classes with these local celebrities are taught in the Market Resource Kitchen of the Dallas Farmers Market (1010 South Pearl Street; 214–939–2808). Classes fill up well in advance, so call ahead for schedules and prices.

pork. (Find this restaurant by traveling southwest from Highway 121 on Bedford Road.)

WINE TASTING

Possibly the best wine-experimenting opportunities in all the Metroplex are found in downtown Fort Worth at the **Grape Escape** (500 Commerce Street; 817–336–9463; moderate), a petite French bistro and tasting room. The unique offerings here are flights of wine—that is, five 1.5-ounce samples of a group of wines—for roughly $5.00 to $15.00. From a lengthy menu, you may choose, for example, reds from the Rhone Valley or syrahs from the Russian River Valley. The servers are extremely helpful and will give opinions if you ask; there's a limited food menu to pair with your flights, consisting of miniature pizzas, cheeses, olives, pâtés, and such.

If you're willing to go a bit farther afield, Grapevine, a once-sleepy town in Northeast Tarrant County—about a 25-minute northeast drive from Fort Worth—is home to four winery tasting rooms. The most scenic is **La Buena Vida** (416 East College Street; 817–481–9463), also the oldest of the North Texas wineries. A $7.00 (per-person) sampling includes tastes of four wines and a keepsake glass. While you're there, enjoy the charming waterfall setting in the vine-covered arbors at La Buena Vida's historic district setting. Tastings are offered from 10:00 A.M. until 4:30 P.M., Monday through Saturday, and from noon until 4:30 P.M. on Sunday.

DINNER

In the 1970s, a Lebanese family immigrated to Texas and called their restaurant "Lebanese Pizza," thinking that the word *pizza* meant *"restaurant."* Their Fort Worth clientele fell in love with the food, and **Hedary's** (3308 Fairfield Avenue; 817–731–6961; moderate) has expanded many times. The best dishes are the kafta, falafel, rib eye sandwich, lamb kabobs, lemony roasted chicken—and now pizza. For vegetable lovers, the *maza* (appetizer) plate offers a dozen small, cold dishes of everything from hummus, tabouli, and eggplant dip to cucumber-yogurt dip and marinated vegetables. Service can be slow and the decor is rather plain, but the food is reliably excellent.

For those craving spicier flavors, **La Playa Maya** (3200 Hemphill Street; 817–924–0698; inexpensive) is sure to please. This authentic Mexican seafood spot does a bang-up job with shrimp, octopus, squid, or whitefish salads in chili-enriched cocktail sauce, as well as grilled shrimp *diablo*—that's devilishly spicy, for you gringos. As charming as the kind servers is the setting inside a renovated older home. The margaritas and beer will help cool your burning lips.

Acquisitions

A TWOSOME'S GUIDE TO COLLECTING AND DECORATING

B Y SPENDING ABOUT FORTY-EIGHT HOURS looking around Dallas and Fort Worth, the two of you will come to understand why the area has become well known throughout the Southwest for art collecting and shopping.

To revel in their wealth of art spaces, Dallas and Fort Worth have each begun a Gallery Night, an evening in September on which thousands of novice and serious art fans prowl the galleries and sip wine in what's become two phenomenal progressive parties. And because the two events often occur on the same night, many patrons cross the 30-mile distance between Dallas and Fort Worth to lap up all the art they can in one evening.

You can create a gallery crawl for two, stopping also in any of the dozens of artful, upscale specialty stores that share neighborhoods with the galleries. It's worth noting that Dallas boasts more shopping square footage than even Manhattan. Thanks to Herbert Marcus Sr. and his sister and brother-in-law, Carrie and Al Neiman, Dallas came to the forefront of the national fashion scene when Neiman Marcus, an "exclusive woman's ready-to-wear store," opened in Dallas in 1907.

This itinerary is designed to allow you a full day exploring each of the city's best art and shopping. Just remember to wear your most comfortable shoes and bring plenty of credit cards. And keep in mind, many galleries are closed on Sunday and Monday.

ITINERARY 9

Two days and one night

63

DAY ONE: *Morning*

Check into **the Adolphus Hotel** (1321 Commerce Street; 214-742-8200 or 800-221-9083; $160 and up), easily one of the most elegant hotels in the Southwest. Built in 1912 by beer baron Adolphus Busch, this gorgeous, twenty-two-floor hotel has lovely rooms and suites, a gift shop, a beauty shop, a barber shop, and the French Room, which is always at the top of national restaurant surveys.

If the two of you would prefer something less expensive, try the **Courtyard by Marriott** (2150 Market Center Boulevard at Stemmons Freeway; 800-321-2211; $99-109). This chain is designed primarily for business travelers, so the rooms are generally well appointed. You may be able to get a good deal on a weekend rate, when many of the business people have gone home and there are empty rooms to fill.

Drop your bags, put on those pairs of comfy shoes, and head to the Cedar Springs-McKinney area of galleries found within gracious older homes and buildings in a lovely, shaded neighborhood now referred to as Uptown.

One of the top galleries in all the Southwest is **Gerald Peters Gallery** (2913 Fairmount Street; 214-969-9410), which is but a three-minute drive (provided there's no traffic) from the Adolphus. Here you'll find work by such contemporary creators as Dallas painter and sculptor David Bates. Sometimes the Peters surprises the old guard with bizarre offerings, such as a Gallery Night performance art event by Texas artist Trenton Hancock, who slept and simulated bodily functions for a couple of hours. The gallery typically is open from noon to 6:00 P.M. Monday through Friday and noon to 5:00 P.M. Saturday.

A short walk away is **William E. Johnson Fine Art** (2525 Fairmount Street; 214-871-1197), which offers seventeenth- through twentieth-century works from American, European, and early Texas artists. It's open from 10:00 A.M. to 5:00 P.M. Tuesday through Friday and noon to 4:30 P.M. Saturday.

Just a block down is **David Dike Fine Art** (2613 Fairmount Street; 214-720-4044). There you'll find paintings from the nineteenth- and early-twentieth-century periods, by American and European artists. There's an emphasis here on Texas Regionalism. It's open from 10:00 A.M. to 5:00 P.M. Monday through Friday and 11:00 A.M. to 5:00 P.M. Saturday.

If you're bibliophiles, you will love **Antiquarian of Dallas** (2609

Routh Street; 214–754–0705), a place for rare and first-edition books, Texana, leather bindings, books on the Civil War and both World Wars, and black history books. You can't miss it—it's right across the street from the Hard Rock Café. It's open from 10:00 A.M. to 5:00 P.M. Monday through Saturday.

DAY ONE: *Afternoon*

LUNCH

This area is packed with great places to eat. For excellent Indian fare in a surprisingly sunny setting, try **Bombay Cricket Club** (2508 Maple Avenue, 214–871–1333; moderate), which is spread along the first floor of a cheery Victorian house. The curry and tandoori dishes are wonderful.

For solid seafood gumbo, barbecued shrimp, and broiled fish head to **S&D Oyster Company** (2701 McKinney Avenue; 214–880–0111; inexpensive). A wonderfully relaxing spot and hugely popular for the past twenty years, S&D will fortify you for more exploring.

A few doors from S&D, you'll find **Gallery Two-O-Nine** (2714 McKinney Avenue; 214–871–9209) in a romantic Victorian building. This Uptown gallery exhibits traditional and contemporary original art by sculptors and painters including David Spence, Eliseo, Desmond O'Hagan, Patrick Coffaro, David Sprague, and Ralph Cooper. It's open daily, but hours vary.

Engaged couples and newlyweds are especially fond of **Crate & Barrel,** which has an enormous, two-story building at the intersection of McKinney and Knox Streets. Register for wedding gifts while

Romance

AT A GLANCE

◆ Check into the **Adolphus Hotel** (1321 Commerce Street; 214–742–8200 or 800–221–9083) or the **Courtyard by Marriott** (2150 Market Center Boulevard; 800–321–2211) and then head to the Uptown neighborhood art spaces, such as **Gerald Peters Gallery** (2913 Fairmount Street; 214–969–9410).

◆ Have lunch nearby at either **Bombay Cricket Club** (2508 Maple Avenue; 214–871–1333) or **S&D Oyster Company** (2701 McKinney Avenue; 214–880–0111) and then browse through more area galleries, such as **Gallery Two-O-Nine** (2714 McKinney Avenue; 214–871–9209).

◆ End your day with dinner at the art-filled **Kathleen's Art Café** (4424 Lovers Lane; 214–691–2355).

you're here, then take an hour to review your purchases over a Texas martini (a handmade margarita) at **Chuy's** (4544 McKinney Avenue; 214–559–2489; inexpensive). An upbeat Mexican restaurant with a wildly colorful interior, Chuy's offers excellent chips and salsa, too.

If you're both bitten by the shopping bug, head north on Preston Road then go left on Lovers Lane. Continue down Lovers Lane a few blocks, then watch on the left for a store called **Cadeaux** (4506 Lovers Lane; 214–363–4500), specializing in eighteenth- and nineteenth-century French furniture and decorative arts. Stop in also at **Anteks** (5814 Lovers Lane at Lomo Alto Avenue; 214–528–5567), the place for furniture and home decor accessories befitting a ranch or lodge look. Antler chandeliers, hand-hewn beds and armoires, and rustic tablewares abound.

DAY ONE: *Evening*

DINNER

Before heading back downtown share a feast together at **Kathleen's Art Café** (4424 Lovers Lane; 214–691–2355; moderate). Here you'll find a blend of fashionable cafe and reliable, creatively wrought foods in a bistro decorated with paintings by local artists. While deciding if you'd like to buy any of the artworks, you'll feast on black bean ravioli in chili-laced cream sauce with grilled chicken, exotically decorated salads, pan-seared sea bass, and desserts that are worth every bit of guilt found in each bite.

Back at the Adolphus have a margarita in the bar and review your day. You'll want to rest up after all that spending—especially with more of the same in Fort Worth tomorrow.

DAY TWO: *Morning*

BREAKFAST

Have coffee and juice at your hotel, then check out and head to Fort Worth (thirty minutes due west on Interstate 30, providing there's little traffic) for one of the best breakfasts either of you has ever enjoyed. It's found at **Jubilee Café** (2736 West Seventh Street; 817–332–4568; inexpensive), a simple diner with loads of good food and friendly service near the Cultural District. Your feast options include buckwheat pancakes (with or without blueberries); Mrs. Tilly's eggs, which are eggs scrambled with tortilla chips, tomatoes, and onions; and outstanding breakfast tacos, which are giant flour tortillas packed with a

A Night Is Born

The origin of Fort Worth's Gallery Night, now more than twenty years old, is traced to Bill and Pam Campbell, a husband-and-wife team who ran a busy custom-framing business to keep them alive while their 1970s-born art gallery—William Campbell Contemporary Art—was emerging. Their perseverance, coupled with their faith in, and love of, art, eventually gave rise to the Fort Worth Art Dealers Association, bringing together area galleries, private dealers, museums, churches, and universities to feature local, regional, and national artists. And in due course, the pair founded Gallery Night in 1979. Fort Worth thanks them.

combination you choose from a list of eggs, black beans, big chunks of potato, bacon, sausage, and cheese.

If you've a shared passion for contemporary art, start your gallery touring at **Evelyn Siegel Gallery Inc.** (3700 West Seventh Street, 817–731–6412), known for contemporary and postmodern work in various media. A typical exhibit was one that featured work by more than thirty ceramic artists. It's open Monday through Friday from 11:00 A.M. to 5:00 P.M. and Saturday from 11:00 A.M. to 4:00 P.M.

For twosomes who enjoy Texas art, a good place to browse is 2 blocks away, **Edmund Craig Gallery** (3550-C West Seventh Street; 817–732–6663). Rather new, the gallery's first show featured the work of twelve regional Texas painters, sculptors, and photographers, including the black-and-white photos of Austin photojournalist Jacquelyn Torbert and Fort Worth artist Randy Phillips. This gallery's hours are 10:00 A.M. to 5:00 P.M. Tuesday through Friday and 11:00 A.M. to 3:00 P.M. Saturday.

A block away find Chicotsky's shopping center, new home to **Carol Henderson Gallery/Artenergies** (3409 West Seventh Street; 817–737–9910). Heavy on contemporary art, with exhibits featuring mixed media works and sculptures, featured artists have included Wayne McKinzie and Marton Varo.

DAY TWO: *Afternoon*

LUNCH

Are you two a pair in search of a leisurely, lavish lunch with wine? Then you'll love **Michaels** (3413 West Seventh Street; 817–877–3413; moderate), next door to Carol Henderson/Artenergies. Washed in tones of cream and tan with a stone floor, the dining room is comfortable and elegant, without being dressy. Dishes range from roasted chicken pizza to pastas and steaks in roasted chili sauces.

Now browse in two wonderful stores, where you can combine wish lists for your home. Next door to Michaels is **Strings** (3425 West Seventh Street; 817–336–8042) a thoughtfully stocked shop with exotic, contemporary lines in lamps and chairs, fabulous martini pitchers and salad bowls, as well as accessories like clocks and picture frames.

A few doors down is **The Market** (3429 West Seventh Street; 817–334–0330), a gorgeous store brimming with classic style in sofa pillows, huge and ornate mirrors, crystal stemware, extravagant chandeliers, and fabrics for that chair you both keep talking about re-covering.

Head west just a few blocks on Camp Bowie Boulevard, stopping at a pair of interesting shops. **Prairie Rose** (3404 Camp Bowie Boulevard; 817–332–4369) and **Kabin Fever** (3408 Camp Bowie Boulevard; 817–338–1912) are great places to find small gift items like picture frames and books, as well as fabulous furniture and decor accessories—all in a Western-lodge-ranch theme.

Continuing west, have a look inside **Out West Down South** (4624 Camp Bowie Boulevard; 817–732–3336). If you're in the market for hand-hewn furniture from Mexico, this is the place. Huge armoires, bookcases, chests, and beds pack the store and are topped with rustic candlesticks, lamps, handwoven Mexican blankets, and Indian gourds. Smaller gift items include American pewter pieces, including spoon rests, key racks, and measuring spoons.

Next door **Leigh-Boyd** (4632 Camp Bowie Boulevard; 817–738–3705) is a wonderful shop, chockablock full of home interior goodies. Silver bud vases, crystal pitchers, antique mirrors, bone picture frames, and thousands of other beautiful items offer a visual feast.

Another few blocks west is **William Campbell Contemporary Art** (4935 Byers Avenue; 817–737–9566), where it's not unusual to find sixty artists showcased in a single show. Those known well to this area have included Ed and Linda Blackburn, Stuart Gentling, J. T. Grant, Luis Jimenez, and Richard Thompson. Other featured artists have included Bruce Webb, an art dealer whose colorful paintings on corrugated steel and salvaged wood indicate his passion for folk art and unconventional people; David Keens, a teacher at the University of Texas at Arlington, whose glass art resembles Venetian glass, with its threads of precious metals; and Japanese-born artist Jun Kaneko, creator of abstract and minimalist-motivated clay works that have human-head shapes as large as 6 feet in diameter.

William Campbell is also the place to find works by Francis X. Tolbert II, the well-known Texas artist whose paintings, drawings, and ceramics frequently present people in caricature-ish fashion. Tolbert has been known, however, to offer landscapes with animals and Texas ranch scenes, lavished with his trademark curving lines and vivid colors.

William Campbell Contemporary Art is open Tuesday through Friday from 10:00 A.M. to 5:00 P.M. and Saturday from 11:00 A.M. to 4:00 P.M.

FOR MORE ROMANCE

In Dallas find still more contemporary European art at **Ivanffy & Uhler Gallery** (4623 West Lovers Lane; 214–350–3500), a space exhibiting paintings, drawings, and sculpture. It's open Tuesday through Saturday from 10:00 A.M. to 6:00 P.M. and Sunday from 1:00 to 6:00 P.M.

In the same neighborhood find **Photographic Archives Lab & Library** (5117 Lovers Lane; 214–352–3167). An excellent small gallery, this one features exhibits from contemporary photographers. Hours here are 10:00 A.M. to 5:00 P.M. Thursday through Sunday.

Because there are few gifts more romantic than antique silver pieces, you'll want to wander through **Lovers Lane Antique Market** (5001 West Lovers Lane; 214–351–5656). Look here for antique Victorian napkin rings, made of sterling and silverplate, that create a gorgeous table setting.

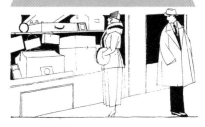

Wheeling and Dealing
Treasure Hunting in the Metroplex

HERE'S A SAYING ABOUT ONE PERSON'S TRASH being another's treasure, or something like that. If the two of you happen to be people who adore sifting through junk at flea markets to find jewels, then you're bound to be soul mates.

This itinerary outlines a fairly succinct trip through the three primary bargain-hunting grounds in the greater Dallas–Fort Worth metro area. Plan to go early and stay long, in order to make good deals on the best finds. Happy hunting.

PRACTICAL NOTE: Some places accept credit cards and local checks, but you're wise to take plenty of cash.

DAY ONE: *Morning*

BREAKFAST

If you're starting out from Dallas, have breakfast en route at **Beckley Grill** (1619 North Beckley Road; 214–948–8484; inexpensive), a fast and friendly coffee shop with good egg-and-bacon dishes, as well as biscuits and hash browns.

If you're bound from Fort Worth, find fortification at **Paris Coffee Shop** (704 West Magnolia Avenue; 817–335–2041; inexpensive), a favorite spot since 1930 for biscuits and gravy, pancakes, and fried eggs.

Head to **Traders Village**, right between Dallas and Fort Worth in Grand Prairie (2602 Mayfield Road; 972–647–2331; free), a gigantic flea market that's quickly approaching its thirtieth birthday. Spreading over 106 acres, Traders Village hosts upwards of 1,600 dealers who set up shop in open lots, beneath covered sheds, and inside enclosed buildings. Open every weekend, crowds numbering up to 60,000 shoppers descend upon Traders Village every weekend in search of antique beds and mirrors, used furniture, imported home furnishings, produce, hubcaps, stereos, clothes, and jewelry.

Be prepared to find some cheap schlock, too, as well as things you can pick up just as easily at Target or another discount department store. Still, it's a lot of fun to browse and people watch, as well as ride the antique carousel and snack on some of the sinful treats, such as cinnamon rolls and corny dogs (as corn dogs are called in Texas).

Special events—such as the Prairie Dog Chili Cook-off in early April and the National Championship Indian Pow Wow on the weekend after Labor Day—mean even larger crowds, so plan accordingly. Traders Village is open every Saturday and Sunday from 8:00 A.M. until dusk. Parking is $2.00.

Romance

AT A GLANCE

◆ *Ply for bargains at **Traders Village** (2602 Mayfield Road in Grand Prairie; 972–647–2331), followed by lunch at **Mariano's** (2614 Majesty Drive in Arlington; 817–640–5118).*

◆ *Wind up the day with deals at **Cattle Barn Flea Market** (3401 Burnett-Tandy Drive in Fort Worth; 817–473–0505), celebrating over steaks at **Hoffbrau** (1712 South University Drive in Fort Worth; 817–870–1952).*

DAY ONE: *Afternoon*

LUNCH

If you didn't eat your fill and you're ready to mark your way west to the next flea market, head north from Traders Village on Highway 360 toward Interstate 30. Watch on the east access road on Highway 360 for **Mariano's** (2614 Majesty Drive in Arlington; 817–640–5118; inexpensive), a local hangout with robust Mexican lunches and dinners. Sizzling chicken and steak fajitas are good bets, as are the huge enchilada dinners. The house specialty is a long menu of margaritas in a rainbow of flavors.

☆ther Bargain-Hunting Spots

*If the weather isn't as conducive to flea marketing as you'd like, think about heading to one of the popular antiques malls in the Dallas–Fort Worth area. These are indoors, of course, with appropriate air-conditioning and heating, and many of the dealers found their goods at flea markets and garage sales. The biggest such place in Fort Worth is **Montgomery Street Antique Mall** (2601 Montgomery Street; 817–735–9685), near the Cultural District. In Dallas, your best bet is **Love Field Antique Mall** (Cedar Springs Road at Mockingbird Lane; 214–357–6500).*

If you're both adventurous and enjoy plenty of driving around, look in the classified ads on Saturday and Sunday in the Dallas Morning News *and the* Fort Worth Star-Telegram *for garage sales. To find sales in the more upscale neighborhoods, look for zip codes 75205, 75225, 75209, and 75220 in Dallas and 76107, 76116, 76109, and 76110 in Fort Worth.*

After lunch, continue north on Highway 360 a mile or two until you reach Interstate 30, which you'll take west to Fort Worth and the **Cattle Barn Flea Market** (3401 Burnett-Tandy Drive; 817–473–0505; free). Tucked inside the cattle barns at the Will Rogers complex in the Cultural District, this twenty-year-old market pulls in around 100 dealers in summer months and around 150 in cooler weather. This is a good place to look for vintage clothing and costume jewelry, used books, a few antiques, guns, collectible dishes and glassware, as well as funky goods like lunch boxes, lamps, and albums.

Rummage to your hearts' content between 8:00 A.M. and 5:00 P.M. Saturday and from 9:00 A.M. to 4:00 P.M. Sunday. Keep in mind, however, that there's no flea market here during the Fort Worth Stock Show and Rodeo, which lasts from the third weekend in January through the first weekend in February.

DAY ONE: *Evening*

Check into the **Courtyard by Marriott** (3150 Riverfront Drive; 817–335–1300; $95 and up), a pleasant, clean lodging about a mile south of Fort Worth's Cultural District via University Drive. There's a heated swimming pool, and some rooms have refrigerators.

DINNER

Walk next door to **Hoffbrau** (1712 South University Drive; 817–870–1952; moderate) for a Texas-size dinner to celebrate your shopping finds. Essentially unchanged from its Austin debut in the early 1970s, Hoffbrau is an extra-casual steak spot where shorts, T-shirts, and sandals are most appropriate. Get the T-bone pan-fried in butter and lemon, or the mesquite-grilled quail or shrimp, all to be washed down with a giant, frosty schooner of Shiner Bock beer.

DAY TWO: *Morning*

BREAKFAST

Fortify yourselves for the big bargain hunting ahead with a big stack of pancakes at **Ol' South Pancake House** (1507 South University Drive; 817–336–0311; inexpensive), right across University Drive from the Courtyard. Known for its diverse breakfast menu as well as its twenty-four-hour crowds, Ol' South is well loved for its pecan waffles, blueberry pancakes, and its Dutch Babies, thin crepes that are dressed with powdered sugar and lemon at your table by the expert staff.

After breakfast, head east on Interstate 30 for a couple of miles, turning north on Interstate 35. About 30 miles ahead is Denton and the **380 Flea Market** (4200 East University Drive/Highway 380; 940–566–5060; free.)

This weekend flea market offers goods from up to 250 dealers, who set up shop in covered sheds, in outdoor stalls, and from the tailgates of their pickup trucks. Goods are primarily garage-sale-type stuff, from furniture and clothes to antiques and electronics—but livestock is sold here, too. The 380 is open on Saturday and Sunday from sunup to sundown; note that Sunday is typically the busier of the two days.

After you've found all your treasures, head home to figure out what to do with it all.

Active
Amour

Getting to First Base
BASEBALL IN ARLINGTON

NLY THE UNENLIGHTENED FAIL TO UNDERSTAND the inherent romance in baseball. It's a complex game of skill and intuition, played at a leisurely pace under the big, open sky, usually in beautiful weather. And in Texas, the very best place to share your enjoyment of the game is at the Ballpark in Arlington—between Dallas and Fort Worth—where the two of you can see the Texas Rangers play some major-league ball.

Opened in 1995, this 49,292-seat stadium is a spectacular creation of red brick and granite with a facade featuring thirty-five cast-stone steer heads and twenty-one cast-stone stars, as well as enormous frieze sculptures illustrating baseball and scenes from Texas history, such as a cattle drive, the Alamo, oil wells, and the Texas Rangers lawmen, the team's namesake. Inside the stadium you'll see, just outside the luxury suite entrances, sixty-seven sepia-toned murals portraying baseball's historic stars.

After struggling for about twenty years, the Rangers have finally become a recognizable force in baseball. In 1996 and 1998, the team captured the American League West pennant, only to lose the World Series both times to the much mightier New York Yankees. But the fans have become fiercely loyal, and the Ballpark is a joyful place to watch a great game together, by sunshine or under the stars.

PRACTICAL NOTE: Buy your tickets well in advance, if possible, to get the best seats.

DAY ONE: *Morning*

Check into the **Arlington Marriott** (1500 Convention Center Drive; 817–261–8200 or 800–442–7275; $79 and up) or the **Courtyard by Marriott** (1500 Nolan Ryan Expressway; 817–277–2774 or 800–321–2211; $94 and up), two nice accommodations within easy walking distance to the Ballpark. The primary difference between the two hotels is that the Arlington Marriott is larger. The Courtyard, which caters to business travelers, has a small desk in the room's sitting area.

BRUNCH *or* LUNCH

Have brunch or early lunch at **Cozymel's** (1300 Copeland Road; 817–469–9595; moderate), conveniently located in front of the stadium on the freeway's access road. This lively, loud chain eatery is styled in a Mexican coastal theme. You'll find a menu full of Tex-Mex specialties, such as enchiladas and tacos, as well as more frivolous dishes, from grilled lamb fajitas to succulent seafood items. Chips and salsa precede the meal. Don't miss one of the numerous, colorful frozen drinks—such as fruit-flavored daquiris and margaritas—meant to transport you to the tropics. But save room for a few goodies at the Ballpark.

Romance
AT A GLANCE

◆ Drop your things at the **Courtyard by Marriott** (1500 Nolan Ryan Expressway; 817–277–2774 or 800–321–2211), and then have lunch at **Cozymel's** (1300 Copeland Road; 817–469–9595).

◆ Take in a Texas Rangers baseball game at the **Ballpark in Arlington** (1000 Ballpark Way; 817–273–5100).

◆ Dine on Cajun and Creole fare at **Pappadeaux Seafood Kitchen** (1304 Copeland Road; 817–543–0545) and then check out **Bobby Valentine's** sports bar (4301 South Bowen Road; 817–467–9992).

DAY ONE: *Afternoon*

Head now to the **Ballpark in Arlington** (1000 Ballpark Way; 817–273–5100), to see the Texas Rangers. The season runs from April

An Intimate Proposal

Let's say you were hoping to pop the question to your sweetheart and you feel that during a baseball game is the right time. You can do just that in elaborate style by contacting the Rangers' main office (817–273–5222) and having your proposal splashed across the enormous JumboTron, the lighted board and big-screen TV perched high atop right field. It happens nearly every day; between innings, a message suddenly appears, such as, "Susan, will you please marry me? Love, Phil." And then a camera operator, who's been apprised of this development, trains the camera on Susan to broadcast her reaction when she sees the board. It's delightful to watch her face, and then see her hug her new fiancé. Needless to say, you won't want to try this tactic unless you're pretty sure you'll get "Yes" for an answer.

through September. Day games are at 2:00 P.M., usually in April, May, and September. Night games from Monday through Saturday are at 7:30 P.M. and. on Sunday at 7:05 P.M. from June through August. Tickets cost $4.00 to $30.00. Buy your mate some peanuts and Cracker Jacks, or a hot dog and a cold beer, and then sit back and enjoy the game.

After the game (or before, if you're taking in a night game) be sure to visit the **Legends of the Game Baseball Museum** inside the Ballpark in Arlington (817–273–5600; $6). Whether you are baseball lovers or just folks wanting to learn more about it, this museum details the history of the sport from an early version of the game in the 1700s to the modern day. Exhibits tell the stories of the Texas League, the Negro Leagues, and the Texas Rangers. There are some 130 artifacts on long-term loan from the National Baseball Hall of Fame and Museum in Cooperstown, New York, such as the jerseys of Ty Cobb and Babe Ruth, bats swung by Lou Gehrig and Ted Williams, and the golden glove of Joe DiMaggio. Have some fun sitting together in a booth and creating a video of the two of you calling a play-by-play of a Texas Rangers game. The video booth is free, but you can't make a copy to take home, so just enjoy it while you're there.

The museum is open Monday through Saturday from 9:00 A.M. to 7:30 P.M. and Sunday from noon to 5:00 P.M., from March through October. Hours from November through February are 9:00 A.M. to 5:00

P.M. Tuesday through Saturday and noon to 5:00 P.M. Sunday; closed Monday. Admission costs $6.00 per person.

Then head to the **Gallery of Sports Art** (inside the Ballpark; free) to see what might be the nation's largest collection of sports paintings, limited-edition lithographs, statues, and autograph memorabilia from all sports. Finish your Ballpark experience with a visit to the large gift shop, where you can buy each other keep-sakes, such as Texas Rangers jerseys and T-shirts.

DAY ONE: *Evening*

DINNER

After a full day of playing around, you're probably both ready for a big meal. Stroll over to **Pappadeaux Seafood Kitchen** (1304 Copeland Road; 817–543–0545; moderate), yet another place specializing in rowdy atmosphere and enormous platters of good food. The theme here is Cajun and Creole, with specialties includ-ing stuffed crab, fried alligator tail, jambalaya, étouffée, "dirty" rice, and excellent red snapper done in any number of delicious, and very rich, sauces. Dixie Beer, made only in New Orleans, is a special brew here, and the Greek salad is simply unbeatable.

If you're a pair of hard-core sports fans and are up for a nightcap, hop in the car and drive to **Bobby Valentine's** (4301 South Bowen Road; 817–467–9922), a sports bar belonging to a former Texas Rangers man-ager and current major-league coach. You'll find plenty of cold beer, as well as every game imaginable on TV, pool tables, and other games.

Finally, it's back to the hotel for a well-deserved night's rest.

DAY TWO: *Morning*

BREAKFAST

Start your day off with a pile of pancakes or a plate of sausage, eggs, and hash browns at the **New Main Street Café** (2023-A South Cooper Street; 817–801–9099; inexpensive).

Before the getaway is over, the two of you could do one of two entertaining things that are perfect if you're both young at heart. **Six Flags Over Texas** (I-30 at Highway 360; 817-640-8900; $26), located almost in front of the Ballpark, is a 205-acre theme park, opened in 1961, that offers every sort of heart-stopping roller coaster you can imagine. There are numerous musical shows, concession games, and cafes, too.

Right across the freeway is option number two, **Six Flags Hurricane Harbor** (1800 East Lamar Boulevard; 817-265-3356; $23), a wild and wet water park. On hot days, it's great for splashing around—but it's often crowded with kids. If you're a pair of thrill seekers, you'll get a kick out of the Black Hole, a spiraling slide of 500 feet of black tubes, and the six-story-high, 300-foot water plunge.

FOR MORE ROMANCE

If you need to take a breather from baseball or just need a pleasant break from the heat pay a visit to the **Arlington Museum of Art** (201 West Main Street; 817-275-4600). After a complete renovation, an old department store in downtown Arlington was transformed into a fine museum housing one large main gallery and a smaller gallery on the mezzanine level. Works here include those of veteran and merging Texas artists. The museum also hosts regional, national, and international contemporary art in visiting exhibits. The museum is open Wednesday through Saturday from 10:00 A.M. to 5:00 P.M. Admission is free.

ℙlaying 𝔾ames

MAJOR-LEAGUE FUN AT REUNION STADIUM

LOVERS WHO ENJOY A GOOD CONTEST OF SKILL have plenty to cheer about around here. Every conceivable professional sport—from rugby to rodeo, soccer to tennis—is presented somewhere, frequently, in the Dallas–Fort Worth area.

For those sharing a passion for fast-paced, even frenetic games, Reunion Arena is the place to be. The Dallas Stars, Texas's only National Hockey League (NHL) team and the 1999 Stanley Cup champions, play from October through April. The Dallas Mavericks present National Basketball Association (NBA) action during the same months. Games are typically played at night, so this itinerary offers area diversions to keep you busy until game time. Hang out together having minor-league fun during the day in order to conserve energy for major-league excitement later on.

PRACTICAL NOTES: Buy your game tickets well in advance, if possible. For Stars tickets, call (214) 467–8277; prices are generally $14.00 to $75.00, and game time is typically 7:30 P.M. For Mavericks tickets, call (972) 988–3865; tickets are $9.00 to $52.00, and the games are at 7:00 or 7:30 P.M.

DAY ONE: *Morning*

Check into the **Hyatt Regency Dallas** (300 Reunion Boulevard;

214–651–1234 or 800–233–1234; $230 and up), which sits imme-diately adjacent to Reunion Arena, home court of the Mavericks and the Stars. The giant Hyatt has nearly 950 rooms on 28 floors and may be, for some, the most glamorous hotel in downtown, thanks to its fifty-story tower with the landmark lighted sphere on top.

Romance AT A GLANCE

◆ Find your room at the **Hyatt Regency Dallas** (300 Reunion Boulevard; 214–651–1234 or 800–233–1234) or **Embassy Suites Hotel Dallas Market Center** (2727 Stemmons Freeway/I–35; 800–362–2779), and then take a spin around **Dallas on Ice** (700 Munger Avenue in the West End; 214–969–7465).

◆ Have lunch at the **Palm** (701 Ross Avenue; 214–698–0470) and wander through the original, world-famous **Neiman Marcus** department store (1618 Main Street; 214–741–6911).

◆ In the evening, it's off to a hockey or basketball game at **Reunion Arena** (777 Sports Street; 214–467–8277 or 972–988–3865).

If the Hyatt exceeds your budget, look up the freeway a short drive at the **Embassy Suites Hotel Dallas Market Center** (2727 Stemmons Freeway/I–35; 800–362–2779; $169). Appealing assets at this attractive all-suite lodging are nonsmoking designa-tion for 214 of the hotel's 240 suites, indoor pool, in-room coffeemaker, and numerous freebies, such as breakfast, newspaper, evening cocktails, and shuttle to Love Field.

After dropping your bags, don some comfortable walking shoes, grab your skate bags (provided you like to ice-skate), and head out to the **Dr Pepper StarCenter** (locat-ed just off MacArthur Boulevard, approxi-mately 3.5 miles north of LBJ Freeway—also called I–635—in Valley Ranch; 214–467–8277). This is the practice home to the National Hockey League's Dallas Stars (for-merly the Minnesota North Stars), so you have a great chance to see the team working out; call to find out their schedule. It's also a fun place to skate yourselves silly when they're not practicing. Admission is $5.50 per person; skate rentals are $3.00 per person.

Otherwise, stay right downtown and head to **Dallas on Ice** (700 Munger Avenue in the West End; 214–969–7465; $6.00 per person). This is Dallas's first outdoor ice rink, open for skating daily from the Friday after Thanksgiving until the end of February. Skate rentals are $3.00 per person.

If the season's not right or your ankles aren't up to skating, why not just buy each other some souvenir jerseys? Inside **West End Marketplace** (603 Munger Avenue; 214–748–4801), a four-story shopping facility in a renovated, Victorian warehouse, you'll find several shops selling logo shirts, jackets, and such for both the Stars and the Mavericks, as well as all other major-league sports teams.

DAY ONE: *Afternoon*

LUNCH

You'll both need plenty of energy to cheer at tonight's game, so get your protein and carbo-loading going now with a big lunch at **the Palm** (701 Ross Avenue; 214–698–0470; expensive), a West End landmark belonging to the famous New York–based chain. In addition to prime steaks and massive burgers, you'll find glorious lobster and calamari. Lunch is offered Monday through Friday.

If it's Saturday or Sunday, another good lunch spot in the West End is **Landry's Seafood House** (306 North Market Street; 214–698–1010; moderate); you can't go wrong with Southern-style fried Gulf shrimp, blackened snapper, gumbo, soft-shell crabs, crab cakes, and fresh fish delights.

The two of you can easily while away the afternoon by exploring the department store that put Dallas on the specialty-shopping map. The original **Neiman Marcus** (1618 Main Street; 214–741–6911), built in 1914 and expanded later, still serves as the flagship store of the chain recognized around the world as the place for lavish service and exquisite taste. During the holiday season, the store is decorated in utter splendor. At any time, this is a delightful place to prowl together, looking at fabulous clothes and perhaps even registering for wedding gifts. Be sure to visit the permanent store history exhibit on the fifth floor and have a look at the acclaimed Zodiac Room on the sixth floor, where Dallas's elite have been doing lunch for decades. The store is open from 10:00 A.M. to 5:30 P.M. Monday through Saturday.

DAY ONE: *Evening*

DINNER

Have a fun early dinner at **Dick's Last Resort** (Record Street at Ross Avenue; 214–747–0001; moderate), another West End spot. This rollicking bar and restaurant specializes in hilariously obnoxious servers, loud but good jazz music, and buckets of beer and food. The barbecued ribs are tasty, the fried catfish is juicy, and the suds are wonderfully cold.

Now it's off to the Stars or Mavericks game at **Reunion Arena** (777 Sports Street). Compared to some stadiums, Reunion Arena almost feels intimate. Seating is arranged so that most fans feel they're right on top of the action—and fans certainly get into the fast-and-furious action. The screaming and cheering at both basketball and hockey games can be deafening, as the fans are intensely loyal. Plenty of cold beer, hot dogs, nachos, and popcorn are available at the numerous concession stands.

If the two of you are up to experiencing Dallas's ultimate nighttime groove after the game, head to the **Starck** (703 McKinney Avenue; 214–922–9677). This nightclub on the northern edge of downtown is partially owned by Dallasite and NBA bad boy Dennis Rodman. It's quite an upscale dance club, with single-malt whisky the drink of choice and Dominican cigars for puffers. The unisex bathrooms are kind of a trip.

DAY TWO: *Morning*

BREAKFAST

After the excitement at last night's game, you'll both probably enjoy a morning to sleep in and wake when the spirit moves you. Why not take advantage of your time together and order in breakfast from room service?

Before heading home, head east to the wonderful, old **Dallas Farmers Market** (1010 South Pearl Street; 214–939–2808). For nearly sixty years, this giant, mostly outdoor market has brought the freshest of all vegetables and fruits to Dallas from Texas farms. Even if you're not buying, it's a wonderful sensory experience to stroll hand in hand past the hundreds of stalls, seeing and often smelling luscious produce.

Adjacent to the fruit-and-vegetable sheds are newer market sections, offering thousands of fresh flowers and plants, as well as locally produced and packaged foods, such as mozzarella cheese, honey, jams, relishes, and more. On many Saturdays during spring and fall, a local culinary group offers gourmet herb and cooking classes, featuring special instruction from the area's celebrity chefs. The Farmers Market is open daily from dawn until dusk, year-round.

FOR MORE ROMANCE

If you're feeling lucky, head about fifteen minutes west of downtown Dallas to **Lone Star Park at Grand Prairie** (Belt Line Road, just north of I–30; 972–263–7223), where you can enjoy watching and betting on the ponies. The fabulous park features live thoroughbred racing from April through August and quarter horse racing in October and November. The grandstand includes a dining section, club house, Jockey Club, bar, and upscale dining room called Silks. The paddock area is open to everyone, and it's a great chance to see the horses up close. Post Time Pavilion airs simulcast racing and has a sports bar and casual dining section. The park is open Wednesday through Monday during racing season. Call for race times. Admission is $2.00 per person for grandstand, $5.00 for clubhouse. Parking is $2.00 to $4.00 per vehicle for self-parking and $5.00 for valet parking.

Retreat at the Four Seasons
AN INTERLUDE IN IRVING

I F YOU SHARE A LOVE OF THE LINKS, by all means spring for a luxurious stay at the Four Seasons Resort and Club in Irving's upscale Las Colinas neighborhood. The 36-hole, TPC championship golf course is home to the prestigious Byron Nelson Golf Classic, a PGA tour stop in May and site of crushing traffic and tournament crowds whenever Tiger Woods makes a tour appearance.

The resort is arguably the finest in North Texas, with a European-style spa, a fitness center with indoor and outdoor jogging tracks, four swimming pools, and eight outdoor and four indoor tennis courts, all in addition to that wonderful golf course. Put your heads together to decide which package to choose, and be sure to leave time to wander around pretty Las Colinas—woven through by the lovely Mandalay Canal, which is lined with trees and cobblestone walkways—and perhaps even ride horses.

PRACTICAL NOTES: Be sure to set up your tee times and spa treatments before your arrival.

DAY ONE: *Morning*

Check into the **Four Seasons Resort and Club at Las Colinas** (4150 North MacArthur Boulevard in Irving; 972–717–0700 or 800–332–3442), a gorgeous spread of 400 rolling acres crowned by the championship golf course.

The resort offers 365 rooms, including 12 suites and 50 new villa-style rooms overlooking the golf course. All rooms have two telephones with message alert, cable TV, am/fm clock radios, writing desk, balcony, walk-in shower and oversize tub, twice-daily maid service, twenty-four-hour room service, complimentary shoe shines, oversize bath towels, wool blankets, down pillows, thick bathrobes, and much more.

Rooms typically start at $280 a night, but you're better off choosing a package deal. Typical examples are the Golf Package, which includes a daily round of golf with a cart, club cleaning and bag storage, access to sports club and spa (no treatments), and lodging, which starts at $350 per night; the Spa/Golf Package, which includes the Golf Package features, plus a facial or massage, starting at $450 per night; and the Romance Package, which includes use of the sports facility, a bottle of champagne, and a full breakfast for two, starting at $340 per night.

If you require a less expensive lodging but still want to play at the Four Seasons, try the **Homewood Suites Las Colinas** (4300 Wingren Road in Irving; 972–556–0665; $125 and up), a very nice all-suite hotel near Highway 114 and O'Connor Road. All suites have living room and kitchen, and some have fireplaces. Breakfast is included, and complimentary cocktails are offered on weekday evenings in the lobby.

Romance
AT A GLANCE

◆ Get your bearings at either the **Four Seasons Resort and Club at Las Colinas** (4150 North MacArthur Boulevard in Irving; 972–717–0700 or 800–332–3442) or **Homewood Suites Las Colinas** (4300 Wingren Road in Irving; 972–556–0665), and then play eighteen holes of golf or get a massage, facial, wrap, and sauna.

◆ Tour the movie studios at the **Dallas Communications Complex** (6301 North O'Connor Road in Irving; 972–869–0700).

◆ Wrap up the day with dinner at **Cool River Café** (105 Hidden Ridge Drive at MacArthur Boulevard in Irving; 972–871–8881).

BRUNCH

After dropping your bags and sending your golf bags to the pro shop, put on your playing clothes and stop for a late breakfast or early lunch at **Café on the Green** (inside the Four Seasons; moderate). This stunning dining room offers views of the pretty golf course, as well as sensational food. Buffet choices number possibly 100 dishes, ranging from omelettes and Mexican egg dishes, Greek salad and marinated mushrooms, poached fish and grilled vegetables to curry chicken and couscous. If either of you wants to be especially healthful, choose items from the spa menu, which offers intriguing and fresh dishes—hot and cold, from salads and sandwiches to full entrees—with notated calorie counts and nutritional information.

Now go play eighteen holes and enjoy one of the most famous, par-70 courses in Texas. If you didn't book a package, the green fee is $130 per person. Equipment rentals are available.

If you're only playing nine holes, your tee time is later in the day or—heaven forbid—you've been rained out, that's OK, too. Here are some other delightful options for two.

If only one of you is a duffer, the other should waste no time heading off to the spa. There, you'll enjoy a massage, facial, herbal wrap, mud and sea kelp treatment, sauna, whirlpool bath, hair styling, manicure, or pedicure. Call ahead for prices.

Couples who like showbiz will get a kick out of touring the **Dallas Communications Complex** (6301 North O'Connor Road in Irving; 972–869–0700), home of the **Studios at Las Colinas.** The enormous film and commercial production complex was the production site for such films as *JFK*, *Leap of Faith*, *Robocop*, and *Problem Child*. On display you'll see the Oval Office used by director Oliver Stone in *JFK*, props from *Addams Family Values*, and *Star Trek* memorabilia that includes Khan's suit, Captain Kirk's uniform, and William Shatner's dummy/stunt double.

After your tour, be sure to buy each other some souvenirs of your visit at the museum's store, where MGM, Paramount, Universal, and 20th Century Fox items are sold. The tours are offered daily from 10:00 A.M. to 4:00 P.M. at a cost of $10 per person.

Another option is the nearby **American Airlines C. R. Smith Museum**, adjacent to the American Airlines Flight Academy (Texas 360 and FAA

Road, immediately southwest of DFW Airport; 817–967–1560). Not an aircraft museum, this wonderful history exhibit, which is named for the "father of American Airlines," offers interactive displays, films, and videos that detail the operation of the Fort Worth–based airline from its beginning in 1930 as American Airways. The centerpiece is a vintage Douglas DC-3, Flagship Knoxville, lovingly restored by retired AMR pilots, mechanics, and employees. The museum is open from 10:00 A.M. to 7:00 P.M. Tuesday through Saturday and from noon to 5:00 P.M. Sunday. Admission is free.

DAY ONE: *Afternoon*

LATE LUNCH *or* SNACK

If the two of you have been golfing or touring, you're bound to want a pick-me-up about now. A charming spot for guaranteed pleasure is **Jinbeh** (301 East Las Colinas Boulevard in Irving; 972–869–4011; moderate). A popular Japanese steak house and sushi bar for more than a decade, Jinbeh has typical dining tables as well as hibachi grill seating and on-the-floor seating in Tatami rooms. We recommend the sushi bar, where you can share the delight in watching skilled sushi chefs put salmon, shrimp, crawfish, fried crab, and myriad vegetables in rice rolls with wonderful garnishes. Even if you're sushi novices, this place will bring your palates to life.

After lunch, spend a few hours playing golf, or take a ride along Mandalay Canal in one of the canopy-covered electric boats (202 Mandalay Canal, O'Connor Road in Irving; 972–869–4321; $3.25). Even better, indulge yourselves in massages and facials. Then retire to your room, suite, or villa for a luxurious snooze.

DAY ONE: *Evening*

DINNER

A new and most popular addition to Las Colinas is **Cool River Café** (105 Hidden Ridge Drive at MacArthur Boulevard in Irving;

972–871–8881; moderate/expensive), a mammoth restaurant done in a stylish lodge theme, complete with western murals, enormous rough wood beams, and iron wheel chandeliers. The fare here is mostly Southwestern and always creative. Choices range from excellent, aged black angus rib eye steak with a Shiner Bock beer sauce and chicken-fried venison to chicken enchiladas and chili-spiked Caesar salad.

After dinner, the two of you can relax around the billiards area, sip margaritas at the bar, or review your day over a snifter of cognac and a cigar in the leather-lavished library area.

Wild Horses

Lest you think Las Colinas is simply a fabulous golf course next to a business community that popped up from the prairie, you'll find that its creators were intent on honoring Texas's rich heritage with one of the most sensational sculptures in the Lone Star State. The **Mustangs of Las Colinas** is a fascinatingly realistic bronze sculpture of nine wild mustangs, whose ancestors brought Spanish explorers through these parts centuries ago. The horses—created by Nairobi-born sculptor Robert Glen, who is known for his African wildlife art—are seen galloping across a granite-based stream in Williams Square Plaza, itself surrounded by shining granite buildings. Sculpted at one and a half times actual life size, the mustangs constitute the largest equestrian sculpture in the world. Find them at 5205 North O'Connor Road in Las Colinas. While you look at the mustangs, the two of you can ponder what this part of Texas was like centuries ago.

DAY TWO: *Morning*

BREAKFAST

Enjoy a splendid brunch at **Café on the Green** (in the Four Seasons Resort) or have a big breakfast at **Le Peep** (4835 North O'Connor Road in Irving; 972–717–0422; inexpensive). For a chain, this is far better than you'd think. The favorite item here is the skillet breakfast, which combines any number of ingredients, from scrambled or poached eggs, potatoes, vegetables, and cheeses to sausage, bacon, beef, and ham. Make it a brunch, and you're set until dinner.

After breakfast you two have a number of choices to consider for the balance of your day. The first, of course, is to play another eighteen holes of golf. Or you could swim some laps or play a set of tennis and then get that herbal wrap that you somehow missed at the spa yesterday.

If it's football season and this is Sunday—and provided that you're sports nuts—then you'll want to head to nearby **Texas Stadium** (2401 East Airport Freeway in Irving; 972–579–5000 or 214–373–8000; $34–$55) to see the famous Dallas Cowboys team put on a pigskin performance. The Cowboys won the Super Bowl in 1993, 1994, and 1996, continuing a championship tradition. Games are often sold out, so you'll want to have secured tickets in advance or take your chances with someone unloading tickets outside the stadium before the game.

Your final option is one that's been shared by lovers for centuries—that of riding horses. At **5 Bar K Stables** (Elm Fork Ranch; 972–579–1140; $20 per hour) you can take a trail ride on more than 100 acres and view either the Dallas skyline or that of the bustling Las Colinas business center. The stables are open daily from 9:00 A.M. until a half hour before sundown. Reservations are a good idea.

FOR MORE ROMANCE

Just about a ten-minute drive west of Irving and Las Colinas is the city of Grapevine, settled in 1850. It was the site of a treaty signing between the Native Americans and Sam Houston in 1849. One of the more entertaining reasons to go there today is to gawk and shop at the mind-blowing **Grapevine Mills** (Hwy 121 at International Parkway; 972–724–4900) outlet mall. More than 200 stores here include Off 5th/Saks Fifth Avenue, Off Rodeo Drive Beverly Hills, bebe Outlet, Brooks Brothers Outlet, Ann Taylor, Liz Claiborne, and much more. The mall is open from 10:00 A.M. to 9:30 P.M. Monday through Saturday and 11:00 A.M. to 8:00 P.M. Sunday.

You can't miss **GameWorks**, a 34,000-square-foot space designed by Steven Spielberg for adventurous types (like you, of course) who enjoy interactive games. Vertical Reality is the one in which you strap yourselves into seats to fight criminals in a skyscraper, rising 24 feet and "falling" to the ground when you're hit.

Unwind afterward at the **Loft**, a full-service bar with pizzas inside GameWorks, or have some wonderful sandwiches, soups, and pastries in the mall at **Corner Bakery.**

Resorting to Romance
AT POSSUM KINGDOM LAKE

HERE'S ANOTHER RETREAT OFFERING PLENTY OF GOLF, as well as a restful refuge beside giant Possum Kingdom Lake. Forget about the lake's silly name—it's said that even FDR laughed when he first heard it—because this 20,000-acre reservoir formed by the damming of the lovely Brazos River is exceptionally pretty, with wooded, hilly shores that stretch 310 miles into four counties. Not only will you two be sharing time at a delightful resort with golf and tennis, but you'll have time to fish, water-ski, and just laze around in the sun. Be sure to make reservations well in advance, if possible.

DAY ONE: *Morning*

Check into **The Cliffs** (940–779–4040 or 888–843–2543; $139 and up). You'll reach it by driving west from the Dallas–Fort Worth area on Interstate 20, then exiting Highway 180 at Weatherford. Continue west on 180 through Mineral Wells and Palo Pinto to the hamlet of Brad. There, take Highway 16 North. The Cliffs is 7.5 miles farther on the left.

This resort offers a stunning eighteen-hole championship golf course, health and beauty spa, tennis and swim center, full-service marina, private white sand beach, casual and elegant dining, and lodging in condominiums. Book a pair of golf lessons, one for each of you, for late morning. PGA professionals here can help with strategy, club selection, swing, and such, for $25 per half hour and up; call the golf pro shop at (888) 843–2543, ext. 4523.

DAY ONE: *Afternoon*

LUNCH

After your lessons, have an early lunch before heading out to the links. For something quick and casual, head to the resort's **19th Hole Grill** at the Pro Shop, where the menu offers deli-style sandwiches. If you want something more elaborate, the **Cliffs Restaurant** in the resort's main building offers fresh fish and prime steaks.

Now it's time to hit the championship golf course designed by renowned golf course architect Robert Von Hagge and touring pro Bruce Devlin; weekday green fee per person (with a cart) is $29 during the week and $55 on weekends. Even if neither of you plays the best golf today, you'll be charmed by the course's 170-foot cliffs, lush fairways, and sensational views. And if either of you has forgotten anything, the **Pro Shop** has all sorts of golf gear, from clubs and accessories to clothing.

If only one of you is playing golf, or you're only playing nine holes, there are plenty of other options for the rest of the afternoon. The resort has two swimming pools with adjoining cabanas, two tennis courts, a fitness center, a sand volleyball court, picnic areas, and hiking trails.

If the weather is gorgeous, consider a guided fishing tour or renting a boat to spend time on the water. An especially romantic idea is a sunset cruise from the resort to Possum Kingdom's famous Hell's Gate, a pair of towering rock cliffs on the southern shore. Check out all possibilities at the **Ship's Store** at the resort marina (940–779–4040), which is open Monday through Wednesday from 8:00 A.M. to 6:00 P.M. and Thursday through Sunday from 8:00 A.M. to 8:00 P.M.

Romance AT A GLANCE

◆ Settle into your room at the **Cliffs** (on Possum Kingdom Lake; 940–779–4040 or 888–843–2543), and then have an early lunch at the resort's **19th Hole Grill** or the **Cliffs Restaurant** before taking a golf lesson or playing eighteen holes.

◆ Swim or take a guided fishing tour or sunset boat tour before driving over to the **Rafters Restaurant on Scenic Point** cove (Highway 16 to Farm Road 2353 to Park Road 36; 940–779–3177) for dinner.

DAY ONE: *Evening*

DINNER

Drive to the **Rafters Restaurant on Scenic Point** cove (940–779–3177) for dinner; it's reached from the Cliffs by driving north on Highway 16, then taking Farm Road 2353 west and north to Park Road 36, which you'll follow west; then follow the signs. The Rafters is a wonderful, casual eating and drinking spot housed in a restored Amish barn that was moved here from Ohio. An impressively crafted rock entryway, made from local stone, was fashioned onto one end of the barn.

Inside the two of you will find rustic wood flooring, giant booths, and several tables that look beyond a simple patio onto the lake. You'll find lots of hearty Texas foods here, from giant burgers and chicken-fried steak to sumptuous homemade pies. If there's a ball game on TV, of which there are several sets, count on finding sports fans enjoying the brews and food while cheering their teams. Be careful with the margaritas, though. That's a winding drive you'll be taking back to the Cliffs for a good night's sleep.

DAY TWO: *Morning*

BREAKFAST

Enjoy a breakfast of eggs and bacon at the Cliffs deli.

Play another round of golf this morning if you're both so inclined. Otherwise, pack up—but keep your swimsuits and hiking boots handy—and check out, and then head west to **Possum Kingdom State Park** (940–549–1803) for the day. You'll be passing through the rough canyon country of the Palo Pinto Mountains and Brazos River Valley, taking Highway 16 south to Highway 180, which you'll take west to the tiny burg of Caddo. Stop there at **Caddo Mercantile** (254–559–6844) to buy picnic supplies for lunch—and to have a big, fresh breakfast if you decided to get an early start and skip breakfast at the resort.

Then head north on Park Road 33, a 17-mile drive that takes you into the park. As you enter the park grounds, watch on the left for one of the state's official herd of longhorn; you'll definitely want to take photos of each other here for souvenirs.

At the park office pay the $5.00 per car entry fee and pick up park maps. Then take time to drive some of the lovely, twisting roads meandering through the park and past some of the rock buildings constructed by the Civilian Conservation Corps in the early 1940s. It's likely that you'll come upon hiking trails you want to explore.

At the park's store and marina (940–549–5612) you can pick up any groceries you might have missed at Caddo Mercantile and look into boat and jet-ski rentals. If either one of you is an angler, the store has bait and tackle to help you catch some of the lake's record striped and largemouth bass. Even if you don't fish, you'll enjoy motoring around the lake to see the scenic, wooded shoreline, and to find just the right cove to stop for a picnic lunch and swim.

A Couple of Critters

While exploring the environs at Possum Kingdom Lake and in the state park, keep watch for two critters that aren't possums. The nine-banded armadillo—which happens to be the state mammal of Texas — is a frequently observed creature, whose body measures from 15 to 17 inches, whose tail can be 14 to 16 inches long, and who weighs 8 to 17 pounds. Sadly, most are seen dead on roadsides, but if you happen to spy one living happily and unharmed in the wild, it's fun to watch it at its incessant digging of burrows and for food.

Another friendly creature you'll see is the carnivora mustelidae, *or striped skunk. In case you're not sure you'd recognize it, look for a fat, waddling critter with thick black fur marked by two stripes on the sides of its back that meet in the neck region. The skunk loves these woods and rocky outcroppings around the lake, but you'll rarely spot one during daylight hours. Don't be surprised if you're grilling steaks over a fire at dusk at one of the park's cabins or campsites and find yourselves suddenly in the company of several skunks. These are relatively tame and are simply hoping for a handout.*

DAY TWO: *Afternoon*

LUNCH

When the two of you agree you've found the ideal spot, have a leisurely picnic. Afterward take a quiet hike in the woods, being watchful for the gentle, white-tailed deer that live in the park. This is the perfect time to enjoy your aloneness together, when the intrusions of your everyday life—urban noise, pagers, wireless phones, car pools—are seemingly millions of miles away. Take your time heading back home, and you'll return feeling refreshed.

FOR MORE ROMANCE

Spend an extra night on Possum Kingdom Lake by booking a cabin in the park. They aren't by any means luxurious, but they're comfortable, sit near the water, and have furnished kitchens. You supply the romance. Call the park office (940–549–1803) to inquire about availability and rates.

Dude Ranch Dalliance

OST OF US AS CHILDREN, at some point or another, wanted to be a cowboy or a cowgirl. There's a romance associated with the West, the frontier, the rugged ranch lands where heroes rode tall in the saddle and then naturally swaggered when they dismounted.

But unless you grew up on a ranch or know somebody with one, chances are you haven't spent a lot of time playing cowboy or cowgirl. But thanks to a ranch close to Fort Worth and Dallas, you can do just that with your sweetheart beside you.

The ranch is for playing dude for a day, and it welcomes individuals, such as yourselves. This is a rarity, as most guest ranches around the state are geared to accommodate group functions only.

So saddle up and have a mighty fine time. Before you know it, you and your honey will be talkin' with a big ole twang.

PRACTICAL NOTE: Your day at Texas Lil's begins at 10:30 A.M. and ends at 4:00 P.M., costs $35 per person, and requires reservations. When you call for reservations, ask for specific directions, which can be faxed to you.

DAY ONE: *Morning*

BREAKFAST

En route to your dude day at the ranch, stop for a robust breakfast at the **Rocking J Café** (417 North Sealy Avenue; Justin; 940–648–2581;

inexpensive). Opened in the late 1980s, the homey cafe is the picture of Texas friendliness and has been used as a backdrop in various movies. Order an omelette with a side of hash browns, or a stack of pancakes with sausage.

Head up to the Denton County town of Justin, home to **Texas Lil's Dude Ranch** (Farm Road 407, just west of Interstate 35W; 800–545–8455). Lil's staff will give you a souvenir bandana, a one-hour horseback ride, an all-you-can-eat barbecue lunch, and plenty of soft drinks. The staff here is really friendly, and you're guaranteed a great time.

You're both welcome to hit some balls on the driving range (golf clubs and balls are provided), fish in two stocked ponds (bring your own gear and bait), swim in the enormous swimming pool, play volleyball, softball, or horseshoes, or just take a quiet hike in the woods.

Romance AT A GLANCE

◆ Be a dude for a day at **Texas Lil's Dude Ranch** (Farm Road 407, just west of Interstate 35W; 800–545–8455).

◆ Feast to your hearts' delight at **Ranchman's Café** (Farm Road 156; 940–479–2221).

◆ Hear music in Denton at the **Groovy Mule** (1131 Fort Worth Drive; 940–383–7674) or **Dan's Bar** (119 South Elm Street; 940–891–1549), then dream sweetly in your room at the **Magnolia Inn Bed & Breakfast** (821 North Locust Street; 940–381–3001).

DAY ONE: *Evening*

DINNER

Have an early feast—all that ranch life must have worked up a fierce hunger—at **Ranchman's Café** in the minute town of Ponder, which is on Farm Road 156 (940–479–2221; inexpensive to moderate), just 7 miles north of Justin. A throwback to the 1940s roadhouses, this legendary steak joint packs in the crowds on weekends, so it's smart to call ahead and reserve a seat and—this is not a joke—your baked potatoes. Dinner choices range from T-bone and rib eye steaks that are cut when you order them (listen carefully and you can hear the saw in the kitchen) to chicken-fried steaks. Do save room for the Ranchman's famous pies and cobblers, made fresh each morning. If you want a beer with your supper, bring it with you.

After you've filled up, make your way north on Farm Road 156 and then east on Highway 380 a short distance to Denton, where you'll check in the **Magnolia Inn Bed & Breakfast** (821 North Locust Street; 940–381–3001; $76–$125). This B&B, which occupies the second story of a historic home, consists of two large suites, each with two rooms, canopy bed, claw-footed bathtubs, cable TV, and Victorian antiques. (An Italian restaurant occupies the first floor.)

If you're up to it, head out to hear some live music in one of Denton's night spots. An eclectic spot to try is the **Groovy Mule** (1131 Fort Worth Drive; 940–383–7674). Cover charge ranges from $2.00 to $5.00, and music acts range from folksy to disco. Another is **Dan's Bar,** right in historic downtown (119 South Elm Street; 940–891–1549), where acts offer blues and pop music. Admission charge at Dan's varies.

Get Gussied Up!

*If your closet doesn't naturally offer up a repertoire of cowboy and cowgirl clothing, then you need to make a stop at **Justin Discount Boots and Cowboy Outfitters** (111 North Farm Road 156 in Justin; 940–648–2797), a bargain store selling world-famous Justin Boots, as well as jeans, cowboy hats, shirts, coats, belts, and saddle blankets. It's also a perfect place to buy great gifts for friends back home, who will no doubt envy your dude experience.*

DAY TWO: *Morning*

BREAKFAST

Start the day off with a big Magnolia breakfast of juice, coffee or tea, bacon or sausage, and buttermilk pancakes with strawberries or breakfast casserole.

Afterward, take a long walk together through Denton's historic district and around the lovely courthouse square, bounded by Locust, Oak, Elm, and Hickory Streets. An hour or two of quiet time together will keep memories of the getaway fresh for a long time.

The Nature
of Love

Return to Eden
The Natural Wonders of Dallas

NE PARTICULARLY APPEALING ASPECT about North Texas's environs for outdoorsy couples is the relative absence of winter. Sure, there's the wildly weird ice storm every few Januarys, but for the most part, the great outdoors is great in and around Dallas. Even when the hundred-degree summer days arrive, the sunshine is still truly inviting—particularly for lovers who want to go outside and play.

So what if Dallas sits in the middle of a plain? Look beyond the skyscrapers and shopping centers and you'll discover that there's a wealth of natural wonders for two to treasure together that are fresh, verdant, and blooming. With plentiful gardens and preserves—as well as a host of joys for animal fans—the pair of you will lose yourselves in nature, right in the city.

DAY ONE: *Morning*

Check into a lovely bed and breakfast that is perfect for this romantic weekend, due to its convenient proximity to the Dallas Arboretum. **Courtyard on the Trail** is a wonderful escape in the woodsy area near White Rock Lake. This B&B has among its offerings a king-size bedroom that opens directly onto the pool and courtyard, as well as an oversize bathtub, where two can enjoy a bubble bath while gazing at the cloud-painted ceiling. Courtyard's rates are $125 to $150, including a full breakfast. Reserve a room through Bed & Breakfast Texas Style; (972) 298–8586 or (800) 899–4538.

Your B&B host will point you toward the **Dallas Arboretum and Botanical Garden** (8525 Garland Road; 214–327–8263), where it's easy to wander away your morning. Sixty-six acres of exquisitely land-scaped grounds with lush blooms and thick foliage overlook White Rock Lake. Do take a camera, because you'll both spot numerous places to cap-ture keepsake photographs. If the day is fine, you'll inevitably see brides having their wed-ding portraits made. Take time to tour the magnificent DeGolyer House, a Spanish Colonial-style mansion built in the 1940s. Its sculpture garden contains fabulous works on loan from the Dallas Museum of Art. A serene place, too, is an ornamental garden with water walls.

During specific seasons the arboretum has specially designed floral displays, always on a grand scale. Look for phenomenal aza-leas in magenta and baby pink in spring, daisies galore in summer, mums in warm autumn colors, and a sea of poinsettias toward the winter holidays. The Arboretum is open daily from 10:00 A.M. to 6:00 P.M. Admission is $6.00; parking is $3.00.

DAY ONE: *Afternoon*

LUNCH

Romance
AT A GLANCE

◆ *Take your room at* **Courtyard on the Trail** *(booked through Bed & Breakfast Texas Style; 972–298-8586 or 800-899-4538), and then wander over to the* **Dallas Arboretum and Botanical Garden** *(8525 Garland Road; 214-327-8263).*

◆ *Have a big Southern lunch at* **Dixie House** *(6400 Gaston Ave-nue; 214-826-2412) that will fortify you for an afternoon at* **Dallas Horticulture Center** *(3601 MLK Jr. Boulevard; 214-428-7476) and* **The Science Place in Fair Park** *(1318 Second Avenue; 214-428-5555), with its* **IMAX Theater.**

◆ *Have dinner at the exotic* **Café Izmir** *(3711 Greenville Avenue; 214-826-7788).*

Right in the Lakewood neighborhood is **Dixie House** (6400 Gaston Avenue; 214–826–2412; inexpensive), a great place for two to load up on good old country cookin', as it's called here. Pot roast, delicious fried chicken, real mashed potatoes, and classic banana pud-ding will definitely fortify you for more nature wanderings.

Head over to Fair Park, just south of the Lakewood area, and take your pick of three excellent diversions for nature lovers. First is the

Dallas Horticulture Center (3601 MLK Jr. Boulevard; 214–428–7476). This marvelous center features seven acres of outdoor gardens containing roses, as well as an herb and scent garden. The center's William Douglas Blachly Conservatory is home to a huge collection of African plants in simulated habitats. The center is open from 10:00 A.M. to 5:00 P.M. Tuesday through Saturday and from 1:00 to 5:00 P.M. Sunday. Admission is free.

Still in Fair Park fish-loving partners will have fun exploring the **Dallas Aquarium** (1462 First Avenue at MLK Jr. Boulevard; 214–670–8443). Particularly exotic is the Amazon Flooded Forest Exhibit, which has thirty fish species, as well as videos and a mural. Otherwise the aquarium features some 400 species of aquatic life. Do try to time your visit for the piranha feedings, held Tuesday, Thursday, and Saturday at 2:30 P.M., or shark feedings, Wednesday, Friday, and Sunday at 2:30 P.M. The aquarium is open from 9:00 A.M. to 4:30 P.M. daily. Admission is $3.00 per person.

Wind up your afternoon over at the **Science Place in Fair Park** (1318 Second Avenue; 214–428–5555), where the **IMAX Theater** offers a 79-foot screen that essentially surrounds you, taking you into the action and making even the bravest souls cling to each other in wonderful tension. Among featured films have been *Mission to Mir*, *Super Speedway: Racing with the Andrettis*, *To the Limit*, and *Mysteries of Egypt*. Admission is $6.00. Show times are throughout the day. Science Place is open from 9:00 A.M. to 5:30 P.M. Sunday through Thursday and from 9:00 A.M. to 9:00 P.M. Friday and Saturday. The Science Place is also a learning-is-fun place where you can delve into electricity, dinosaur robotics, and the magic of the human body. Admission to the museum is $6.00, a fee separate from the admission for the IMAX Theater.

Head back to your B&B for a swim or to rest up for dinner.

DAY ONE: *Evening*

DINNER

Spend a leisurely few hours over a rewarding repast at **Café Izmir** (3711 Greenville Avenue; 214–826–7788; moderate). This family-run, Middle

Eastern jewel on bustling Greenville (convenient to White Rock neighborhoods) has no printed menu, but the charming, friendly servers will help the pair of you navigate your way through a steady flow of fresh, flavorful grilled meats (beef, lamb, chicken), savory vegetables, and cool, herbed salads. The cozy rooms are washed in earthy colors and warm lighting, making you want to stay awhile.

After dinner, take in some live jazz at **Terilli's** (2815 Greenville Avenue; 214–827–3993), an Italian bistro where music is offered after 9:00 P.M. Tuesday through Sunday. There's no cover charge.

Another option for live music after dinner, right in the same neighborhood, is **Poor David's Pub** (1924 Greenville Avenue; 214–821–9891). This is a good choice for lovers of Texas rockabilly and folksy tunes from such artists as Monte Montgomery, Shake Russell, and Dana Cooper. The music starts around 9:00 P.M. Wednesday through Saturday. Cover charges range between $7.00 and $12.00.

DAY TWO: *Morning*

BREAKFAST

Plan to spend time this morning over a delightful breakfast at Courtyard on the Trail. From the menu left in your room, you'll be able to choose from several

Becoming "Parents"

Partners can seal their shared love of animals by joining the Dallas Zoo's Adopt-An-Animal program. For $25 and up you help provide for improvements to the animals' habitats and the acquisition of animals for the collection. By adopting you receive a personalized adoption certificate with a color photo of your animal; a zookeeper's report, providing information about your animal; mailings from the zoo; an invitation to the annual adopting parents' party; and a listing on the honor roll posted at the main entrances to the zoo. Contact Adopt-An-Animal, Dallas Zoological Society, 650 South R.L. Thornton Freeway (I–35E); (214) 942–3678, extension 14.

offerings; the signature dish is a French toast complemented by a fresh raspberry compote. There are about ten different omelettes available, as well as specialty breads, coffee, teas, and juices.

If you've chosen a hotel, head to the hugely popular coffeehouse, **Café Brazil** (2221 Abrams Road; 214–826–9522; inexpensive) in

Lakewood for an astounding breakfast. Eggs come any way you can think of, and many you'd never considered. Try an omelette packed with chilies and cheeses and with black beans, or a crepe loaded with fresh veggies. The pastries are fabulous, too, and the house coffee selection will keep you motoring for hours.

Fortified from breakfast head south on I–35 to the Marsalis exit, just 3 miles from downtown, to the **Dallas Zoo** (650 R.L. Thornton Freeway; 214–670–5656), considered by experts to be one of the nation's top animal research facilities. You'll know you're there when you see the giant giraffe at the zoo entrance—at 67½ feet, it's the tallest statue in Texas. Founded in 1888 the excellent zoo is home to 2,000 specimens of 400 species. It's also an integral part of the national Species Survival Plans for twenty-nine species, including gorillas, snow leopards, tigers, chimps, lemurs, okapis, and Bali mynahs.

Treat yourselves to the wonderful Wilds of Africa exhibit, a twenty-five-acre spread that includes six natural habitats, a nature trail, an aviary, a chimpanzee forest, and a surprisingly good, twenty-minute monorail tour. Climb aboard, and the two of you will view simulated African habitats—a steal at $1.50.

You can act like kids at Primate Place, imitating the cute titi monkeys from South America, African Colobus monkeys, and Asian white-cheeked gibbons.

As you can tell, you'll need some time to experience all that this lush zoo has to offer, so you should plan to spend the bulk of your day here.

The zoo is open from 9:00 A.M. to 5:00 P.M. daily. Admission is $6.00 per person.

DAY TWO: *Afternoon*

LUNCH

Before heading home have a late lunch at **Las Mananitas** (4444 West Illinois Boulevard at Cockrell Hill Road; 214–339–7151; inexpensive). Not far from the zoo, this very simple, no-frills spot is perfect for a great Tex-Mex fix. Be warned that the salsa is fiery hot but makes a good complement to the crazy nachos, which is an oversized platter of chips piled with refried beans, chicken, ground beef, fajita steak, cheese, and jalapeños. For more authentic Mexican fare, indulge yourselves with a plate of *guisado de puerco*, tender pork tips bathed in a deeply red chili gravy.

FOR MORE ROMANCE

If you have an extra day, head downtown to the **Dallas World Aquarium** (1801 N. Griffin Street; 214–720–2224; $10.95), a privately owned and particularly contemporary aquarium with twelve saltwater tanks featuring coral reef ecosystems and marine life from around the world. In addition there's a wonderful exhibit called "Rainforest: Orinoco-Secrets of the River." A two-story escalator ride takes you through the Venezuelan, multilevel rainforest to see its emerald tree boa, poison dart frog, squirrel monkeys, toucans, and the endangered Orinoco crocodile. "The Cape of Good Hope Exhibit" features a black-footed penguin and South African plains exhibit. The aquarium is open daily from 10:00 A.M. to 5:00 P.M.

Or if you've been given a sunny day and you're hikers, head southwest of downtown to the **Dallas Nature Center** (7171 Mountain Creek Parkway; 972–296–1955). This 630-acre preserve offers 7 miles of woodsy trails that pass a pond pricked with cattails and lead to sensational viewing points. Do bring water, because hikes take two or three hours. If you're butterfly lovers, stop at the Mary Alice Bland butterfly garden. The nature center is open from 7:00 A.M. to sunset Tuesday through Sunday. There is no admission charge.

Wild Things
A Wilderness Escape in Fort Worth

NLY TRUE LOVERS OF NATURE AND WILDLIFE need consider this retreat. Although Fort Worth's wildness was long associated with cowboys hootin' it up on Saturday night in the saloons, or gunfighters shooting each other in the streets, today the city has a romance with gardens, wilderness, and beasts that you're invited to share together.

You'll spend your first day exploring a sensational wilderness refuge, where you can even learn to canoe, and then you'll explore one of the nation's leading centers for rescue and rehabilitation of large cats. The second day is occupied again with gorgeous and exotic animals, and then an escape into soothing, green environs.

PRACTICAL NOTES: Both activities for Day One require some advance planning; the visit to the Texas Exotic Feline Foundation requires an appointment.

DAY ONE: *Morning*

Check in at your lodging of choice. The first recommended accommodation is **Bed & Breakfast at the Ranch** (8275 Wagley Robertson Road; 817–232–5522 or 888–593–0352; $75–$159), a newer addition to Fort Worth lodgings, located north of the city in a countryside setting. There are four guest rooms: the Lazy B Ranch Room, with barnwood paneling; the Wrangle Room, with its own private patio; the Cattle Baron's Quarters, with a whirlpool tub and western mural; and the Hideaway, with a vaulted ceiling, private balcony, and 100-gallon, antique, claw-footed tub. Each room has a private bath, and all guests enjoy a large den area with sauna, wet bar, and wood-burning stove, as well as tennis courts and a putting green. Huge country-style breakfasts are included with your stay; typical offerings include bacon, eggs, and biscuits.

Or you can stay downtown at **Radisson Plaza Hotel Fort Worth** (815 Main Street; 817–870–2100; $120 and up), which in an earlier incarnation was the Hotel Texas, the place where John F. Kennedy spent his last night before his tragic Dallas visit.

The graceful, old red-brick hotel has 502 guest rooms and 15 suites that have been recently given a contemporary, Southwestern redecoration. Each room has cable TV, PC hookup, desk, and sitting area. The Plaza Club level offers evening beverages and snacks, concierge service, and more. The bed-and-breakfast package ($120 and up) includes an extensive breakfast buffet for two in the hotel's Café Texas, and the Sweetheart Package ($160) includes an oversize king bedroom, valet parking, chilled champagne upon arrival, chocolate-covered strawberries, and a giant breakfast buffet for two at Café Texas.

After the two of you have dropped your bags and put on your favorite hiking boots or walking shoes, you're ready for a thirty-minute drive northwest to the **Texas Exotic Feline Foundation** (north on U.S. 81/287 from Fort Worth, then west on Texas 114 toward Bridgeport; 940–433–2378); which you have called well in advance to schedule a tour. Founded in 1983, the nonprofit organization is a thirty-six-acre, outdoor sanctuary for more than sixty lions, tigers, cougars, leopards, and other big cats that have been rescued from abusive situations or have been abandoned

Romance AT A GLANCE

◆ Drop your belongings at **Bed & Breakfast at the Ranch** (8275 Wagley Robertson Road; 817–232–5522 or 888–593–0352) or **Radisson Plaza Hotel Fort Worth** (815 Main Street; 817–870–2100), and then make tracks to the **Texas Exotic Feline Foundation** (north on U.S. Highway 81/287 from Fort Worth, and then west on Texas Highway 114 toward Bridgeport; 940–433–2378), followed by a visit to the **Fort Worth Nature Center and Refuge** (Texas Highway 199, 2 miles west of the Lake Worth Bridge; 817–237–1111).

◆ Finish the day with a stylish Lebanese dinner at **Byblos** (1406 North Main Street; 817–625–9667) or steaks in an elegant setting at **Del Frisco's Double Eagle Steakhouse** (812 Main Street; 817–877–3999).

by people who realized these beautiful creatures don't make good house pets. TEFF does not breed or sell cats, but simply provides a permanent, wonderful home for these magnificent animals.

Among the cats you'll see on this two-to-three-hour tour are three hearty, healthy lions that were rescued from a zoo in Mexico. There, they had been kept in tiny, cramped concrete shelters, where they were starving and virtually unable to move. The rescue mission, which was partially funded by private individuals and American Airlines, brought the trio to TEFF, where they gained appropriate weight and learned to walk and roam again.

The stories you'll hear as you wander through the hilly, wooded refuge are both heartbreaking and uplifting. You'll both be delighted to see tigers playing in their marvelous watering holes, crafted from native Texas limestone, and volunteers who come daily to clean out the cages and spend time with the animals—the latter a critical measure for many of these cats, which were raised by humans before being abandoned.

Tours are available at 10:00 A.M. Monday and Friday and between 8:30 A.M. and 1:00 P.M. on Saturday and Sunday. The center is closed in extreme weather, and no tours are given after 11:00 A.M. in the hottest part of summer. There is no admission charge, but donations are welcome.

DAY ONE: *Afternoon*

LUNCH

Two places are worth your combined consideration for lunch; neither is fancy, but both are good and put you in easy proximity to the Fort Worth Nature Center. Either one is an escape from the many dull fast-food offerings in the area.

The first option is **Ginger Brown's** (6312 Lake Worth Boulevard; 817–237–2114; inexpensive), a nondescript cafe in a strip shopping center next to the supermarket. The reason for going is solid, old-fashioned, home cooking, such as chicken-fried steak with cream gravy, big cheeseburgers, and unbelievable cinnamon rolls.

If the two of you share a taste for Tex-Mex fare, head a few blocks back toward downtown along Texas Highway 199, also known as the Jacksboro Highway, to **Arizola's** (6055 Jacksboro Highway; 817–237–0020;

inexpensive). Overlook the fact that this fine, family-owned operation is in a renovated McDonald's; the fresh, homemade food makes this a local favorite. Try the fajitas, taco salad, or cheese enchiladas.

Walk off your full bellies at the **Fort Worth Nature Center and Refuge** (Texas Highway 199, 2 miles west of the Lake Worth Bridge, 817–237–1111). To make the most of your afternoon there, stop en route at the Albertson's supermarket you'll see before you reach the Lake Worth Bridge to pick up water and soft drinks.

This 3,500-acre nature sanctuary, owned by the city of Fort Worth and managed by its parks department, is not only a place for the layperson's pleasure but also a center for environmental education and natural science training and research, so you'll likely see groups in learning situations during your visit.

You can simply traipse together along the myriad trails and enjoy the thick foliage, or—if you two visit on a springtime Saturday—take one of the forty-five-minute wildflower walks. Naturalists will lead the two of you along the caprock and along the edge of the prairie in search of spring wildflowers; in April and May, you'll be able to enjoy and photograph the state's wonderful bluebonnet, as well as a spread of other wild blooms. Hand the naturalist your camera, and then put your arms around each other and smile for a beautiful souvenir of your fun with the flowers.

On scheduled Saturdays, the nature center offers a number of different canoeing courses for all levels of experience. Guides take visitors on interpretive canoe tours on some of the refuge waterways, explaining the area's natural history and ecology. There are also courses in the American Red Cross Fundamentals of Canoeing Course, which qualifies you to become a canoeing guide. If the two of you are experienced canoeists, you can sharpen your skills and learn to navigate white water with skilled instructors who also take a classroom session and a weekend trip to the San Marcos River in central Texas. Or simply sign up for an interpretive float down the West Fork of the Trinity River; call well in advance to see when these are offered.

In the fall, it's a nice time to wander around the sanctuary together during the cooler days and enjoy the changing leaves—provided there's been no summer drought.

At the refuge's Hardwicke Interpretive Center, you'll find a gift shop, trail maps, a bird-watching courtyard, an herbarium, a nature library, and rest rooms. The nature center is open from 9:00 A.M. to 5:00 P.M. Tuesday through Saturday and noon to 5:00 P.M. Sunday. Admission is free.

Head back to your lodging for a long bath, if you have one of the rooms with a special tub, and some quiet time alone.

DAY ONE: *Evening*

DINNER

You have two excellent dinner options this evening. The first is **Byblos** (1406 North Main Street; 817–625–9667; inexpensive to moderate), a delightful family operation serving delicious Lebanese fare, including stuffed eggplant, lemony grilled chicken, and various lamb dishes. On weekends, there's belly-dancing entertainment.

Another fine choice is **Del Frisco's Double Eagle Steakhouse** (812 Main Street; 817–877–3999; expensive). This clubby, elegant dining room is a temple of exquisite beef, as well as perfectly prepared veal *osso bucco*, lobster, and shrimp. Do make reservations in advance; the restaurant is right across the street from the Radisson.

DAY TWO: *Morning*

BREAKFAST

You can have your morning meal to be savored at both B&B at the Ranch and at the Radisson.

If you've chosen another lodging, head to **Ol' South Pancake House** (1509 South University Drive; 817–336–0311; inexpensive) to fill yourselves. This old-fashioned landmark is a favorite diner among cowboys, business folks, and college students. Best breakfast bets are the Dutch babies, crepes that are finished with powdered sugar and lemon at your table; and the Spanish omelette, full of cheese and salsa.

Thus fortified, the two of you are ready for more animal appreciation. Head just a couple of blocks south on University to the **Fort Worth Zoo** (1989 Colonial Parkway; 817–871–7050), named one of the best five or ten zoos in the nation, depending on whose poll you read. What's outstanding about this one is not just its more than 5,000 native and exotic animals, but also its numerous natural habitat exhibits—mostly cageless—that keep visitors separated from the animals by only a river or a waterfall. The landscaping is a treat, too, if you're lovers of botany.

The gorillas, bears, hippos, elephants, birds, and big cats are wonderful, but you and your mate will be particularly charmed by the Koala Outback exhibit. Home to koalas—some of which came from the San Diego Zoo—as well as red kangaroos and yellow-footed rock wallabies, this exhibit is one of ten in the United States and the only one in Texas with koalas. You'll be able to view the koalas, who sleep something like eighteen hours each day, from a partially covered boardwalk, which also affords views of the kangaroo and wallaby yard.

Rasha Rules

The Fort Worth Zoo's reigning celebrity is Rasha, the elephant who has been entertaining football fans with her careful consideration in picking winning football teams. Every Tuesday throughout football season, Rasha is presented with an easel displaying logos of competing teams; she makes her predictions—usually successful choices—by touching the logos of her choice with her trunk. You're invited to attend this Pachyderm Pickin', held in the Elephant Yard of the Fort Worth Zoo at 1:00 P.M. every Tuesday of football season.

Other exhibits you'll enjoy seeing are those of meerkats, penguins, Komodo dragons, flamingoes, Malayan sun bears, and Sumatran tigers. A herpetarium and an aquarium are on site, as well. The zoo is open daily from 10:00 A.M. to 5:00 P.M. Admission costs $7.00 per person, and parking is $3.00 per vehicle.

Before leaving the zoo area, you'll both enjoy a ride on the **Forest Park Miniature Train** (facing the zoo; 817–336–3328), the longest miniature train ride in Texas. The delightful ride takes less than thirty minutes, winding through the green, shady expanse of Trinity Park. It's lots of fun. The train operates from noon to 5:00 P.M. on Saturday and Sunday, weather permitting. Tickets cost $3.00 each.

DAY TWO: *Afternoon*

LUNCH

Just a few blocks north of the zoo, the two of you can have a feast at **Blue Mesa** (in the shopping center at 1600 South University Drive;

817–332–6372; moderate), Fort Worth's only restaurant with New Mexican cuisine. The interior is done in a stylish adobe design, with stucco walls, cactus, and heavy woods, and the food offers a wonderful blend of mild and hot chilis. Stacked, blue-corn enchiladas, adobe pies (corn-meal domes stuffed with chicken), and cheese-packed *chilies rellenos* are outstanding. If you're game, the house margaritas—which come in their own shakers—are fabulous. And if you happen by on Sunday, the brunch is huge and delicious.

You'll probably both welcome the opportunity to walk off that enormous lunch at **Fort Worth Botanic Garden** (3220 Botanic Garden Boulevard; 817–871–7686), just a couple of blocks north on University Drive. The state's oldest botanic garden, opened in 1933, this spread of 109 acres displays more than 2,500 species of native and exotic plants, with twenty-one specialty gardens that feature roses, perennials, cactus, and other plant kingdom miracles. As you wander arm in arm down numerous pathways, you may easily see a wedding in progress or bridal portraits being taken, especially in the terraced Rose Gardens, which have gorgeous arbors and trellis work.

Do take your camera along, as there are hundreds of photogenic spots where you'll want to take keepsake pictures of each other. You'll find these places in the the series of lagoons at the site of the original Rock Springs; the Fragrance Garden; and the Test Garden, which features All America Selections of annuals and roses. You'll want at least one photo with both of you in it, so look for another couple with a camera and offer to snap a shot of them together if they'll do the same for you.

Within the Botanic Garden is the Japanese Garden, more than seven acres of serene, lush plantings, meandering paths, pools filled with colorful koi fish, and a variety of gate, teahouse, and pavilion designs. Frequently, you'll find special festivals with tea ceremonies here.

Botanic Garden, which is home to the International Begonia Species Bank, includes a 10,000-square-foot Conservatory, exhibiting tropical plants from Central America, South America, Africa, and Asia. Behind the Conservatory are still more gardens, ponds, and pathways for restorative hand-in-hand strolls. Before leaving Botanic Garden and ending this retreat, stop in the gift shop at the Conservatory to buy a book on flowers or a set of wind chimes as remembrances of your visit here.

Botanic Garden grounds are open from 8:00 A.M. to 11:00 P.M. daily.

The Conservatory is open from 10:00 A.M. to 9:00 P.M. Monday through Friday, 10:00 A.M. to 6:00 P.M. Saturday, and 1:00 to 6:00 P.M. Sunday, from April to October. From November to March, the closing time is 4:00 P.M. on Saturday and Sunday.

The Japanese Garden is open from 10:00 A.M. to 5:00 P.M. Tuesday through Sunday. Admission is free to the Botanic Garden grounds; Conservatory admission is $1, and Japanese Garden admission is $2.50.

FOR MORE ROMANCE

Right across the street from Botanic Garden is **Trinity Park**, which the miniature train travels through from the zoo. If the weather's inviting and you've come equipped, the two of you can practice your in-line skating or go bicycling along the paved trail that follows the Trinity River's path. There are lovely picnic areas throughout the park, too. The park is always open.

Another great place for drinking in the fresh air and taking in a bit of nature study is **River Legacy Park and Living Science Center** (703 Northwest Green Oaks Road in Arlington; 817–860–6752; $3.00). There are self-guided nature trails (pick up maps at the center), as well as trails for hiking, biking, and skating. Naturalist-led walks are offered at 10:00 A.M. on Saturday.

Tracking Together
THROUGH TIME

BOUT NINETY MINUTES SOUTHWEST OF DALLAS and an hour southwest of Fort Worth is the town of Glen Rose, the seat of Somervell County. The small hamlet (population 3,000 or so) sits at a wonderfully picturesque place on the Paluxy River, just above its confluence with the meandering Brazos River. Nearly a century ago this was a popular spot for sanitariums where people with various medical problems would come take the waters to heal whatever ailed them.

The rolling, often rocky landscape of Somervell County and a lovely little town square—full of nooks and crannies for two to explore—in Glen Rose makes this area a favorite getaway for North Texans. During the spring wildflower season, the hills and riverside bluffs of the area are covered in carpets of blue, yellow, and pink.

Clear evidence shows that millions of years ago, dinosaurs roamed this land. In very recent years, however, Glen Rose has become known as a place to see some of the world's most endangered critters. All in all, it's a great place to look to the past and see the future of the animal kingdom.

DAY ONE: *Morning*

Check into **Hummingbird Lodge** (Farm Road 203, just off U.S. Highway 67; 254–897–2787; $85–$115), a comfortable retreat 2 miles from Glen Rose in the rolling countryside of Somervell County. The lodge's rustic-but-contemporary buildings of stone and cedar are surrounded by 140 wooded acres with walking trails, a fishing pond stocked with black bass and channel cat, and plenty of bird-watching and wildlife watching.

Large porches and decks have rocking chairs, and the hot tub area has a swinging hammock—what could be better when the two of you are ready to relax together or read?

The lodge has six guest rooms, all with private baths. Guests share a roomy library that has a TV with VCR, as well as a living area and dining room with wood-burning fireplaces, antiques and period Texas pieces, Mexican tile detail, and Oriental rugs. A generous breakfast buffet is offered with your stay.

Another popular lodging choice a block away from Glen Rose's charming, historic square is **Inn on the River** (205 Barnard Street; 254–897–2101 or 800–575–2101; $115–$165). Built in 1914 and restored in 1993, this pretty inn offers Adirondack chairs on the patio beside the Paluxy River, beneath 200-year-old oak trees. There are twenty-two rooms with private baths, each with antiques, feather beds, and down comforters. A full breakfast is included with your stay here, too.

You'll both be tempted to hang around and relax at your lodging, but you'll need the full day to explore. Set off as early as you can to **Fossil Rim Wildlife Center** (3 miles southwest of Glen Rose via U.S. Highway 67; 254–897–2960), as that's when your best

Romance AT A GLANCE

◆ Find your room at either **Hummingbird Lodge** (Farm Road 203, just off U.S. Highway 67; 254–897–2787) or **Inn on the River** (205 Barnard Street; 254–897–2101 or 800–575–2101) and then spend time at **Fossil Rim Wildlife Center** (3 miles southwest of Glen Rose via U.S. Highway 67; 254–897–2960) before exploring **Dinosaur Valley State Park** (north 4 miles from Glen Rose on Farm Road 205, then 1 mile north on Park Road 59; 254–897–4588).

◆ Dinner is an unforgettable event at **Rough Creek Lodge** (County Road 2013, south of Glen Rose via U.S. 67; 800–864–4705).

chances are to see the animals moving around this 2,700-acre refuge.

Fossil Rim's heavy involvement in the global network of conservation organizations concerned with preserving endangered species and their habitats sets it far apart from the typical drive-through wildlife experience. Its staff is always working on economic, scientific, and humanistic agendas in an effort to provide a model for private initiatives in worldwide conservation. All proceeds from public visitors such as yourselves help fund Fossil Rim's operation and conservation programs.

There are three touring opportunities, so put your heads together to figure out what interests the two of you most. The Scenic Wildlife Drive ($12.95 per adult) starts at the Visitor Center and takes in a petting pasture, the Nature Store, and a stop at the cafe. The paved, winding road you travel on this tour allows you to drive your vehicle at your own pace along almost 10 miles of savannas, wooded hills, and valleys. You'll have a chance to see more than sixty species of exotic and endangered wildlife—about 1,100 animals in all—living in conditions that closely approximate their normal environments.

In addition to wild turkeys and armadillos, which have wandered here on their own, you're likely to see rhinos and cheetahs (in protected areas), as well as curious giraffes and zebras—which will probably come right up to your car—plus aoudads and gazelles, kudus and wildebeests, and countless other animals in the wild.

By calling ahead you may be able to hook up with a Behind-the-Scenes Tour ($25 per adult). In this tour a small group is taken in an open-air vehicle by a Fossil Rim naturalist who answers questions and provides in-depth information. You're able to see Fossil Rim's protected areas not open to the general public, where you'll view wolves, coatis, black rhinos, and other animals. This tour includes a Scenic Wildlife Drive pass.

If you're cyclists, inquire about guided Mountain Bike Tours ($30 per person), allowing you to explore the wild side of Fossil Rim and glimpse some of the rare and endangered animals seldom seen by the casual visitor. The half-day tours begin at 9:00 A.M. and 3:00 P.M., are customized to your level of experience, and include snacks and a souvenir T-shirt.

During certain seasons Fossil Rim offers special events, such as a wolf howl, a moonlight safari, an owl prowl, and other activities. Call ahead to inquire.

Fossil Rim also has a half-mile nature trail, offering a moderately strenuous hike along a hillside, where you'll see cacti, fossils, wildflowers, and beautiful vistas. If you like, the Overlook Café—reached on the Scenic Drive—offers burgers and turkey sandwiches, light salads, and such for lunch.

Before you leave Fossil Rim, stop in the Nature Store to pick up gifts for each other to remind you of your visit. There are books and educational materials pertaining to wildlife, as well as art and unusual handcrafts, many of which come from Texas artisans.

Fossil Rim is open daily from 9:00 A.M. until two hours before sunset.

DAY ONE: *Afternoon*

LUNCH

If you didn't have a burger at Fossil Rim, and if you're visiting Monday through Friday, have a midday repast at the **Bluebonnet Café** inside the **Glen Rose Emporium** (102 West Walnut Street; 254–897–4855; inexpensive) on the town square. If you're in the mood for brunch items, try the breakfast burrito or Irish potatoes and Polish sausage. Otherwise the two of you can share a chicken Caesar salad and a spicy, grilled Cajun chicken sandwich, or tuck into a plate of pasta primavera or a plate lunch of chicken, gravy, and potatoes. After lunch browse through the emporium's selection of antiques, handcrafts, and gourmet coffees.

If it's Saturday or Sunday, however, stop for barbecued brisket or a burger at the **Western Kitchen** (509 U.S. Highway 67; 254–897–2310; inexpensive). This is a good old country diner with few frills but big plates of good eats.

After filling up tighten the laces on your hiking boots and head over to **Dinosaur Valley State Park** (north 4 miles from Glen Rose on Farm Road 205, then 1 mile north on Park Road 59; 254–897–4588), an adventure that will take the rest of your day.

This rolling, tree-filled park spreads over 1,523 acres and encompasses a meandering bend of the clear, comforting Paluxy River. More than an excellent state park, it's been designated as a National Natural Landmark by the National Park Service.

If you're geologically inclined explorers, you'll appreciate that the park's natural history consists of limestones, sandstones, and mudstones, deposited from 110 million to 105 million years ago along the shorelines of an ancient sea. These layered formations have been dissected and sculpted by the Paluxy River over the past few million years to plane off large exposures of rock in the river bottom where footprint molds show the dinosaur tracks that were discovered in 1909.

Most common are the three-toed, giant birdlike prints, measuring from 12 to 24 inches in length and from 9 to 17 inches in width, that are believed to be the Acrocanthosaurus—a 20- to 30-foot-long, two-legged carnosaur, from a group that later produced the larger Tyrannosaurus rex.

Another category of prints you'll see are saucerlike depressions, ranging to over 3 feet in length and 2 feet in width, with stride lengths from 7 to 10 feet, that are thought to have been made by the sauropods, plant-eating creatures with serpentine necks, massive bodies on pillarlike legs, and long tails. Scientists believe that the Glen Rose sauropod was a Pleurocoelus. This dinosaur measured from 30 to 50 feet long and had a relatively short neck and tail. Look to see its saucer-shaped prints from its four-toed, clawed hind feet, as well as its rather horseshoe-shaped tracks made when its sheathed front feet sank into the mud.

Finally, look for the third, mysterious category of prints, thought to be made by an early ornithopod, which was one of the two-legged plant-eaters whose later descendants included the duckbilled dinosaurs. These prints are large, three-toed and birdlike, but the toes are not as elongated, and the "heel" tends to be more rounded. Experts say that a 1985 Texas discovery of Iguanodon bones—belonging to a 30-foot-long ornithopod that had previously been thought to live only in Europe—suggests that this dinosaur could be the culprit, because it has the right sort of stubby, three-toed foot structure to match these prints. Take a moment to share some thoughts of what the world must have been like when these huge creatures roamed the land.

Throughout the park you can hike areas covered with Ashe juniper, live oak, Texas red oak, and Texas ash, with some post oak and mesquite and various grasses and shrubs. Trees in the bottomlands are mainly American elm, cedar elm, Texas sugarberry, bur oak, and green ash. Areas along the river offer pecan, walnut, cottonwood, sycamore, black willow, and several kinds of shrubs and vines.

Bird-watchers will enjoy spotting, at times, wild turkey and various waterfowl near ponds, and you're likely to see—particularly at dusk—white-tailed deer and the occasional coyote, bobcat, raccoon, beaver, skunk, opossum, armadillo, fox squirrel, and rabbit. If the weather's inviting, take a swim in the river.

Boning Up
on the Trackway

The Glen Rose Trackway was first documented in 1938 by Roland T. Bird, who came to Texas looking for dinosaurs and other fossils for the American Museum of Natural History in New York. One of the three trackways Bird excavated with a large work crew remains in Dinosaur Valley State Park, and the others are the University of Texas in Austin and the Smithsonian Institution. Read more about his work in Bones for Barnum Brown, by Roland T. Bird, published in 1985 by Texas Christian University Press. Another good resource for dinosaur lovers is The New Dinosaur Dictionary, by Donald Glot, published by Citadel Press in 1982.

Remember your cameras, as you'll want to capture on film the rather kitschy dinosaurs donated by the Atlantic Richfield Company in 1970. You'll see—in a fenced area—a 70-foot Brontosaurus (more correctly called Apatosourus) and a 45-foot Tyrannosaurus rex, which were fiberglass models for the Sinclair Oil Corporation's 1964–65 New York World's Fair Dinosaur Exhibit. The Apatosourus head was reconstructed in 1985 to reflect more accurate paleontological information on this dinosaur.

The park also has sixteen primitive campsites, as well as forty-six campsites with water and electricity. You'll find picnic tables, restrooms with showers, and a park store that sells dinosaur books, models, posters, T-shirts, and other goods. The park's visitor center has a dinosaur exhibit, open daily from 8:00 A.M. to 5:00 P.M. The park itself is open daily from 7:00 A.M. to 10:00 P.M. Park admission is $5.00.

DAY ONE: *Evening*

DINNER

After taking time to freshen up, head out to **Rough Creek Lodge** (County Road 2013, south of Glen Rose via U.S. 67; 800–864–4705; expensive). This extraordinary place is on Chalk Mountain Ranch and was built by the rancher as a bird-hunting retreat. The restaurant and very pricey lodgings are open to the public.

The restaurant is something to behold: Polished wood floors, huge chairs covered in leather and cowhides, and antler wall sconces add a rustic elegance, and an enormous limestone fireplace serves as the room's centerpiece. Mouth-watering dishes include grilled quail with Parmesan cheese grits, steamed clams in a garlic-saffron broth, roasted pork tenderloin with garlic mashed potatoes, pan-roasted duck in a chunky fig sauce, and for dessert, shortbread layered with plums and nutmeg cream. The wine list is heavy with California varietals. It's a dinner neither of you will forget.

FOR MORE ROMANCE

You two can take a room at **the Lodge at Fossil Rim**, crafted from Austin stone and cedar in 1985 and set in a secluded area of the preserve. There are five elegant guest rooms furnished with antiques, and a giant living area with a massive stone fireplace and glass walls overlooking sunny decks and a spring-fed swimming pool. The rates are $125 to $225 per room per night and include breakfast.

Fossil Rim also offers an unusual escape in its **Foothills Safari Camp**, in which you stay in a safari-style luxury tent outfitted with two twin beds, fresh linens, private bathroom, heating and air conditioning, ceiling fans, and your own small patio. There's a pavilion nearby, where you and other campers meet for breakfast and snacks or have a drink at the bar. Evenings are filled by sitting around the campfire. Throughout the day you're likely to see a host of exotic animals gathering at the water hole just below the tents. The tents are $150 per night, including breakfast.

Rendezvous with History

The Fall of Camelot
AND OTHER HISTORICAL HAPPENINGS

HATEVER CONTRIBUTIONS DALLAS AND ITS PEOPLE have made to the world will be forever eclipsed by a single moment in time. Just as Dallas was becoming accepted as something more than a hick town or a gathering place for a bunch of lucky oilmen, but rather as a major player in the areas of finance, energy, and fashion merchandising, a tragic few seconds in November 1963 devastated the nation.

The assassination of President John Fitzgerald Kennedy in Dallas has long been called the fall of Camelot. It was an abrupt, horrific end to an era bursting with hope and youth, and the obliteration of a union of two inspiring, beautiful people to whom an entire generation looked with admiration and pride.

In the course of this itinerary, the two of you will share sites relevant to Camelot's end. But you'll also explore the places associated with much happier points in time, such as the graceful Swiss Avenue Historic District, containing exquisite homes built by city pioneers in the late nineteenth century.

DAY ONE: *Morning*

Check into the venerable **Fairmont Hotel** (1717 North Akard Street; 214–720–2020; $119–$200) for a luxurious stay right in the Arts District. Inside the twenty-four-story hotel are 550 rooms, an

Olympic-sized pool, health club, barber, beauty shop, retail shops, and three restaurants.

If you'd like something less costly, try the **Paramount Hotel** (302 South Houston Street; 214–761–9090; $69–$89), a smaller, simpler hotel downtown near Union Station.

Stash your bags and freshen up, and then head west just a few blocks to **Dallas County Historical Plaza** (Main and Market Streets), where you'll find the **John F. Kennedy Memorial**. This stark, simple space was designed as a spot for meditation, an open-air structure with high walls to block noise and provide time for reflection.

On an adjacent space a few feet away, the **John Neely Bryan Cabin** is the restored structure of the town founder. It sits in the shadow of the **Old Red Courthouse** (Main and Houston Streets), an overwhelming 1892 structure crafted of red sandstone in a particularly ornate Richardsonian Romanesque design. Note the gargoyles on its corners—pretty scary. Neither building is open to the public. For more detail, call the Dallas Convention and Visitors Bureau at (214) 746–6677.

Another block northwest, you'll find the **Sixth Floor: JFK and the Memory of a Nation** (411 Elm Street; 214–653–6666), a museum dedicated to the nation's thirty-fifth president. Situated inside the building formerly known as the Texas School Book Depository, from which Lee Harvey Oswald is said to have assassinated Kennedy, the exceptional museum is a historical, educational exhibit that documents the dreadful events of November 22, 1963.

The corner of the room where Oswald supposedly stood is just as it was on that date, except the window is permanently closed. Throughout

*R*om*aN*ce
AT A GLANCE

◆ *Check into the* **Fairmont Hotel** *(1717 North Akard Street; 214–720–2020) or the* **Paramount Hotel** *(302 South Houston Street; 214–761–9090), and then walk west a few blocks to see the* **John F. Kennedy Memorial** *(Main at Market Streets) and, in the next block, the* **John Neely Bryan Cabin,** *followed by the* **Sixth Floor: JFK and the Memory of a Nation** *(411 Elm Street; 214–653–6666).*

◆ *In the afternoon have a drink or an espresso at* **Walt Garrison Rodeo Bar** *in the Adolphus Hotel (1321 Commerce Street; 214–742–8200), followed by dinner at the sensational* **Morton's of Chicago** *(501 Elm Street; 214–741–2277).*

the museum, you'll find more than 400 historic photographs, artifacts, and forty minutes of documentary films that illustrate both Kennedy's presidency and death. The thirty-five-minute audio tour has won awards, so be sure you both spring for the extra $2.00 each.

The Sixth Floor is open daily from 9:00 A.M. to 6:00 P.M. Admission costs $5.00 per person. No photography is allowed. Do plan on spending at least an hour here to see it all.

When the two of you exit the building, you'll want to walk across the street together to Dealey Plaza. You'll be among the thousands of people who wander around this spot each week (you'll see people here at all hours, in any kind of weather), looking at the presidential motorcade route down Elm Street and at the infamous grassy knoll, from which some people believe other shots were fired.

If the two of you love history, head over to the **Conspiracy Museum** (110 South Market Street; 214–741–3040). Tucked into the first floor of the historic Katy Building, this museum delves into assassinations throughout American history and political motivations that could have been relevant. Particularly interesting, of course, is that the creators of this museum say Oswald did not kill Kennedy. What do *you* think? The museum is open daily from 10:00 A.M. to 6:00 P.M. Admission is $7.00 per person.

DAY ONE: *Afternoon*

LUNCH

Here's something wonderful that you don't find too often—a terrific restaurant at the top of a skyscraper, but it's not a private hangout. The **Yorkshire Club** (325 North St. Paul Street; 35th floor of the Republic Tower II; 214–871–2001; moderate) is strictly a lunch spot on weekdays, with a powerful view of the city. Excellent food includes lemon-seared shrimp, salmon in a honey glaze, and grilled beef tenderloin.

If it's the weekend, go Italian at **Avanti Café** (1445 Ross Avenue in Fountain Place; 214–965–0055; moderate), a little sister to a same-named restaurant in Uptown. This is a charming, cheery spot for wonderful soups, which change daily, as well as handmade ravioli, fine linguine, and good Caesar salad.

So fortified, continue exploring Dallas's past by taking a trip just south of downtown to **Old City Park** (1717 Gano Street; 214–421–5141). Shadowed by skyscrapers, this lovely, quiet park offers delightful refuge from urban stress. Dallas life from about 100 years ago is showcased in a collection of thirty-seven period structures in the park. You'll walk through a school, a church, a Victorian bandstand, a dentist's office, a general store, an antebellum house, and a tepee (which probably predates the others), all of which has been renovated and relocated from throughout North Texas. This charming place is often the scene of weddings and receptions. You'll find it open Tuesday through Saturday from 10:00 A.M. to 4:00 P.M. and Sunday from noon to 4:00 P.M. Admission costs $5.00 per person.

On your way back to your hotel stop for a cold beer

What's In a Name?

While it is certain that John Neely Bryan was the first permanent Dallas resident, no one has definitely established for whom Dallas is named— although it seems that the township was always called Dallas. The possibilities, according to the Texas State Historical Association, are George Mifflin Dallas, vice president of the United States, 1845–49; his brother, Commodore A. J. Dallas, United States Navy; their father, Alexander James Dallas, secretary of the treasury, 1814–16; Joseph Dallas, a settler near this new hamlet in 1843; and a trio of brothers, James R., Walter R., and Alexander Janes Dallas, who served in the Army of the Republic of Texas. If the two of you have had enough of discussing the Kennedy conspiracy theories, you can ponder which of these Dallases might have been the city's namesake.

or an espresso at the **Walt Garrison Rodeo Bar** in the Adolphus Hotel (1321 Commerce Street; 214–742–8200). It's a nice place to unwind together and consider the evening's options. You can't help but be entertained at this sophisticated version of an Old West barroom inside such an extravagant, beautiful hotel—which was built as the baroque mansion for beer baron Adolph Busch.

DAY ONE: *Evening*

DINNER

If you're seafood lovers, there's no other consideration than **Fish** (302 South Houston Street; 214–747–3474; expensive). An elegant dining room attached to the Paramount Hotel, Fish does an excellent job with steamed sea bass, grilled salmon, and bountiful fish soups. Live piano music adds to the romantic charm.

But if you've a taste for prime beef, head to **Morton's of Chicago** (501 Elm Street; 214–741–2277; expensive). Definitely another romantic choice, the refined mood here is set with dark woods, etched glass, starched linens, and soft music from Tony Bennett and Frank Sinatra. Have one of thirty martini varieties, exceptional dry-aged steaks, and a bottle of robust red wine.

After dinner, you can listen to more music in the bar over a snifter of cognac. If you're both feeling like moving around, however, head a few blocks north to the **Pyramid Room in the Fairmont Hotel** (1717 North Akard Street; 214–720–5249). On Friday and Saturday night, the Julie Mondanaro Trio plays jazzy mood music until 1:00 A.M.

DAY TWO: *Morning*

BREAKFAST

Have breakfast at your leisure at **Norma's Café** (1123 West Davis Street; 214–946–4711 in the Oak Cliff neighborhood, immediately west of downtown. While the diner is somewhat short on décor, it's long—and famous—for mounds of comforting home cooking, such as biscuits, sausage, gravy, buttermilk pancakes, and omelettes cooked to order. When you're finished with breakfast, head over to the **Swiss Avenue Historic District** to walk off some of the meal. You'll find this exquisite neighborhood northeast of downtown, east of Central Expressway on Swiss Avenue between La Vista Drive and Fitzhugh Avenue (which is an exit off of Central Expressway). In the early 1900s, this was the town's prestigious address; about a half mile of the street is listed on the National Register of Historic Places for its restored mansions.

The most noted blocks are those numbered 2800 and 2900, called the Wilson Blocks after Frederick P. Wilson, who built several of the homes in the late 1890s. Dallas's Preservation League (214–821–3290) offers free, guided tours at noon on Tuesday, Wednesday, Thursday, and Saturday.

What you'll learn on the tour (and what you can already know if just showing yourselves around) is that Henrietta Frichot Wilson and her husband, Frederick, built their wonderful abode in 1899 on a city block that she inherited from her uncle Jacob Nussbaumer, a settler from the ill-fated La Reunion colony of European pioneers. The Wilsons built six more houses on their land, which gave them the opportunity to select their neighbors.

Although people moved away from the central area in later years, and many of the Victorian homes were replaced by or converted to commercial buildings, Wilson Block withstood the changes. Henritetta and Frederick's son, Laurence Wilson, lived in the family home until the late 1970s. Though the houses on his block needed repair, they had survived.

A commercial developer bought up most of the neighborhood but donated Wilson Block to the Preservation League. The league then restored the Arnold House and others, with the help of local philanthropists. Some thirty nonprofit organizations now occupy Victorians in the district, rent-free.

FOR MORE ROMANCE

If you're a pair sharing a love of airplanes, check out the **Frontiers of Flight Museum** at Love Field's Terminal LB-18 (Cedar Springs Road at Mockingbird Lane; 214–350–1651). The History of Aviation collection, formerly kept at the University of Texas at Dallas, chronicles the age of flight, from primitive balloon launches in the 1800s to today's Stealth bomber and space shuttle. Exhibits include a fur parka worn by Admiral Richard E. Byrd during his first South Pole flight in 1929, engines from early airplanes, and a Hindenberg collection, complete with an original radio operator's chair and silverware recovered from the crash. The museum is open Monday through Saturday from 10:00

A.M. to 5:00 P.M. and Sunday from 1:00 to 5:00 P.M. Admission costs $2.00 per person.

Another place to let your love take wing is the **Cavanaugh Flight Museum** (4572 Claire Chennault Drive; 972–380–8800), in far north Dallas. Inside four hangars, you two can examine more than thirty fully restored vintage war planes from World Wars I and II, the Korean War, and the Vietnam War. It's open Monday through Saturday from 9:00 A.M. to 5:00 P.M. and Sunday from 11:00 A.M. to 5:00 P.M. Admission costs $5.50 per person.

Courting Adventure
AT THE STOCKYARDS HISTORIC DISTRICT

*I*F YOU AND YOUR BELOVED HAVE THE SPIRIT of adventure and wish to enjoy the days of the Old West, a retreat to the Stockyards National Historic District is made for you. From a refurbished train to an elegant mansion, there are touches that bring alive the turn of the century—the *last* century—in Fort Worth.

If not for a military camp established toward the end of the Mexican War by General Winfield Scott and named for General William Jenkins Worth, who served in the war, there might not have even been a Fort Worth. Established in 1849, Fort Worth became the Tarrant County seat in 1860 and then a post–Civil War shipping and supply depot for cattlemen.

As demand for beef in the East exploded, millions of cattle were driven through Fort Worth along the renowned Chisholm Trail. Fort Worth was considered the last chance for rest, gambling, and partying before tackling the arduous weeks driving north through lonely prairies in Indian Territory.

DAY ONE: *Morning*

Check into the **Texas Hotel** (2415 Ellis Avenue; 817–624–2224; $59–$129), a 1930s hotel that was renovated and reopened in 1996. Among the twenty-one rooms is what owners call the honeymoon suite, the one with a king-size bed and an in-room Jacuzzi. Other rooms have either double or queen beds and showers. A continental breakfast of juice, coffee, and pastries comes with all stays.

Your other lodging options include **Miss Molly's,** a hotel that used to be a bordello, and the **Stockyards Hotel,** an inn that has rooms decorated in different period motifs. Both of these hotels are described in greater detail in Itinerary 7.

After dropping your bags and putting on your most comfortable walking shoes, the two of you can set about roaming the historic Stockyards area. To get your bearings, mosey down the street a block to the **visitor information center** (130 East Exchange Avenue; 817–624–4741), where you can pick up maps and brochures. Ask about guided walking tours, which are usually offered daily.

Next, wander over to **Stockyards Station** (140 East Exchange Avenue; 817–625–9715), a vast structure built in 1911–1912 to house hogs and sheep during the livestock days. Throughout what's now a bustling retail center of art galleries, souvenir shops, and restaurants, you'll see much of the original wooden railings and all the original brick flooring.

Romance AT A GLANCE

◆ Get settled into **Miss Molly's** (109 ½ West Exchange Avenue; 817–626–1522) or the **Stockyards Hotel** (109 East Exchange Avenue; 817–625–6427) before heading down to **Stockyards Station** (140 East Exchange Avenue; 817–625–9715), where you'll lunch at **Riscky's Bar-B-Q** (140 East Exchange Avenue; 817–626–7777) and then board the **Tarantula Train** (817–625–7245).

◆ Shop at **Fincher's Western Store** (115 East Exchange Avenue; 817–624–7302) and **M. L. Leddy's Boot & Saddlery** (2455 North Main Street, at Exchange Avenue; 817–624–3149).

◆ Have a huge meal at either **Cattleman's Steak House** (2458 North Main Street; 817–624–3945) or **Joe T. Garcia's Mexican Dishes** (2201 North Commerce Street; 817–626–4356).

DAY ONE: *Afternoon*

LUNCH

Right in Stockyards Station is one of Fort Worth's oldest and most popular purveyors of smoked meats, **Riscky's Bar-B-Q** (140 East Exchange Avenue; 817–626–7777; inexpensive). Settle in with your pardner for a thick beef brisket sandwich or a pile of rich pork ribs, washed down with an icy-cold brew.

Stockyards Station is also where the two of you will board the **Tarantula Train** (817–625–7245), which makes round-trips daily to

Eighth Avenue (in south Fort Worth) and to Grapevine. It departs at noon and returns at 1:00 P.M. Monday through Saturday, and departs at 3:00 P.M. on Sunday, returning an hour later. It's best to arrive thirty minutes before departure.

The Tarantula's name is credited to the appearance of an 1873 railroad map that showed Fort Worth in the center of a circle with proposed rail lines radiating out in all directions. As city leaders learned of a proposed railroad being built across Texas, they encouraged railroad builders to consider routing the new line through Fort Worth; with the addition of various tracks, the map began to resemble a *tarantula*.

The Tarantula's trains include steam locomotive No. 2248, built in 1896 and called a "heavy mountain-class" locomotive. No. 2248 was purchased by the Texas State Railroad, became Engine No. 200 and was painted blue with red and white trim in honor of the United States Bicentennial. In 1990, No. 2248 was purchased by today's Tarantula company. "Puffy," as the engine is fondly called, was fully restored, to the tune of $1 million, and placed in service in 1992; it's the only operational steam locomotive in Texas that dates from before 1900.

The train's passenger coaches include four 1925 day coaches, purchased from the Strasburg Railroad in Strasburg, Pennsylvania. The coaches' period decor dates to approximately 1908 but is outfitted with new upholstery, wooden doors and trim, light fixtures, brass appointments, art glass windows, and window shades. Each car also has a ceiling fan and rest room.

The 10-mile trek alongside the famous Chisholm Trail passes through the western edge of downtown Fort Worth, crossing both the West and Clear Forks of the Trinity River on large trestles that offer spectacular views of the Fort Worth skyline that you won't see from city streets. You'll travel through pretty Trinity Park, near Fort Worth's Cultural District and the Fort Worth Zoo.

Upon the train's return, take an arm-in-arm stroll through the shops and galleries inside Stockyards Station. In the **Stockyards Station Gallery** (817–624–7300), you'll be tempted to empty your wallets on Western art, including original oils and bronzes, Remington and Russell prints, specialty dinnerware by artist Till Goodan, ranch photography, travel bags, gift items bearing the Texas State Seal, books,

Shootout at the White Elephant Saloon

While the two of you are having a drink at the White Elephant Saloon, you can think about the saloon's place in Texas history. Each year on February 8, historians in the Stockyards celebrate the most famous—and last—Old West gunfight to take place in the district. Actors recreate the incident that occurred in front of the White Elephant Saloon (then located nearby on Main Street) on February 8, 1887. Because the area had become a dangerous place, thanks to the outlaws who loved to spend time here, the town hired T. I. "Longhair Jim" Courtright—who was a marksman, Civil War hero, former marshal, and private detective—to keep order. His illustrious career ended in a duel with gambler Luke Short, who owned the White Elephant and was a friend to Wyatt Earp, Bat Masterson, and Doc Holliday. Courtright's gun jammed, costing him his life, but a subsequent investigation declared the duel legal.

Courtright was buried near the Stockyards at Oakwood Cemetery (Grand Avenue at Gould Street), as was Short, who died in 1893 of natural causes. Other notables buried there include General Winfield Scott, Jim Miller, the gunman who killed the famous lawman Pat Garrett, and various cattle barons who settled Fort Worth.

jewelry, and more. Other shops sell everything from Texas souvenir T-shirts and posters, candy, and food gifts, such as salsas, chili mustards, jams, and other goodies.

Right across the street is the **Stockyards Museum**, inside the Livestock Exchange Building (131 East Exchange Avenue; 817–625–5087), a lovely 1902 building that once headquartered one of the world's greatest livestock markets. Among the Stockyards memorabilia you'll see Western and Indian artifacts pertaining to the district. It's open Monday through Saturday from 10:00 A.M. to 5:00 P.M. Admission is free, but donations are appreciated.

Now wander back along Exchange Avenue to see more shops housed in historic buildings. **Fincher's Western Store** (115 East Exchange Avenue; 817–624–7302) occupies the 1910 structure that was the Stockyards National Bank until 1933. For more than fifty years, it's been a great place to buy cowboy boots, hats, and the like.

The two of you can find still more fine Western wear, as well as saddles and tack (which makes for good decor, if you're doing Old West at home) at **M. L. Leddy's Boot & Saddlery** (2455 North Main Street at Exchange Avenue; 817–624–3149), in business since 1941 at this location. The building is a 1907 work by architects A. J. Long and C. A. O'Keefe, with a rough-wood exterior.

Across the street is another 1907 Long-O'Keefe work, the **General Store** (101 West Exchange Avenue; 817–625–4061) has been a dry-goods outlet for most of its existence. It's an ideal place to pick up Texas souvenirs, housewares, books, and Indian rugs.

DAY ONE: *Evening*

DINNER

Two excellent dinner options await the two of you tonight. First is **Cattleman's Steak House** (2458 North Main Street; 817–624–3945; moderate to expensive), a landmark since 1947. Every sort of heavy beef steak you can imagine is here; you choose the exact cut you desire, and the cooks grill it over an open fire to your specifications. If you're daring, have the calf fries—a tasty, tender delicacy from the calf's most tender area. This is an old-fashioned, friendly spot, with a saloon setting and walls covered with pictures of past champion cattle from the Fort Worth Stock Show.

The other great choice this evening is **Joe T. Garcia's Mexican Dishes** (2201 North Commerce Street; 817–626–4356; moderate), a favorite Fort Worth tradition for nearly seventy years. This family operation began as the tiny house that is now but one corner of the enormous spread of Mexican-tiled dining rooms and a succession of lush patios. Meals consist of sizzling platters of beef or chicken fajitas, as well as the standard Mexican dinner, which is an ample supply of cheese nachos, beef tacos, cheese enchiladas, guacamole, refried beans, rice, and chips and salsa.

Some folks go simply to sip the lethal margaritas and enjoy a nice evening on the landscaped patios. Don't be surprised if you have to wait in line for a table.

Your post-dinner options are numerous. Put your heads together and decide what sounds like the most fun. If it's Friday or Saturday night, you'll want to take in a rodeo at **Cowtown Coliseum** (123 East Exchange Avenue; 817–625–1025; $5–$12). Home of the world's first indoor rodeo, the 1907–1908 building also hosted such cultural gatherings as an opera performance by Enrico Caruso. Wild West shows are offered during the summer, too.

If it's live music you two crave, wander a block north to **Billy Bob's Texas** (2520 Rodeo Plaza; 817–624–7117; cover charge varies), widely known as the world's largest honky-tonk. Slightly more low-key is the **White Elephant Saloon** (106 East Exchange Avenue; 817–624–1887; cover varies), an Old West barroom that occupies a 1930 building. It has a small dance floor and traditional, boot-scootin' music nightly. Both of these nightspots are described in greater detail in Itinerary 7.

DAY TWO: *Morning*

BREAKFAST

Have coffee and juice at your B&B or hotel, and then head down Main Street to **Esperanza's** (2140 North Main Street; 817–626–5770; inexpensive). Because it's owned by the same Garcia family, lots of locals just call this Joe T.'s Bakery; you'll both call it wonderful for its filling, delightful morning feasts. Beneath an array of Mexican piñatas, you'll chow down on *migas*, which are plates of eggs scrambled with tortilla strips, ranchero sauce, and chicken; or *huevos y chorizo con papas*, eggs scrambled with spicy Mexican sausage and potato chunks. It's authentic and sensational.

Thus fortified, the two of you can leave the Stockyards now and head south to the downtown area. Your passions will be stirred as you imagine yourselves living a life of wealth and luxury in a cattle baron mansion. There are two fine old homes to see here.

You can tour the exceptional **Eddleman McFarland House** (1110 Penn Street; 817–332–5875; $2.50) between 9:00 A.M. and 4:00 P.M. Monday through Friday. Otherwise, it's still a wonderful house to view from the outside, if just for its architecture and setting. Sitting on a bluff overlooking the Trinity, this gorgeous 1899 home is one of few remaining examples of Fort Worth's famed cattle baron homes. Designed by English architect Howard Messer, of the firm Messer, Sanguinet and Messer, the home has belonged only to two families and is mostly unchanged from its original bearing. Carrie (Mrs. Frank Hays) McFarland lived in the house for seventy-five years. She inherited the grand home—noted for turrets, gables, copper finials, a slate-tile roof, and a porch of red sandstone and marble—from her father, William H. Eddleman. Weekend tours are arranged by appointment.

Nearby, find **Thistle Hill** (1509 Pennsylvania Avenue; 817–336–1212; $4), known as the last of the fabulous cattle baron mansions. Meticulously restored to its 1910 opulence, the home represents the wealth that populated an area once called Quality Hill. Built by Albert Buckman Wharton, who married Electra Waggoner, the daughter of North Texas rancher W. T. Waggoner, the home was designed by the famous Texas architect Marshall Sanguinet; it cost $42,000. The interior features bog oak, white oak, curly maple, bird's-eye maple, mahogany, and local soft pine. Marvel at the public rooms, a parlor, a library, a billiard room, a dining room with a conservatory, as well as a wide staircase with a stained-glass window, and you'll understand why a huge number of weddings and wedding receptions are held here, year-round. Thistle Hill is open Monday through Friday from 10:00 A.M. to 3:00 P.M. and Sunday from 1:00 to 4:00 P.M.

FOR MORE ROMANCE

Visit the **Cattle Raisers Museum** (1301 West Seventh Street; 817–332–7064; free). Operated by the Texas and Southwestern Cattle Raisers Foundation, this small but delightful museum captures the romance of the Old West with displays in colorful exhibits, film, photographs, and cowboy memorabilia—such as barbed wire, branding irons, and saddles. This museum represents the history and significance of the Texas ranching industry. You can visit the museum Monday through Friday from 8:30 A.M. to 4:30 P.M. Admission is free.

Flirting on the Frontier
A WEATHERFORD GETAWAY

EATHERFORD IS BECOMING THE PERFECT getaway home for people who work thirty minutes east in Fort Worth. The town grew from its creation in the 1850s as the seat of Parker County and was named for Jefferson Weatherford, a member of the Texas Senate when the county was created.

A western frontier settlement located on the wagon-train route between Fort Worth and Fort Belknap, Weatherford has a rich, romantic cattle drive history, too. Today, it's a peaceful town with a welcoming, restful attitude. The two of you can poke through antiques shops, tour a beautiful garden or a historic cemetery, and take long walking (or driving) tours of historic neighborhoods filled with Victorian architecture. Or you can do nothing in great comfort, tucked into your lovely bed-and-breakfast hideaway.

PRACTICAL NOTE: Pop into the visitors' center on Highway 180, inside the restored, 1909 **Santa Fe Depot** (401 Fort Worth Street; 817–596–3801) to get some maps of the historic neighborhoods. It's open from 8:30 A.M. to 5:00 P.M. Monday through Friday.

DAY ONE: *Morning*

BREAKFAST

On your way into Weatherford, stop for a tummy-filler at **Jack's Family Restaurant** (3503 Fort Worth Highway; Weatherford; 817–594–6464; inexpensive). Take advantage of the bountiful breakfast buffet—laden with eggs, sausage and bacon, pancakes, hash browns, and biscuits—or just order toast and save room for lunch.

Check into your bed-and-breakfast. The first of my two favorites is the **St. Botolph Inn Bed & Breakfast** (808 South Lamar Street; 817–594–1455; $80–$165), found within a meticulously restored Queen Anne–style mansion built in 1897. All rooms and suites have private baths; four rooms open onto a second-floor ballroom. Especially romantic are the King David Suite, with a sitting room and breakfast nook tucked into a turret that offers astounding views; and the Song of Solomon Suite, with a private entrance and giant tub for two.

Another marvelous B&B choice is the **Angel's Nest & Breakfast** (1105 Palo Pinto Street; 817–599–9600 or 800–687–1660; $90–$270). There are ten guest rooms in this exceptional, century-old home, all with private baths; some have Jacuzzis, and all are decorated in elaborate style. Breakfast is served in three courses on silver, china, and crystal.

After dropping off your overnight bags, put on your favorite walking shoes and head downtown. The first thing you'll want to examine—and which you surely saw heading into town—is the magnificent **Parker County Courthouse** (junction of Highways 180 and 171). Three previous structures were destroyed by fire, but the

Romance

AT A GLANCE

◆ Find your cozy room at **St. Botolph Inn Bed & Breakfast** (808 South Lamar Street; 817–594–1455) or **Angel's Nest & Breakfast** (1105 Palo Pinto Street; 817–599–9600 or 800–687–1660), and then take photographs of the **Parker County Courthouse** (junction of Highways 180 and 171) and do some browsing through **First Monday Trade Days** (junction of Highways 80 and 180).

◆ Explore the history-rich **Greenwood Cemetery** (Elm and Front Streets; 817–596–3801) and wrap up the day with a feast at the **Mesquite Pit** (1201 Fort Worth Street; 817–596–7046).

one you see now was built from locally quarried limestone and erected at a cost of $55,555.55. Dedicated in 1886, it's the design of Waco architect Wesley Clarke Dobson, who designed nine other Texas courthouses. Be sure to take keepsake photos of each other here.

If it's the weekend prior to the first Monday of the month, walk arm in arm across the street to the giant flea market known as **First Monday Trade Days.** Dating back to the days when farmers and ranchers would come to town just before the beginning of monthly court sessions, the regular event offers every sort of treasure and junk you can imagine. Anything from a pair of old cowboy boots, a shovel, homemade jam, an antique mirror, and just-weaned puppies can be yours.

DAY ONE: *Afternoon*

LUNCH

Mosey back to the courthouse together and look south a few feet. There's the **Downtown Café** (101 West Church Street; 817–594–8717; inexpensive), a friendly little family diner. If the blue plate special is chicken-fried steak or meat loaf, get it. Be sure to have pecan or cherry pie, too. Whatever's on special is what you should have.

If the two of you feel like poking through some of the shops around the cute, old downtown, head north along Main to the **Treasure Chest Boutique** (303 North Main Street; 817–594–2220). This not-for-profit resale shop, open Tuesday through Saturday, supports Freedom House, a center for local domestic violence victims. Another little spot to hunt for antiques is **Miss B's** (311 North Main Street; 817–596–0902).

Just northeast of the courthouse, you'll find quiet pathways to stroll in the beautiful and history-rich **Greenwood Cemetery** (Elm and Front Streets; 817–596–3801; free). Broadway actress Mary Martin (star of *Peter Pan* and *South Pacific*, among many shows) is buried in the cemetery, as is English painter Douglas Chandor. The oldest grave here is dated 1859. Buried in the cemetery are soldiers from Texas's war for independence, as well as Civil, Spanish-American, Korean, Vietnam, and both world wars.

You'll see a state historical marker at the grave of Oliver Loving, affectionately known as the "Dean of Texas Trail Drivers," who moved to Parker County from Kentucky around 1855. Loving was wounded by Indians during a drive with Charles Goodnight and died in 1867 at Fort Sumner, New Mexico, after traveling in secret without food for five days. The story of his burial was romanticized in West Texas author Larry McMurtry's Pulitzer-winning novel *Lonesome Dove.* Loving's son and Goodnight kept Goodnight's promise to Loving, returning Loving's body more than 600 miles by wagon for burial in his hometown of Weatherford.

Just southwest of downtown, the two of you will find **Heritage Gallery** in the Weatherford Public Library (1214 Charles Street; 817-598-4150; free), with exhibits detailing the life and career of a favorite hometown daughter, the late actress Mary Martin. The library was a beneficiary of the Broadway star, whose image as Peter Pan is exhibited in a striking bronze statue by Texas artist Ronald Thomason. The gallery features a rich Mary Martin Collection, augmented since her death by family donations, including those by her son and star of TV's *Dallas*, Larry Hagman. The gallery is closed on Sunday. It's open from 10:00 A.M. to 6:00 P.M. Monday, Wednesday, Friday, and Saturday and from 1:00 P.M. to 9:00 P.M. Tuesday and Thursday.

Wind up your touring with a walking (or driving) tour past some of Weatherford's most interesting private residences. In the southwest quadrant of town, you'll see possibly the most gorgeous home in town at **508 Davis Street**, which runs parallel to South Main Street. Including a basement and attic, the red-brick Victorian with green trim is a four-floor beauty designed by Barker and Barker of Knoxville, Tennessee, and was completed in 1899.

Around the corner at **604 South Alamo Street** is a spectacular cream-and-white home built in 1872 by S. W. T. Lanham, a schoolteacher who went on to become an attorney, U. S. Congressman, and Texas governor. He was also the father of Fritz Lanham, also a U. S. Congressman.

And at **202 West Oak Street** is a lovely Queen Anne–style home, surrounded by an ornate iron fence, painted cream, detailed in blue,

In an English Country Garden

A place of phenomenal beauty in Weatherford is Chandor Gardens (710 West Simmons Street; 817–613–1700). Begun in 1936, its creator was English artist Douglas Chandor, who gained international fame by painting extraordinary portraits of Winston Churchill, Franklin D. Roosevelt, Queen Elizabeth II, Sam Rayburn, and others. In 1934 he married Ina Hill of Weatherford where he crafted a showplace of their estate grounds in her hometown. He named it White Shadows and designed a complex network of plants, trees, Chinese pagodas, Japanese water gardens, and even a small replica of Mount Fujiyama to surround their home.

Chandor died suddenly in 1953 of a brain hemorrhage, just before seeing his and Ina's dream home completed. The gardens were open to visitors from the 1940s through the 1960s, then closed and left to ruin. Bought and restored by a local family in 1994, the gardens—and English lawn bowling green, streams crossed by stepping-stones, courtyards blanketed by roses—are again a gorgeous place to visit, meditate, and wander. It's also a lovely place to have a wedding.

Chandor Gardens are open from March through November. Hours are 1:00 to 5:00 P.M. Sunday, or by appointment. Admission costs $6.00 per person.

and crowned with a red roof. This is fitting for the childhood home of Jim Wright, who became the youngest mayor in Weatherford's history and then a U. S. Congressman and Speaker of the House.

DAY ONE: *Evening*

DINNER

Take a great, big appetite along with the two of you to dine at the **Mesquite Pit** (1201 Fort Worth Street; 817–596–7046; inexpensive/ moderate). One of the busiest, most dependable places in town, the Pit offers mesquite-grilled steaks as well as smoked brisket, ham, pork ribs, and sausage, plus burgers, chicken-fried steak, and grilled chicken breast.

Weatherford isn't known for its nightlife. Your best bet is to head back to the B&B and spend some time in the Jacuzzi. Maybe you could also give each other a back rub.

DAY TWO: *Morning*

BREAKFAST

At Angel's Nest, your breakfast will probably include sausage, eggs, biscuits, fruit salad, and coffee. At St. Botolph, you'll be able to choose from a menu listing a dozen selections. The gourmet spread is likely to offer egg dishes, Belgian waffle with fruit compote, multigrain pecan pancakes, bacon, and sausage. You can dine in the formal dining room, on the veranda, or in your room.

On any day of the week, the town **Farmers Market** (2 blocks east of the courthouse on Highway 180) is a good place for the two of you to browse. Inside an open-air, vintage stucco building are the bounties of area farmers. Choose from among the beautiful produce, including fresh tomatoes, corn on the cob, peppers, onions, and the legendary Parker County peaches. Locally made honey, jelly, and jam are offered, too, as are dozens of tropical and bedding plants, at bargain prices.

FOR MORE ROMANCE

If the weather is as nice as usual, take a picnic along when the two of you go exploring **Holland Lake Park** (exit 409 off Interstate 20 to Clear Lake Road). A ten-acre nature preserve, the city park has a marked nature trail that details three different ecosystems in a relatively small area. The park is also where you'll find G. A. Holland's double-log cabins, awarded a Texas Centennial Historical Marker in 1936.

ᵖPIONEER ᵖPASSION

HISTORIC DENTON

ERHAPS THE GREATEST CHARM HELD BY THE DENTON County seat—like most of the other towns in this group of itineraries—is its function as an instantaneous antidote to city life. For denizens of Dallas or Fort Worth, Denton offers perfect escape and utter relaxation just minutes away, sitting 35 miles north of each city.

Denton was founded in 1857 and is a place known for producing more educators than any other spot in the nation. Such a distinction is credited to the existence of the University of North Texas (UNT) and Texas Woman's University (TWU), both of which offer powerful education departments. The college atmosphere, as well as a hearty historical flavor, makes Denton a delightful place for a couple to kick back and share valuable downtime, wandering together through quaint museums and antiques shops.

DAY ONE: *Morning*

BREAKFAST

Before heading to Denton, fill up on breakfast. If you're driving from Dallas, stop first at the **Mecca** (10422 Harry Hines Boulevard, Dallas; 214–352–0051; inexpensive). A truckstop-ish diner straight out of Hollywood, this longtime favorite makes excellent omelettes and waffles. The cinnamon rolls cover an entire plate, and they're delicious.

If you're en route from Fort Worth, stop at **Cactus Flower Café** (2401 Westport Parkway, Fort Worth; 817–491–9524; inexpensive). A branch of the popular morning spot in Fort Worth's Cultural District, this friendly diner has wonderful pancakes, steak and eggs, Spanish omelettes, and giant, homemade cinnamon rolls with gooey icing.

Drive to Denton straight up Interstate 35 and check into the **Redbud Inn** (815 North Locust Street; 940–565–6414; $56–$100), a warm and comfortable 1910 Tudor Revival home near TWU. Five rooms—named Brass, Wicker, Walnut, Oak, and Country—all have private baths and antique furnishings. Breakfast is included at the inn.

Put on comfortable walking shoes and head to the historic center of town, revitalized in recent years under the Main Street Program. You'll make your first stop at the beautiful **Denton County Courthouse,** home to the **Denton County Historical Museum** (110 West Hickory Street; 940–565–5667; free), a collection of area and Old West artifacts, including pressed blue glass, dolls, guns, pottery, and wonderful historic photos. The museum is also a genealogy research center.

Be sure to bring your cameras, if architecture interests you. The Denton courthouse was completed in 1897 of native stone—including marble from Burnet in Central Texas, limestone, and carved sandstone—in a freeform style combining various Victorian influences. There's a marvelous clock tower, as well as several turrets, giving this sort of a fairy-tale appeal.

You'll see on the courthouse lawn the burial site of John B. Denton, the pioneer lawyer, preacher, and soldier for whom the town

Romance
AT A GLANCE

◆ *Drop your belongings at* **the Redbud Inn** *(815 North Locust Street; 940–565–6414) and then wander over to the* **Denton County Historical Museum** *(110 West Hickory Street; 940–565–5667).*

◆ *Browse at* **Longhorn Gallery** *(101 North Elm Street; 940–484–8778) and* **Recycled Books, Records and CDs** *(200 North Locust Street; 940–566–5688).*

◆ *Have a leisurely dinner at the* **Texican Grill** *(111 West Mulberry Street; 940–381–6722), and then hear live music at* **Rick's Place** *(125 Avenue A; 940–382–4141).*

The Bad Dude of Denton

Denton's most notorious resident was surely Sam Bass, who introduced train robberies to Texas. Bass, an Indiana native, was a teenage farmhand in Denton in 1870, but he quit his job four years later after some wins at the horse races. Later he joined a cattle drive headed for North Dakota but wound up robbing some stagecoaches. He eventually scored a big hit on a Nebraska train robbery and moved back to Denton County. With his riches he bought fancy clothes down in Fort Worth, where he also outfitted his gang of eight with new rifles. Sam Bass & Co. robbed several trains in North Texas before the Texas Rangers, William Pinkerton, and others went after him. He was finally ambushed in Round Rock (near Austin) just two days shy of his twenty-seventh birthday, July 21, 1878. Today Sam's name lives on in cowboy songs.

was named. He died—with his boots on, as they say—on horseback while fighting Indians.

On the courthouse square are diversions to fill what's left of the morning. **Evers Hardware** (109 West Hickory Street; 940–382–5513) remains unchanged since its opening in 1885, and it's been in the same family all along. Merchandise is stacked floor to ceiling, and clerks still use rolling ladders to access higher shelves. It's a delightful blast from the past. It's closed on Sunday.

If you share a love for rummaging for treasures, pop into the numerous antiques shops facing the square. Among choices with stashes of coins, books, jewelry, glassware, furniture, old postcards, lace, and such are minimalls at 108 North Locust Street and 118 North Locust Street. Another shop to explore is called **Sleeping Lizards** (708 North Locust Street; 940–484–4056), brightly painted on the exterior and with an interior stocking zany greeting cards, dangling earrings, baskets of incense, homemade birdhouses crafted from doorknobs and bent spoons, and fresh flowers. Just down the block, there's **This Old House** (809 North Locust Street; 940–565–0667), selling such housewares as ivy topiaries, framed illustrations and paintings, colorful tableware and pottery, and handmade furniture such as cupboards and sideboards crafted from old doors.

Even if you decide to skip the shops, don't miss a visit to the impressive **Longhorn Gallery** (101 North Elm Street; 940–484–8778). Unusual in that it's not a historic building, it was designed specifically to blend in with its vintage neighbors. The beautiful, 4,500-square-foot gallery features oil, watercolor, pencil, and mixed media paintings; sculpture in bronze, woods, welded steel, and clay; modern glass sculpture, including pieces from Venice; hand-etched crystal; gourd art; handmade jewelry in sterling with semiprecious stones; and limited edition prints and serigraphs.

Many of the artists whose work is exhibited at Longhorn are either established or emerging creators from west of the Mississippi. The gallery is open from 10:00 A.M. to 5:00 P.M. Tuesday through Friday and 10:00 A.M. to 4:00 P.M. Saturday.

DAY ONE: *Afternoon*

LUNCH

Get a healthy but wonderfully tasty fix at **Cupboard Café**, inside Cupboard Natural Foods store (200 West Congress Street; 940–387–5386; inexpensive). The dishes here are so delicious, you'll have trouble believing that they're good for you. Spicy lentil soup goes nicely with wrap sandwiches, such as the whole wheat tortilla rolled around natural turkey, avocado, jack cheese, and sprouts. There's terrific jalapeño-apple pie for dessert and lots of natural drinks and teas.

Before leaving the historic downtown area, spend some time at **Recycled Books, Records and CDs** (200 North Locust Street; 940–566–5688) on the northeast corner of the square. The three-story, 17,000-square-foot store counts some 200,000 books in its inventory, as well as 12,000 or more CDs, and thousands of record albums. Look around—maybe you'll find the music you fell in love to, whether it was Frank Sinatra, Stevie Wonder, or K. C. and the Sunshine Band.

While away your afternoon together strolling the campuses. At UNT check out the **Rare Book Room and Texana Collections** (in the Willis Library; 940–565–2769; free). If you're bibliophiles, you'll relish the Rare

Book Collection's holdings in eighteenth-century English literature—especially the Romantic poet William Blake—travel, and the history of printing and illustration. Travel literature, includes more than 200 titles from the Orient, across Europe, and into the Americas. There's also a fascinating collection—more than 500 titles here—of miniature books.

If you are history buffs, linger in the Texana Collection, with artifacts ranging from documents such as the constitutions of 1824 and 1836 and the laws of colonization, to more than one hundred important maps dating from 1597 to 1900. In addition this collection houses books from the private library of Anson Jones, the last president of the Republic of Texas. It's open from 8:00 A.M. to 5:00 P.M. Monday through Friday.

At the nearby TWU campus, have a look in the lovely **Little Chapel-in-the-Woods** (Bell and University Streets; 940–898–3642; free). Designed by O'Neil Ford, the chapel has been named one of Texas's twenty most outstanding architectural achievements. The chapel dates from 1939, and its dedication ceremony was attended by First Lady Eleanor Roosevelt. In the stained-glass window design—created by TWU arts students—you'll find a theme called, "Woman Ministering to Human Needs." A place for meditation and for weddings, the chapel is open during school hours.

Also at TWU visit the **Gowns of the First Ladies of Texas** exhibit in the Human Development Building (117 Bell Avenue; 940–898–3201; free). This collection is the only one of its kind, offering either the actual garments or true copies of the gowns worn by the wives of the governors of Texas and presidents of the Republic of Texas. Created in 1940 the exhibit has been updated with gowns worn by former first ladies Mamie Eisenhower and Lady Bird Johnson during their husbands' terms in the White House. Open from 8:00 A.M. to 5:00 P.M. Monday through Friday during fall and spring semesters. Call for an appointment during summer sessions.

DAY ONE: *Evening*

DINNER

Put on your feedbags at the **Texican Grill** (111 West Mulberry Street; 940–381–6722; inexpensive), found about 2 blocks south of the courthouse square in a renovated blacksmith shop. The setting involves light fixtures crafted from old wagon wheels and decor wrought from farm equipment, as well as exposed brick walls. Your feast can be anything from crab claws in hot garlic butter and delicious fried catfish to grilled chicken with black beans and sautéed peppers in tortillas or linguine topped with salmon. And ooh, dessert—try the apple caramel crisp.

Denton is a town well known for its emerging alternative music scene. If you're the adventurous types, head to **Rick's Place** (125 Avenue A; 940–382–4141), a very casual, no frills, upstairs/downstairs club with local talent and cheap beer. A very contemporary and hugely popular regional band called Brave Combo plays here at times. Cover charge varies from $5.00 to $8.00.

Another idea is **Rubber Gloves Rehearsal Studios** (411 East Sycamore Street; 940–387–7781), a simple band rehearsal joint for touring and hometown punk and underground shows that lets the public in, too. Cover charges at these are usually $5.00 to $8.00.

Finally, wend your way back to the B&B, and snuggle in for a good night's rest.

DAY TWO: *Morning*

BREAKFAST

Talk about your visit to Denton over breakfast at Redbud Inn—always a gratifying meal. Choices might include buttermilk-blueberry pancakes, Belgian waffles, or an egg casserole, with lots of juices, coffee, and tea.

FOR MORE ROMANCE

Your history-loving souls will enjoy the **Hangar 10 Flying Museum** (Denton Municipal Airport, 1945 Matt Wright Lane; 940–565–1945). The four planes displayed here are the Lockheed 10A, which has been owned by child movie star Margaret O'Brien, among others; the Stagger Wing, used mainly for VIPs; the Army Air Corps' PT-22, used primarily as a trainer for new pilots; and the sporty-looking Piper L-4, a World War II reconnaissance plane. The museum is open from 8:00 A.M. to 2:00 P.M. Monday through Saturday. Admission is free.

Cozy Countryside B&B Getaways

Cuddling in Collin County
A MCKINNEY RESPITE

ITY REFUGEES WITH THE FORTITUDE TO CHARGE north-ward through the suburban congestion known as Plano will find relief just beyond that in the charming and infi-nitely quaint heart of McKinney. About 30 miles north of down-town Dallas and some 60 miles north of Fort Worth, the Collin County seat was settled in 1845 and named for Collin McKinney, a signer of the Texas Declaration of Independence.

McKinney is becoming known as a delightful place to run away to for a day or two, with more than 1,700 historic homes and buildings and a lovely courthouse square provided to help the two of you erase—at least temporarily—mental images of skyscrapers and freeways. In this itinerary, you'll both be downshifting to a much slower gear than the one you use in the city. There are vintage homes to tour, antiques shops to peruse, a nature center to explore, and bed-and-breakfast comforts to exhaust. Reach McKinney from Dallas driving due north on Highway 75. From Fort Worth, drive north of Highway 121.

PRACTICAL NOTE: Reservations are advised for weekend dinners at the Goodhues Wood-Fired Grill.

DAY ONE: *Morning*

BREAKFAST

As you set out toward McKinney, stop first for sustenance. If you're leaving from Dallas, stop en route at **Corner Bakery** (2401 Preston Road in Plano; 972–398–1955; inexpensive), the Chicago export that offers a huge selection of excellent pastries.

A good place to stop on the way out of Fort Worth is **Einstein Bros. Bagels** (2200 Airport Freeway/Highway 121 in Bedford; 817–354–5773; inexpensive). A cranberry bagel spread with honey walnut cream cheese or a lemon poppyseed muffin should keep you for awhile.

Park your car and drop your bags at **Dowell House Bed & Breakfast** (1104 South Tennessee Street; 972–562–2456; $85–$95), a lodging that occupies a Federal/Classical style home that was built in 1870. Guest rooms have private baths, and there's a full breakfast provided with stays on Friday or Saturday night. Weeknight stays include a continental breakfast the following morning.

Another inviting option is the **Bingham House** (800 Chestnut Street; 972–529–1883; $79–$149), a gorgeous retreat within a Georgian Italianate mansion built in 1883. Each of four guest rooms has a queen-size bed, private bath, a wealth of period antiques, and color TV. Guests are not only treated to an elaborate breakfast, but are also offered evening cordials and hors d'oeuvres. If you'd like to arrange for flowers and champagne, just ask.

Now wander down to **Chestnut Square** (311 South Chestnut Street; 972–562–8790) to explore some wonderful examples of peri-

Romance
AT A GLANCE

◆ After dropping your bags at **Dowell House Bed & Breakfast** (1104 South Tennessee Street; 972-562-2456) or **Bingham House** (800 Chestnut Street; 972-529-1883), head down to tour the historic buildings at **Chestnut Square** (311 South Chestnut Street; 972-562-8790).

◆ Have a snack at **Backstage Coffee Company** (103 East Virginia Street; 972-542-1289) and take a walk through the **Heard Museum and Wildlife Sanctuary** (Farm Road 1378; 972-542-5566).

◆ Celebrate in the evening with a lavish dinner at **Goodhues Wood-Fired Grill** (204 West Virginia Street; 972-562-7570).

A Picnic in the Shadow of History

If the two of you are looking for a relaxing time alone together, pack a lunch and head over to Finch Park, a 25-acre, wooded expanse on the south side of McKinney. Drive south from downtown on Kentucky Street; at the southern end of town, you'll run into Finch Park.

If he hadn't been born in New Jersey and lived in Virginia, Kentucky, and Arkansas before traveling to Texas with his second wife, Betsy Coleman, and their six children, Collin McKinney might have been the most Texan of any state native in history. He was one of the drafters of the Texas Declaration of Independence, as well as a signer, and he is said to have boasted about living under eight flags before his death at ninety-five—the British, Colonial, Spanish, Mexican, Texas Provisional, Texas Republic, United States, and Confederate. He died a Confederate in 1861 and is buried about 15 miles north of McKinney in the burg of Van Alstyne. He's credited with having been the lawmaker who decided that counties in central North Texas should have straight lines. In 1936, the Texas Centennial Committee moved his family cabin to Finch Park, where you're enjoying your picnic more than sixty years later.

od buildings from the area. Among the seven Victorian and Greek Revival houses, built between 1853 and 1910, is the **Dulaney House**, a 1910, prairie-style, two-story family home built by Joseph Dulaney. Inside you'll see an unusual collection of home furnishings and cultural artifacts, such as vintage clothing dating back to the 1860s. The home is frequently used for private parties and luncheons and by the Heritage Guild, the organization that runs Chestnut Square.

Chestnut Square is open for touring at 11:00 A.M. on Tuesday, Thursday, and Saturday, and by appointment. Admission costs $3.00 per person.

Now head to the downtown square, surrounded by old buildings filled with every sort of shop. Among the places where you can buy quilts for your new home or just simple keepsakes for each other are **Remember This Antique Mall** (210 Tennessee Street; 972–542–8011); **Town Square Antiques** (113 East Virginia Street; 972–542–4113); and **Treasures from the Past** (115 East Virginia Street; 972–548–0032).

DAY ONE: *Afternoon*

LUNCH

Take time out to just enjoy the lazy day, and to get your batteries recharged with soups and salads, sandwiches or blue plate specials at the **Opera House Restaurant** (107 North Kentucky Street; 972–562–3818; inexpensive). If you'd like something to spice up your day, try **Café Juarez** (311 East Louisiana Street; 972–548–9181; inexpensive). It's a merry little cantina serving simple Tex-Mex specialties, such as cheese or chicken enchiladas, chilies rellenos, beef tacos, and guacamole salad.

After lunch, pick up a couple of cappuccinos at **Backstage Coffee Company** (103 East Virginia Street; 972–542–1289) and head for the great outdoors. The best place to spend a nice day outside is the **Heard Museum and Wildlife Sanctuary**, a 287-acre refuge found by driving 2 miles south of McKinney on Highway 5 and east 1 mile on Farm Road 1378 (972–542–5566). Opened in 1967, the natural history museum grew from an extensive butterfly collection belonging to Miss Bessie Heard (1884–1988), who was dedicated to preserving the native wildlife and vegetation of Collin County. Inside the museum you'll find a 4,000-square-foot raptor rehab center, as well as collections of seashells, gems, and minerals.

The wildlife sanctuary offers 5 miles of trails the two of you can explore either by yourselves or with an interpreter. Living in the complex land, which consists of woodland, prairie, and wetlands types as well as an outcropping of Austin chalk limestone in the hilltops, are more than 240 species of birds, mammals, reptiles, and amphibians. In the 50-acre wetlands area, you'll find an outdoor learning center, observation deck, a floating laboratory, and a boardwalk. Inquire, too, about canoe tours through the sanctuary.

In any season, and especially in spring—when the wildflowers are exploding with color—you'll enjoy the sanctuary's Texas Native Plant Garden. This marvelous exhibit of regional trees, shrubs, grasses, vines, ground covers, and perennials native to the Lone Star State provides plenty of lovely scents, as well as picturesque settings in which you can photograph each other.

The Heard Museum and Sanctuary are open from 9:00 A.M. to 5:00 P.M. Monday through Saturday and from 1:00 to 5:00 P.M. Sunday. Guided nature trails are available on a first-come, first-served basis; trail times are at 11:30 A.M. on Saturday, and every half-hour from 1:30 until 3:30 P.M. on Sunday. Admission to the facility costs $3.00 per person.

DAY ONE: *Evening*

DINNER

For a sumptuous end to a soothing day, head to **Goodhues Wood-Fired Grill** (204 West Virginia Street; 972–562–7570; moderate/expensive), a newish bistro near the town square. Chef Chong Boey, who spent nearly two decades at the divine Jennivine in Dallas, is doing gorgeous things at this spot with escargots, roasted garlic with goat cheese, and pan-fried shrimp as appetizers. For entrees, you might consider a veal chop dressed with wild mushrooms and port wine; grilled salmon with Dijon sauce; or a center-cut filet with a buttery topping of blue cheese with roasted walnuts and apple-smoked bacon. Rhubarb custard pie and chocolate hazelnut pie are signature desserts. Some nice chardonnays and cabernets are included on a small wine list. The restaurant is open for dinner nightly, except Tuesday. Reservations are advised on weekends.

Have a decaf coffee with dessert, and then wander back to your B&B for a cozy night of cuddling.

DAY TWO: *Morning*

BREAKFAST

Breakfast at Dowell House, served in the formal dining room, generally consists of an egg dish, a breakfast meat, fruit, breads, coffee, and juice. At Bingham House, you'll have a choice of two or three house specialties. One favorite is a croissant stuffed with ham, egg, cheese, and spicy mustard, then baked; another is a casserole of egg, sausage, cheese, and potato. You won't be disappointed.

FOR MORE ROMANCE

If you're equestrian types, head over to **Jolabec Riding Stables** (Highway 380 at Custer Road; 972–562–0658). Experienced riders can take mounts unsupervised on trails, but you can easily take a guide along if that's what makes you both more comfortable. Do call ahead for reservations. Hourlong trail rides are $20 per person.

East Texas Escapade
COMFORTS IN ATHENS

T O THE EAST OF DALLAS/FORT WORTH lies the irresistible comforting region of Texas known as the Piney Woods, where romance is the natural by-product of the area's relaxing, rejuvenating powers. Winding, two-lane roads, fields of wildflowers, and dense stretches of evergreens characterize the territory, as do quaint burgs such as Athens.

The two of you will rediscover together what it means to unwind, tucked away in your bed-and-breakfast or touring the charming seat of Henderson County. If you share a love of hamburgers, you'll be pleased to know that this is where the treat is said to have been invented in the late 1880s. And if you're a pair who likes a country fair, you'll love the Uncle Fletch Hamburger Cook-Off and the Black-Eyed Pea Festival, both in October.

On this itinerary, the two of you will visit a haven for animals that is guaranteed to touch a spot deep in your souls. You'll also browse through what may be the largest flea market in all of the South, be pampered at a country-estate B&B, and generally recall what's it like to truly unwind.

PRACTICAL NOTE: Be sure to schedule your visit for a Saturday and Sunday during the weekend prior to the first Monday of the month.

DAY ONE: *Morning*

BREAKFAST

On the way to Athens, stop along Highway 175 at the community of Crandall to eat at **Crandall Cotton Gin** (1500 East Highway 175; 972–427–3883; inexpensive). Spreading out inside a former cotton gin, this homey restaurant serves solid country cooking. Get your day started with pancakes, eggs, and ham.

The very best reason—that's if you're animal lovers, and you soon will be, otherwise—for visiting Athens is found about 18 miles east of town at **Black Beauty Ranch** (off Highway 31 East, via Farm Road 1803 and County Road 3806; 903–469–3811; donations welcome). Open to the public on Saturday only from 9:00 A.M. to 4:00 P.M., the ranch is a wondrous, 1,150-acre refuge for unwanted and abused animals, including chimpanzees, burros, elephants, dogs, cats, horses, and many more. Founded in 1979 by the late author, Cleveland Amory, and the Fund for Animals, the ranch is a nonprofit facility supported primarily by private donors like yourselves.

During your tour at Black Beauty Ranch, you'll hear heartwarming stories of rescued animals who have befriended other rescued inhabitants here, and how the staff has become devoted to these creatures. Among the several hundred animals enjoying a safe, healthy home for the rest of their lives at this sanctuary are burros from Grand Canyon National Park, who had outlived their usefulness as pack animals. If the two of you are as swept away by the living stories at the ranch as most visitors are, you can "adopt" one of the burros together. Your sponsorship of the beast's upkeep will make you part of the ranch legacy.

Romance

AT A GLANCE

◆ See the heartwarming animals living at **Black Beauty Ranch** (off Highway 31 East, via Farm Road 1803 and County Road 3806; 903–469–3811), and then have a delicious lunch in town at **Danny's Smokehouse Bar-B-Q** (650 East Corsicana Street; 903–675–5238) or **Garden of Eating** (400 North Prarieville Street; 903–675–5181).

◆ Visit the **Texas Freshwater Fisheries Center** (5550 Flat Creek Road; 903–676–2277), then wind up the day with dinner at **Jubilee House Restaurant & Club** (114 East Corsicana Street; 903–675–1795).

◆ Dream sweet dreams at **the Carriage House** (Farm Road 753; 903–677–3939).

DAY ONE: *Afternoon*

LUNCH

Today's lunch can take on one of two distincly different personalities, depending on what yours are at the moment. If you'd like something hearty and purely Texan, then head over to **Danny's Smokehouse Bar-B-Q** (650 East Corsicana Street; 903–675–5238; inexpensive), a down-home, friendly, and rustic spot where you'll feast on barbecued pork ribs, beef brisket, and spicy sausage.

But if you'd like something lighter in a setting nearly as soft and sweet as the country mornings around these parts, head for the **Garden of Eating** in the Athens Alley Antique Mall (400 North Prairieville Street; 903–675–5181). Here your choices are a mix-and-match menu of sandwiches, soups, salads, and desserts.

Now for some more critters, these of the swimming variety. Even if neither of you thinks fish are interesting, you owe it to yourselves to visit the new **Texas Freshwater Fisheries Center** (5550 Flat Creek Road; 903–676–2277). Covering 106 acres and serving as the flagship operation of the Inland Fisheries Division of the Texas Parks and Wildlife, the fisheries center hosts the "sharelunker" program, designed to increase the production, size, and quality of Florida largemouth bass in Texas waters. By seeing such backstage workings, the two of you could fall in love with a new hobby together.

You'll enter through the massive visitors' center—named for Athens native Edwin L. Cox, Jr., a former chair of the Parks and Wildlife Foundation of Texas, rancher, and conservationist—offering an excellent introduction to a fascinating aquarium and hatchery complex that houses more than 300,000 gallons of more than forty fishy representatives from the state's freshwater streams, ponds, and lakes. Among hundreds of things to see (and often, to catch) are some of the heftiest largemouth bass in the world and the American alligator.

On your tour, you'll see divers hand-feeding lunker bass in a 26,000-gallon dive tank and, if either of you chooses, you can fish at a 1.5-acre casting pond stocked with rainbow trout or channel catfish.

You Want Fries with That?

Although the hamburger-creation story is disputed by some, Athens's claim to the crown is honored by no less than McDonald's Hamburger University, as stated on a historical marker you'll find on the north side of the Henderson County Courthouse Square, next to the 1927 First National Bank Building. The plaque explains that at Fletcher Davis's cafe there on the square, customers were wild about the creation of ground beef between two pieces of bread—generally called "steak sandwiches"—sold there. The town's gentry were so impressed with his dish that they collected money to send Uncle Fletch and his invention to the St. Louis World's Fair and Exposition in 1906. A New York reporter at the fair interviewed Fletch on the midway, which is said to have resulted in the first published account of the hamburgers. The two of you can debate whether the original burger had mustard or ketchup, pickles, or onions.

Before leaving the fisheries, have a prowl around the Flat Creek Bait 'N Goods gift shop, where you'll buy each other fun themed souvenirs, such as T-shirts, caps, fish-shaped lamps, and the always-romantic rubber frogs.

The fisheries center is open from 9:00 A.M. to 4:00 P.M. Tuesday through Saturday and from 1:00 to 4:00 P.M. Sunday. Admission costs $4.00 per person.

When you've had enough roaming around, check in at the **Carriage House** (3 miles outside of town via Highway 19 and Farm Road 753; 903–677–3939; $95–$120), a bed-and-breakfast lodging sitting on a 50-acre, country estate called Hickory Hill Farm. Your stay here—in either one of two downstairs rooms or the roomy upstairs suite, which has a sensational view—includes afternoon snacks, evening dessert, and a lavish Southern breakfast. All bedrooms have private baths, velour bathrobes, fluffy down comforters, pressed linens, and feather pillows.

If that one's full, try **Oak Meadow Bed & Breakfast** (2781 Farm Road 2495; 903–675–3407 or toll-free 877–675–3407; $85), a cozy little escape on a former quarter horse ranch. The two guest rooms have private baths and nice views, and the home's Great Room features a large fireplace, books by Texas legends, such as J. Frank Dobie; and an artwork collection by Texas artists, including A. D. Greer, Bill Zaner, Lil Mitchell, Roger Simmons, and Larry Prellop, thanks to the owners, who once owned an art gallery in San Antonio. An extravagant breakfast is included with your stay, of course, and you're encouraged to lose yourself in the rural wonders on a walk through oak groves on Oak Meadow's nine acres.

DAY ONE: *Evening*

DINNER

After a good rest, head over to the courthouse square to eat at **Jubilee House Restaurant & Club** (114 East Corsicana Street; 903–675–1795; moderate). Considered one of the top spots in town, this charming restaurant occupies a renovated period building and offers a diverse menu of grilled and blackened fish, prime steaks, Cajun dishes such as jambalaya, and a variety of pizzas and pasta. Because Athens is dry, you have to buy a "club membership" (it's cheap) to share a bottle of wine with dinner.

Athens isn't the place for nightlife, so you'll have to create your own excitement back at your B&B.

DAY TWO: *Morning*

BREAKFAST

At Carriage House, your full Southern breakfast will include eggs, sausage or bacon, biscuits or pastries, as well as fruits, juices, and coffee. At Oak Meadow, expect a country breakfast of eggs, bacon, grits, biscuits and gravy, and perhaps a fruit cup. Other choices might include orange French toast, blueberry muffins, or Belgian waffles with strawberry sauce.

After that sensational feast at your bed-and-breakfast, check out and head to **First Monday Trade Days** in Canton, 25 miles due north of Athens via Highway 19. Held on the Friday, Saturday, and Sunday prior to the first Monday of each month, this 150-year-old tradition takes place on a 100-acre marketplace where some 5,000 vendors sell anything you can think of—and a lot of stuff you've never thought of.

Goods may be very old, slightly used, or brand-new and usually range from ancient rocking chairs and baby carriages and iron beds to contemporary things like hand-crafted wooden toilet seats, quilts, jewelry, and clothes. Collectors will be happy to find old kitchenware, china, and depression glass. In terms of snacks, you'll be tempted by barbecue, fresh-roasted peanuts, popcorn, fudge, burgers, roasted corn, and pastries.

FOR MORE ROMANCE

If you're furnishing a home together or are looking for nice keepsakes of your trip, do so in style at some of the terrific antiques shops on and around the square. Our favorite collection of antiques dealers is found at the **Alley Antique Mall** (400 North Prairieville Street; 903–675–9292), where excellent European and American pieces include china cabinets, sideboards, beds, dressing tables, buffets, chairs, and much more. There's plenty of quality glassware, linens, and framed artwork, too.

Granbury

AND HOOD COUNTY VICTORIANA

*W*HEN FOLKS IN FORT WORTH AND DALLAS want to make a fast getaway from urban burdens, they'll often choose Granbury for its simple charms. About a half-hour drive southwest of Fort Worth and less than an hour from Dallas, Granbury straddles the lovely Brazos River (dammed, actually, to form Lake Granbury).

Settled in 1854 by Thomas Lambert, the town and county were named in 1866 for Civil War heroes General Hiram B. Granberry (the spelling was changed for the community's name) and General John B. Hood. Now the home to about 5,000 relaxed souls, Granbury stays busy every weekend with bed-and-breakfast guests and antiques hounds. It's the ideal place for two to revel in a rural spirit.

DAY ONE: *Morning*

BREAKFAST

As you reach the northern outskirts of Granbury, watch on the right side of Highway 377 for **Niester's** (4426 East Highway 377; 817–573–0211; inexpensive), a German deli with sensational weekend

164

breakfasts. Your choices include thick pancakes that cover an entire dinner plate and eggs with your choice of bratwurst or knackwurst.

Check into a bed-and-breakfast, such as the **Iron Horse Inn** (616 Thorp Spring Road; 817–579–5535; $90 and up), a grand, Craftsman-style home built in 1907 and renovated to accommodate plenty of guests. Among six bedrooms with private baths in the main house are the Baron's Balcony Suite, with French doors leading to a private balcony, and the Cogdell Suite, with its own solarium. The separate carriage house offers bedroom, sitting room, clawfoot tub, fireplace, cable TV, microwave, and refrigerator. Breakfast at this home is a special, multi-course affair, featuring egg-and-sausage casseroles, pastries and biscuits with homemade jam, and mixed fresh fruits.

Another fine choice is the **Arbor House** (530 Pearl Street; 817–573–0073; $95 and up), a lovely new structure fashioned after other Queen Anne homes of the town's Victorian period. Seven guest rooms have private baths, and some have Jacuzzi tubs. The inn faces Lake Granbury and is just a 3-block walk to the courthouse square.

After stashing your bags put on your favorite old tennis shoes and set out to spend the morning roaming the courthouse square. Surrounding the restored Hood County Courthouse, a wedding cake sort of structure that was built in 1891, are oodles of shops tucked into wonderful historic buildings. So remarkable is this collection of Victorian architecture that the Department of Interior noted, when naming this square to the National Register of Historic Places, that it's "one of the most complete examples of a late 19th century courthouse square in Texas."

Romance
AT A GLANCE

◆ Settle in at the **Iron Horse Inn** (616 Thorp Spring Road; 817–579–5535), and then stroll downtown to browse through the goods at **Brazos River Trading Company** (115 East Bridge Street; 817–573–5191), **Wagon Yard Antiques** (213 North Crockett Street; 817–573–5321), and **Books on the Square** (124 North Houston Street; 817–573–9672).

◆ Lunch at **Pearl Street Pasta House** (132 East Pearl Street; 817–279–8669), then resume your browsing and also visit the **Old Jail and Hood County Historical Museum** (208 North Crockett Street; 817–573–5135).

◆ Dine on Thai stir-fried prawns or stacked New Mexican enchiladas at **Hennington's Texas Café** (121 East Bridge Street; 817–573–9362) before taking in a musical at the **Opera House** (116 East Pearl Street; 817–573–9191).

A Wife Waits

About 5 miles north of Granbury along Highway 377 is a teensy town called Acton, where you'll find Acton Cemetery, the smallest of all of Texas's state parks. Inside the cemetery is the grave of Elizabeth Crockett, widow of Alamo hero Davy Crockett. Inside an aging little iron fence is a tall pedestal bearing a statue of Elizabeth, who appears to be scanning the horizon with her hand shading her brow, watching to see if her husband is heading home from fighting for Texas's independence.

Of the four dozen or so shops—many of them are antiques stores—facing the courthouse, one of the most interesting is **Brazos River Trading Company** (115 East Bridge Street; 817-573-5191). This shop blends old pieces of furniture and home accessories, such as lamps, bowls, and boxes, with new decor items, including blankets, rugs, and tableware.

For anything from old music boxes, hall clocks, and vintage magazines to reproduction pieces—including desks, dining tables, and rockers—you'll want to stroll through the sprawling **Wagon Yard Antiques** (213 North Crockett Street; 817-573-5321).

A small, charming bookstore that you can both be happily lost inside for a while is **Books on the Square** (124 North Houston Street; 817-573-9672).

Most of the courthouse square antiques shops, gift shops, and art galleries are open from 10:00 A.M. to 5:00 P.M. Tuesday through Saturday and noon until 5:00 P.M. on Sunday.

DAY ONE: *Afternoon*

LUNCH

Settle in for a plate of penne with vegetables or a pasta salad at **Pearl Street Pasta House** (on the south side of the square at 132 East Pearl Street; 817-279-8669; inexpensive). If the day is warm, the two of you can sit outside on the sidewalk patio and bask in the sun.

After lunch step next door to the **Coffee Grinder Espresso Bar** (129 East Pearl Street; 817–279–0977; inexpensive) for a cappuccino or cafe mocha.

There's plenty more browsing to be done on and near the square. The **Red Elk** (114 West Pearl Street; 817–573–3355) is a 1917 building that was once the assembly site for Ford Model Ts. Today's interior holds twenty-five antiques and gift dealers selling home decor items in lodge and Western styles, mirrors, glasswares, and jewelry.

At **Earth Harvest Market** (208 North Houston Street; 817–579–7335), you'll find some 400 varieties of bulk herbs, spices, and teas, as well as aromatherapy oils, and a huge selection of vitamins, homeopathic remedies, and books.

Before heading back to your B&B, visit the **Old Jail and Hood County Historical Museum** (208 North Crockett Street; 817–573–5135). As you tour the 1885-built jail, you'll see its original cell blocks and hanging tower, as well as collections of area artifacts and memorabilia from Hood County's early days. It's open from 1:00 to 4:00 P.M. Saturday and Sunday and by appointment on other days.

DAY ONE: *Evening*

DINNER

Mosey over to the Nutt House, an 1893 former store and longtime country inn, and have supper inside at **Hennington's Texas Cafe** (121 East Bridge Street; 817–573–9362; moderate). A physical and spiritual facelift in 1998 turned this tired little dining room into an excellent restaurant serving such delights as Thai stir-fried prawns, chicken and dill dumplings, stacked enchiladas with New Mexico chili sauce, and hot smoked salmon in avocado with tropical fruit on top. The interior is done in a hunting-lodge theme, and a good wine list is offered.

After dinner head across the square to the **Opera House** (116 East Pearl Street; 817–573–9191). Built in 1886 and completely restored in 1975, the theater offers year-round entertainment in such productions as Broadway-style musicals, popular theater, and musical revues. Call ahead to reserve seats. Performances are usually at 8:00 P.M.

DAY TWO: *Morning*

BREAKFAST

Enjoy a leisurely breakfast at your lodging. Typical offerings include egg casserole or pancakes with sausage or bacon, sinful pastries, fruit, and gourmet coffee and tea.

If you're a couple of history nuts, take a short hike north on Crockett Street to its intersection with Moore Street to the **Granbury Cemetery**. As you wander around the pastoral site, look for headstones marking the final resting places of General Hiram Granberry and the legendary outlaw Jesse James.

FOR MORE ROMANCE

On nice days you can take a **two-hour cruise** on a pontoon boat on Lake Granbury/Brazos River with boat captain John Hubbard. He charges $12 per person and can share lots of insight as to area scenery. Give him a buzz at 817–279–6556.

Gingerbread Bliss
IN WAXAHACHIE

A S MORE PEOPLE BECOME WEARY OF TRAFFIC SNARLS and other city hassles, plenty of them find that living just a half hour away makes life cheery once again. And so it's going with Dallas and Waxahachie (pronounced *WOCKS-a-hatch-ee*). The Ellis County seat, situated 30 miles south of downtown Dallas in rolling farmland, has become a permanent retreat for folks who require a slower pace in their lives away from the office. The town's heritage as a prolific cotton production center, as well as its inherent architectural charms, made Waxahachie the natural choice as the setting for the Academy Award–wining movie *Places in the Heart*, starring Sally Field, Danny Glover, and John Malkovich.

Waxahachie is the ideal place for unwinding on a wee retreat from things urban. Well known by those interested in Victorian architecture as a repository of intricate home design detail, Waxahachie is also a great place to roam the antiques shops.

This itinerary is tailor-made for a pair in search of a place that's friendly, quaint, and quiet. Count on spending this time together poking around some stores and historical sites, checking out an assortment of beautiful architecture, and perhaps just catching up on those novels that neither of you finds time to read at home.

DAY ONE: *Morning*

BREAKFAST

Romance
AT A GLANCE

◆ *Take photographs at the **Ellis County Courthouse**, a spectacular, 1895 work in red sandstone and granite, and then wander across the street to the Victorian-style **Ellis County Museum** (201 South College Street; 972–937–0681) before having a sensational lunch at the **Dove's Nest** (105 Jefferson Street; 972–938–3683).*

◆ *Take in the remarkable art at the **Webb Gallery** (209–211 West Franklin Street; 972–938–8085), and have a good night's sleep at either the **BonnyNook Inn** (414 West Main Street; 972–938–7207 or 800–486–5936) or the **Chaska House** (716 West Main Street; 972–937–3390 or 800–931–3390).*

Before leaving town for Waxahachie, stop en route for breakfast. Dallasites can get a great fill of eggs with bacon and grits at **Vern's Place** (3600 Main Street at Exposition Street in Dallas; 214–823–0435; inexpensive) an old-fashioned, Southern soul food haven with a loyal following.

If you're heading southeast from the Fort Worth area, stop at **Calloway's** (1001 South Bowen Road in Arlington; 817–277–1672; inexpensive), where great waffles have been keeping customers happy for years.

Check into your bed-and-breakfast. Our favorite has long been the **BonnyNook Inn** (414 West Main Street; 972–938–7207 or 800–486–5936; $100 and up), a six-room lodging within a renovated, 1895 home. An ideal choice for lovers would be one of the suites with whirlpool tubs. Bring your own wine if you like, as the hosts will gladly provide you with an ice bucket and wine glasses. Breakfast here is an elegant, three-course affair of eggs or crepes, hot fruit dish, and inventive baked goods.

Another lovely accommodation is found at the **Chaska House** (716 West Main Street; 972–937–3390 or 800–931–3390; about $100), a National Historic Landmark built in 1900 and updated to offer two rooms with private baths. There's also a very private three-room guest house. Breakfast is included with your stay.

Drop off your overnight bags, put on your tennis shoes, and set out for the courthouse square, an easy block from either B&B. Just on Main Street alone, you'll see marvelous examples of the gingerbread architecture celebrated heavily on the first weekend of June each year.

The **Ellis County Museum** (201 South College Street; 972–937–0681), right across the street from the courthouse in the Old

A Love Carved in Stone

Your first stop on Main Street in Waxahachie will be the **Ellis County Courthouse,** a spectacular, 1895 work in red sandstone and granite. Many of the elaborate stone carvings were created by artisans brought from Italy. One sculptor in particular, it's said, became enamored of a local woman, Mabel Frame; you'll see her face depicted in beautiful and then horrible images, thought to reflect the artisan's feelings when Mabel didn't return his affection.

Inside the building are spiral stairways and thirty-four rooms. The tower clock requires the use of a 250-pound winding mechanism, and its bell-striker weighs more than 800 pounds. Be sure you've brought your cameras—this is the most-photographed courthouse in the state.

Masonic Lodge Hall, is a wonderful example of the High Victorian Italianate Style popular in the late 1880s. Inside are historical artifacts and photos detailing local history. You'll learn a little about Atlanta native Bessie Coleman, who grew up here in Waxahachie and in 1921 became the world's first black person to become a licensed pilot. The U.S. Post Office issued a commemorative stamp in her honor in 1995.

The museum chronicles the life of Paul Richards as well. The late Waxahachie resident was a longtime player and manager for the Chicago White Sox, Baltimore Orioles, Houston Astros, and Atlanta Braves; he also served as special advisor to former Texas Rangers' owner Eddie Chiles.

The Ellis County museum is open from 9:00 A.M. to 5:00 P.M. Tuesday through Saturday and 1:00 to 5:00 P.M. Sunday. No admission fee is charged.

DAY ONE: *Afternoon*

LUNCH

Settle in for a sumptuous meal at the **Dove's Nest** (105 Jefferson Street; 972–938–3683; moderate). Far more than the typical antiques shop tearoom, this charming spot offers delightful surprises such as tequila-cured salmon and *chilies rellenos* stuffed with apricot-laced chicken. Open for lunch, Monday through Saturday. Open for dinner also on Friday and Saturday. You're welcome to bring your own wine.

If you're in the mood to hunt, spend the rest of the afternoon digging for treasures in the numerous antiques shops downtown. Some dependable stock can be found at **Waxahachie Crafters and Antique Mall** (315 South Rogers Street; 972–938–1222) and **Courthouse Antiques** (200 South Rogers Street; 972–938–2777). Maybe you'll find the perfect old-fashioned keepsake for your loved one.

But if the two of you love history or architecture, you'll want to wander through the **Sims Library** (515 West Main Street; 972–937–2671; free). One of the first libraries in Texas when opened in 1904, the building's exterior is noted for enameled brick, copper cornices, and a carved replica of the Greek torch of knowledge. Inside you'll find gold leaf detail and Carrara marble, as well as some 33,000 volumes. The library, open from 9:00 A.M. to 5:30 P.M. Tuesday through Saturday, is closed Sunday and Monday.

The point of this little trip was to relax, right? So stroll hand in hand back to your B&B, have a nice long soak in the whirlpool tub, and even indulge yourselves in a cuddly nap.

DAY ONE: *Evening*

DINNER

Catfish Plantation (814 Water Street; 972–937–9468; inexpensive/ moderate) is not only a good place to eat, it's one of the better area legends. A vintage cottage renovated into a series of dining rooms, this popular eatery offers a catfish-rich menu and a history of ghost stories. Fried shrimp, onion rings, and dill pickles are very good here, too, as are the tales of late-night ghost sightings. Often filled to capacity, this place serves lunch on Saturday and Sunday, dinner from Thursday through Sunday.

The sidewalks roll up early in Waxahachie. Plan on spending some quality time together at your B&B for the rest of the night.

DAY TWO: *Morning*

BREAKFAST

At the BonnyNook, breakfast will likely include a hot fruit dish, followed by a baked egg entrée with pastries. It's always a lovely, thoughtful series of creations. At Chaska House, the full Southern breakfast ranges from stuffed French toast strata served with an apple cider syrup to huevos rancheros or another of what the owners call "six or seven killer recipes." At both B&Bs, you'll find silver, fine linens, and china used, as well as stimulating conversation with other guests.

After breakfast the two of you can do some exploring around the square and along the little streets leading away from it. Right on the square is one of the better regional art spaces, the **Webb Gallery** (209–211 West Franklin Street; 972–938–8085), opened in 1987. Begun as sort of a curio shop, with old collectibles from fraternal lodges and country markets, the gallery grew into one of the Southwest's leading folk art venues as the owners have amassed works by self-taught artists from across Texas, the South, and the Midwest.

Webb Gallery is now an important folk art source for schools and museums nationwide. It is home, too, to the Webb Photo Archive and Library. The gallery also hosts numerous events throughout the year. Regular gallery hours are 1:00 to 5:00 P.M. Saturday and Sunday and by appointment.

FOR MORE ROMANCE

From late April through mid-June, one of the most spectacular annual events in Texas happens just outside the Waxahachie city limits. **Scarborough Faire** is an enormous Renaissance fair with loads of medieval-style entertainment, from jousting and juggling to acts by jesters and puppeteers. Participants dress as royalty, urchins, poets, peasants, and so on, and there are dozens of diversions in the form of arts and crafts, sheep dog shows, and merchants selling all sorts of trinkets. Food booths are plentiful. For details call (972) 938–3247. Admission is $16 per person.

Love That Crazy Water

Rejuvenating in Mineral Wells

BSOLUTELY ONE OF THE BEST-KEPT SECRETS in all of North Texas is the Palo Pinto town of Mineral Wells. The town lies in a scenic, rough, and rolling landscape that rivals some of the most gorgeous in all of the fabled Hill Country near Austin. The twisting terrain, in fact, afforded ideal hiding places for Indians and outlaws even after the county had several established pioneer communities.

You reach Mineral Wells by making an hour's drive west of Fort Worth or a ninety-minute drive west of Dallas via Highway 180. The town today offers but a glimpse of its glory of a century ago when water from the Crazy Well—discovered in 1885—was reputed to cure "hysterical manias" and numerous other disorders. By 1920 there were 400 mineral wells in town, making Mineral Wells a significant health resort attracting visitors from across the United States.

On this itinerary the two of you will explore a quaint town with fabulous period architecture, see the last of the wells, roam the antiques shops, visit an herb farm, paddle the lovely Brazos River, and take the ultimate hike. Bring your most comfortable shoes and plenty of film.

DAY ONE: *Morning*

BREAKFAST

As you're heading west in the morning toward Mineral Wells, make a stop for breakfast at **La Madeleine** (6140 Camp Bowie Boulevard in Fort Worth; 817–732–4656; moderate). This ever popular French bakery and cafe provides a boost with scrambled eggs, bacon, potato cakes, and baguette, or you can have a spinach quiche with fresh fruit. Don't miss La Mad's phenomenal French roast coffee.

Get to town as early as you can to enjoy as much as you please. Drop your bags at **Silk Stocking Row Bed & Breakfast** (415 Northwest Fourth Street; 940–325–4101; $85 and up). This stately, 1904 home was originally built as a boarding house and had several owners before winding up in the hands of talented innkeepers who are helping Mineral Wells with its rediscovery process.

Four guest rooms include a suite with a bedroom and a separate parlor. All rooms have private baths, television, and either king, queen, or twin beds. In a shared hospitality area, you'll find an ice maker, snacks, a stocked refrigerator, and freshly ground coffee. A full gourmet breakfast is served on weekends, and a generous continental breakfast is served on weekdays. Both are included with your room tariff.

The best place to begin exploring the vintage downtown is at the **Crazy Water Hotel and Pavilion** (401 North Oak Street; 940–325–4441). Built in 1912, destroyed by fire in 1925, and soon rebuilt, the grand old hotel hosted big-name entertainers. Now it's a retirement hotel, but the lobby is still worth a look.

Along North Oak Street are a few antiques shops worth poking through. One of the places to make a point of visiting is **Hanchey Leather Goods** (200 North Oak Street; 940–325–1843), a quality

Romance
AT A GLANCE

◆ Take your room at **Silk Stocking Row Bed & Breakfast** (415 Northwest Fourth Street; 940–325–4101), and then head downtown to shop at **Hanchey Leather Goods** (200 North Oak; 940–325–1843) and **W. D. Woodworks** (221 North Oak Street; 940–328–0424).

◆ Have a sumptuous lunch at **Shotguns** (215 Northeast Twenty-Seventh Avenue; 940–325–4242), which you'll work off by paddling down the Brazos River, thanks to **Rochelle's Canoe Rentals** (Highway 4 at the Brazos River; 940–659–3341 or 940–659–2581).

◆ Work up an appetite for dinner at **Baris Pizza & Pasta** (2805 Highway 180 West; 940–325–0333).

shop selling handcrafted leather items, from wallets and belts to earrings and watch bands. **W. D. Woodworks** (221 North Oak Street; 940–328–0424) allows you to view talented craftspeople producing all sorts of furniture, which you can order or buy on the spot.

Before leaving Oak Street be sure to pop in to **Garrets** (301 North Oak Street; 940–325–2207), a wonderfully weird assortment of collectibles housed in a converted grocery store. Everything from jewelry and chintz-covered furniture is here among the used goods. One local fan says everyone should ask to explore the downstairs, where it's a good bet that Elvis could be hiding.

Then wander over to the old **Baker Hotel** (201 East Hubbard Street), the most famous of the original thirteen hotels that boomed during the crazy water craze. Modeled after the Arlington Hotel in Hot Springs, this 1929 hotel is a lonely, empty shell of a place once frequented by such celebrities as Judy Garland, Will Rogers, Clark Gable, and Lord Mountbatten. The old Baker is only open for tours occasionally. Call the chamber of commerce office (511 East Hubbard Street; 940–325–2557) for details.

DAY ONE: *Afternoon*

LUNCH

Hop in the car and drive west just a bit on Hubbard, which is also Highway 180, until you reach **Longhorn Bar and Grill** (3501 Highway 180 West; 940–325–9882; inexpensive). What makes this place distinctive is its longhorn beef, which—contrary to the rumors—is lean and flavorful. Have a brisket sandwich or burger, along with big, greasy curly fries and a frosty beer.

Another favorite among Palo Pinto County denizens is **Shotguns** (215 Northeast Twenty-Seventh Avenue; 940–325–4242; moderate). Here you'll find a menu laden with good smoked barbecue, steaks, and fish. The interior ranges from the typical diner chairs and tables to unique chandeliers crafted from shotgun shells attached to old wagon wheels. Big ol' glasses of iced tea or cold beer will quench your thirst.

But if tearooms better suit your combined style, have a lunch of soups, salads, and freshly made sandwiches at **Palace Tea Room** (113 North Oak

Street; 940–325–9508; inexpensive). Tucked into a historic downtown building that was restored by the Palo Pinto Historical Foundation, the Palace is also known for sensational desserts. It's open only for lunch, Monday through Friday.

The afternoon's options depend on how active you both want to be. If you feel like enjoying the deliriously beautiful Palo Pinto Mountains scenery, by all means head out to **Rochelle's Canoe Rentals** (Highway 4 at the Brazos River; 940–659–3341 or 940–659–2581). Reach the outfitter by driving west of Mineral Wells on Highway 180 about 12 miles to the town of Palo Pinto. Then turn north on Highway 4 and drive another 6 miles to the river. This is a very gentle river, unless rains have been heavy. Little experience is necessary. Rochelle's is one of the oldest, friendliest, and most reputable canoe outfitters in the state. They'll charge you $10 to $20 per person, depending on how long you're keeping the canoe, and they'll pick you up at a designated spot along the river when you're finished canoeing.

Speaking of **Highway 4,** the twisting ribbon of road that stretches from Interstate 20 to Highway 180 is truly outstanding. If the two of you have chosen to visit in spring, you'll find several places to stop and take photos of each other amidst blankets of wildflowers on the roadsides. The same goes for your visit in the fall, when the thickets of trees offer stunning palettes of reds, oranges, and golds.

On the other hand, if you feel more like just sticking around town, take a stroll along Northwest. Fourth Avenue to see examples of the extraordinary homes that marked the former wealth of Mineral Wells. Some to note are at 401 Northwest Fourth Avenue, built by the popular Bock family; 503 Northwest Fourth Avenue, built in the 1920s by the lumberyard owner's wife, who chose the design after examining those in Hollywood; and the Belcher home at the corner of Northwest Fourth Avenue and Northwest Twenty-first Street, built as a replica of FDR's summer home in Warm Springs, Georgia.

At 300 Northwest Fourth Avenue, have a look at the **First Presbyterian Church**, founded in 1890. The 1894 building was destroyed in 1907, and the current structure was built in 1983 to replace the 1908 church. On the south and west sides, you can see the stained glass from the 1908 church. Inside is the original Esty pipe organ installed in 1910.

DAY ONE: *Evening*

DINNER

Make your way over to **Baris Pizza & Pasta** (2805 Highway 180 West; 940–325–0333; inexpensive), the reigning favorite among locals and visitors for excellent freshly baked breads and homemade pastas by a family relocated from New York. The portions are astounding, and guests are absolutely welcome to bring their own wine, beer, or liquor.

Alqua Viva

*Founded in 1913 the **Famous Water Company** (209 Northwest Sixth Street; 940–325–3853) is the sole mineral water well operating today. In the well's heyday owner Edward P. Dismuke made his fortune with Dismuke's Pronto-lax, Dismuke's Famous Mineral Crystals, Dismuke's Eye Bath, and Dismuke's Residuum. None of the products is offered today, but the two of you can sample chilly restorative waters inside this delightfully restored building between 8:00 A.M. and 1:00 P.M. Tuesday through Saturday.*

DAY TWO: *Morning*

BREAKFAST

Your hosts at Silk Stocking will fill you with a sumptuous breakfast before you check out. Weekday mornings, there is a choice of three juices, a plate of fresh-cut fruits and yogurt, cereals, and muffins. On weekends, you're served all that plus a hot entree, such as an omelette with hash browns and sausage or French toast (cut into the shape of Texas) with fresh strawberry topping. The setting is special too, with pewter chargers, linen napkins, and Fiesta table wares.

You'll have ample opportunity to work off the morning feast at **Lake Mineral Wells State Park** (Highway 180, 3 miles east of town; 940–328–1171). This wooded and rocky park features a sparkling 650-acre lake and excellent hiking trails and rock-climbing settings. Many of the screened shelters and other facilities bear the unmistakable crafts-manship of the 1930s Civilian Conservation Corps. Check in at the park office and get maps of the various trails and scenic areas, as well as a checklist of wildlife you're likely to see, including white-tailed deer, turkeys, raccoons, ducks, and squirrels.

The park also marks the western end of the fabulous **Rails-to-Trails** pathway. This 22-mile linking of Mineral Wells and charming Weatherford to the east is built on an old rail bed. The trail is open to hikers, cyclists, and horseback riders who enjoy beautiful, rolling scenery.

FOR MORE ROMANCE

In town visit **Woodland Park Cemetery** (2600 South Oak Street). Little known to outsiders the cemetery is beloved by area residents for its sunken gardens that are filled with thousands of roses of hundreds of varieties, bursting with color from spring through fall.

Just 6 miles north of town, find **Boudreau Gardens Herb Farm** (5545 North Highway 281; 940–325–8674), a working, organic herb farm atop Sage Hill. The historic farm was settled by a local legend known as Hellfire Morgan, who's buried on the northwest hillside of the farm. Today visitors come in search of 250 culinary, decorative, and medicinal herbs in the gardens and greenhouse. Herb products are sold in the Country Herb Store. It's open from 10:00 A.M. until 5:00 P.M. Wednesday through Saturday, from March through September; and Wednesday through Friday, October through February.

Appendix of Events

YEAR-ROUND

Rodeo. Friday and Saturday evening, unless special event; Cowtown Coliseum, Fort Worth; (817) 625-1025. Home of the world's first indoor rodeo. Wild West shows during the summer.

JANUARY

Southwestern Exposition and Livestock Show & Rodeo. Third weekend of January through the first weekend of February; Will Rogers Memorial Complex, Fort Worth; (817) 877-2420. Thousands of livestock, horse shows, and exhibitors of ranch and farm wares, a parade, plus a midway, live entertainment, and the world's largest indoor rodeo.

FEBRUARY

Last Great Gunfight. Held annually on February 8; Fort Worth Stockyards; (817) 624-9712. Reenactment of the last great gunfight of the Old West, with Luke Short and Marshal "Long Hair" Jim Courtright. Slide show and festivities held in White Elephant Saloon following the 7:00 P.M. gunfight.

Cowtown Marathon and 10K Run. Last Friday of February; Fort Worth Stockyards; (817) 735-2033.

Texas Golden Gloves. Last week of February and first week of March, Wednesday through Saturday; Will Rogers Memorial Center; (817) 871-8150.

MARCH

Wine and Food Festival. Held in March; Delaney Vineyards in Grapevine and Fairmont Hotel in Dallas; (214) 887-9915. Wine food, awards, winner of Dallas's National Wine Competition announced.

Cowtown Goes Green. Week of March 17; Fort Worth Stockyards; (817) 625-9715. St. Patrick's Day street party and parade.

Coca-Cola 300 and NASCAR Winston Cup Race. Last weekend of March; Texas Motor Speedway; (817) 215-8500.

APRIL

Cardboard Boat Regatta. River Legacy Park in Arlington; (817) 459–5474.

Denton Arts & Jazz Festival. (940) 565–0931.

Arbor Daze. Fourth weekend in April; Euless; (817) 685–1821. Largest nonalcoholic, free, family-oriented festival in Texas. Music, arts and crafts, business exposition, and free tree giveaways.

Main Street Fort Worth Arts Festival. Third weekend in April; Downtown Fort Worth. Over 200 artists, live music on five stages, children's events.

Scarborough Faire. Saturdays and Sundays beginning the third weekend in April through the first weekend in June, including Memorial Day; Waxahachie; (972) 938–3247 or 938–1888. Thirty-five acres of fun, food, and fantasy including music, magic, juggling, and jesting on ten stages throughout the day. Full-armor combat jousting, knighting ceremonies, art exhibits, and falconers.

MAY

Mayfest. Four-day festival held the first weekend of May; Trinity Park; (817) 332–1055. Many activities in different areas: teen area, sports area, free children's area; 200 artists, live entertainment on five stages, Garden Run, parade, and more.

Autofest/Pate Swap Meet. First weekend of May; Texas Motor Speedway; (817) 215–8500.

GTE Byron Nelson Golf Classic. Second week of May; Four Seasons Resort and Club in Las Colinas; (972) 717–0700.

Mastercard Colonial Golf Tournament. Third week of May; Colonial Country Club; (817) 927–4278. The world's top golfers on the PGA tour compete in this nationally televised event.

Mayfair. Three stages, arts and vintage cars, crafts, food. McKinney; (972) 562–6880.

National Polka Festival. Third weekend of May; Ennis (888) 366–4748. Featuring 250 arts and crafts booths, Czech food, dancing, thirteen polka bands playing four venues.

JUNE

Texas Scottish Festival and Highland Games. University of Texas at

Arlington's Maverick Stadium; (817) 654–2293. Celebration of Scottish and Celtic culture. Highland dancing, bagpipes, drumming, Scottish clan tents, caber toss, authentic Scottish food and ale.

Shakespeare in the Park. Two productions—one begins first week of June through third week of June, one begins last week of June through first week of July. Trinity Park, Fort Worth; (817) 923–6698.

Concerts in the Garden. Second week of June until July 4, Thursdays through Sundays; Botanic Gardens in Fort Worth; (817) 665–6000.

Chisholm Trail Round-up. Second weekend of June; Fort Worth Stockyards;
(817) 625–7005. Festival and rodeo celebrating Fort Worth's history as the last major stop on the legendary Chisholm Trail.

International Summer Music Festival. Mid-June to first weekend of July; Meyerson Symphony Center, Dallas; (214) 692–0203.

Shakespeare Festival of Dallas. Mid-June through end of July; Samuell-Grand Park; (214) 559–2778. Country's second oldest Shakespeare festival.

JULY

Fort Worth Fourth! Fourth of July; Downtown Fort Worth. Fireworks over the Trinity River.

Miss Texas Pageant. Second week of July; Fort Worth Convention Center; (817) 884–2222.

Parker County Peach Festival. Second Saturday in July; Weatherford Courthouse square; (817) 594–3801. Celebrates the harvest of the Parker County peaches in a country fair atmosphere.

Taste of Dallas. Second weekend of July; West End Historic District; (214) 741–7185. Live music and food booths from more than thirty local restaurants.

National Cutting Horse Association Summer Cutting Spectacular. Last week of July; Will Rogers Equestrian Center, Fort Worth; (817) 244–6188.

AUGUST

American Quarter Horse Association World Championship Show. Second week of August; Will Rogers Memorial Center, Fort Worth; (817) 871–8150.

SEPTEMBER

National Championship Indian Powwow. First weekend after Labor Day; Traders Village; (214) 647–2331. Salute to Native American heritage features championship dance competitions, Indian arts and crafts show, teepee contest, storytelling and demonstration tent, and Native American food.

Gallery Night. Second Saturday in September; galleries in Fort Worth. Most galleries, especially those on West Seventh Street and Camp Bowie Boulevard, are open this afternoon and evening for open houses.

State Fair of Texas. Last weekend of September through the second weekend of October; Fair Park, Dallas; (214) 421–8713 or 565–9931. One of the largest annual expositions in the world. Midway, featuring North America's largest Ferris wheel. Free, live musical entertainment on various stages, art exhibits, livestock shows, fireworks, and car show. Legendary Texas-Oklahoma football game at the Cotton Bowl.

Harvestfest. Fourth weekend in September; McKinney; (972) 562–6880. Bed races, fiddling, and arts and crafts.

Pioneer Days. Third weekend of September; Fort Worth Stockyards; (817) 626–7921.

OCTOBER

Black-Eyed Pea Festival. Athens; (800) 755–7878.

Uncle Fletch Hamburger Cook-off and American Music Festival. Athens; (800) 755–7878.

Oktoberfest. First weekend of October; Fort Worth Convention Center; (817) 332–2560.

International Air Show. Second weekend of October; Alliance Airport; (817) 870–1515.

Fright Fest. Weekends beginning the first weekend in October through October 31; Six Flags Over Texas; (817) 640–8900. Halloween events.

Dallas Race for the Cure. Third Saturday of October; Northpark Center; (214) 750–7223. Run or walk 5K or 1-mile route to benefit the Dallas County Chapter of the Susan G. Komen Breast Cancer Foundation.

Fort Worth Film Festival. Third week of October; Sundance Square; (817) 237–1008. Will show up to 50 features, documentaries, and shorts; premieres, screenwriters' panels, and more.

Boo at the Zoo. Last week of October; Fort Worth Zoo; (817) 871–7050.

NOVEMBER

SMU Literary Festival. Weekends in November; Hughes-Trigg Student Center, Dallas; (214) 768–4400. Features authors reading from their work.

Parade of Lights and Annual Tree Lighting Ceremony. Friday evening after Thanksgiving. Downtown Fort Worth and General Worth Square (817) 336–2787 or 926–3262. Floats, carriages, marching bands, and more.

National Cutting Horse Association Futurity. Thanksgiving weekend through second week of December; Will Rogers Memorial Center, Fort Worth; (817) 871–8150 or 244–6188.

DECEMBER

Holiday in the Park. Weekends only, beginning Thanksgiving through the end of the year, with the exception of school vacation week, when park is open daily; Six Flags Over Texas; (817) 640–8900. Special holiday programming at Six Flags Over Texas, with lights, shows, decorations, a real snow hill for sledding, and more.

Neiman Marcus Adolphus Children's Parade. First Saturday in December; Downtown Dallas; (214) 640–8383. Celebrities, clowns, floats, marching bands, and more.

Special Indexes

ROMANTIC LODGING

Inexpensive—$100 or less

Amelia's Place, Dallas, 48–49

Arbor House, Granbury, 165

Arlington Marriott, 77

Bed & Breakfast at the Ranch, Fort Worth, 108–9

Bingham House, McKinney, 153

Courtyard by Marriott, Dallas, Fort Worth, 17, 64, 72

Dowell House Bed & Breakfast, McKinney, 153

Hummingbird Lodge, Glen Rose, 117

Iron Horse Inn, Granbury, 165

La Quinta, Dallas, 32

Magnolia Inn, Denton, 99

Miss Molly's, Fort Worth, 52–53, 132

Oak Meadow Bed & Breakfast, Athens, 161–62

Paramount Hotel, Dallas, 125

Redbud Inn, Denton, 145

Silk Stocking Row Bed & Breakfast, Mineral Wells, 175, 178

Moderate—$101–$199

Adam's Mark, Dallas, 57

Adolphus Hotel, Dallas, 13, 64

Angel's Nest & Breakfast, Weatherford, 139

Azalea Plantation, Fort Worth, 39

BonnyNook Inn, Waxahachie, 170

Carriage House, Athens, 161

Chaska House, Waxahachie, 170

Cliffs, Possum Kingdom Lake, 92

Courtyard by Marriott, Arlington, 77

Courtyard on the Trail, Dallas, 102

Embassy Suites Hotel Dallas Market Center , 82

Etta's Place, Fort Worth, 17

Fairmont Hotel, Dallas, 124–25

Foothills Safari Camp, Glen Rose, 122

Homewood Suites Las Colinas, 87

Inn on the River, Glen Rose, 117

Lodge at Fossil Rim, Glen Rose, 122

Melrose Hotel, Dallas, 32

Radisson Plaza Hotel Fort Worth, 109

St. Botolph Inn Bed & Breakfast, Weatherford, 139

Southern House, Dallas, 32

Stockyards Hotel, Fort Worth, 53, 132

Stoneleigh Hotel, Dallas, 11

Texas White House, Fort Worth, 23–24

Worthington Hotel, Fort Worth, 16–17

Expensive—$200 and up

Four Seasons Resort and Club at Las Colinas , 87

Hotel St. Germain, Dallas, 10–11

Hyatt Regency Dallas, 81–82

Mansion on Turtle Creek, Dallas, 30–31

ROMANTIC RESTAURANTS

Barbeque

Danny's Smokehouse Bar-B-Q, Athens, inexpensive, 160

Railhead Smokehouse, Fort Worth, inexpensive, 27

Brunch and Breakfast

Beau Nash, Dallas, moderate, 14
Beckley Grill, Dallas, inexpensive, 70
Breadwinners, Dallas, inexpensive, 35
Bridge, Fort Worth, moderate, 21
Brownie's, Dallas, inexpensive, 14
Cactus Flower Café, Fort Worth, inexpensive, 42, 145
Café on the Green, Las Colinas, moderate, 88, 90
Calloway's, Arlington, inexpensive, 170
Dream Café, Dallas, inexpensive, 37
Einstein Bros., Bedford, inexpensive, 153
Jack's Family Restaurant, Weatherford, inexpensive, 139
Jubilee Café, Fort Worth, inexpensive, 27, 67
La Madeleine, Fort Worth, inexpensive, 21, 175
Le Peep, Las Colinas; inexpensive, 90
Mecca, Dallas, inexpensive, 144–45
Niester's, Granbury, inexpensive, 164–65
Paris Coffee Shop, Fort Worth, inexpensive, 70
Vern's Place, Dallas, inexpensive, 170

Cajun and Creole

Pappadeaux Seafood Kitchen, Arlington, moderate, 79
Razzoo's, Fort Worth, moderate, 22

Coffee

Backstage Coffee Company, McKinney, inexpensive, 155
Café Brazil, Dallas, inexpensive, 105–6
Coffee Grinder Espresso Bar, Granbury, inexpensive, 167
Starbucks Café, Fort Worth, inexpensive, 45

Continental

Reflections, Fort Worth, expensive, 44

Dessert

Back Porch, Fort Worth, inexpensive, 27

Filipino

Filipiniana Bakeshop and Café, Fort Worth, inexpensive, 60–61

French

Saint-Emilion, Fort Worth, expensive, 26

Indian

Bombay Cricket Club, Dallas, moderate, 65

Italian

Avanti Café, Dallas, moderate, 126
Baris Pizza & Pasta, Mineral Wells, inexpensive, 178
Pearl Street Pasta House, Granbury, inexpensive, 166

Japanese

Jinbeh, Las Colinas, moderate, 89
Tei Tei Robata Bar, Dallas, expensive, 59
Teppo, Dallas, expensive, 60

Latin American

Gloria's, Dallas, inexpensive, 58

Lebanese

Byblos, Fort Worth, inexpensive to moderate, 112
Hedary's, Fort Worth, moderate, 62

Mediterranean

Mediterraneo, Dallas, moderate to expensive, 13
Sambuca, Dallas, expensive, 50

Mexican

Arizola's, Fort Worth, inexpensive, 110–11

Cabo Mix-Mex Grill, Fort Worth, inexpensive, 54

Café Juarez, Mckinney, inexpensive, 155

Chuy's, Dallas, inexpensive, 66

Cozymel's, Arlington, moderate, 77

Esperanza's, Fort Worth, inexpensive, 136

Javier's Gourmet Mexicano, Dallas, moderate to expensive, 34

Joe T. Garcia's Mexican Dishes, Fort Worth, moderate, 135

La Familia, Fort Worth, inexpensive, 28

La Playa Maya, Fort Worth, inexpensive, 62

Las Mananitas, Dallas, inexpensive, 106–7

Loredo's, Fort Worth, inexpensive, 55

Mi Cocina, Fort Worth, inexpensive to moderate, 19

Nuevo Leon, Dallas, moderate, 49–50

Sol's Taco Lounge, inexpensive, Dallas, 49

Uncle Julio's, Fort Worth, inexpensive to moderate, 43

Middle Eastern, African

Bistro A, Dallas, moderate, 33

Café Istanbul, Dallas, moderate, 59

Café Izmir, Dallas, moderate, 104–5

Marrakesh, Dallas, moderate, 59

Queen of Sheba, Dallas, moderate, 59

New American

Al Biernat's, Dallas; expensive, 34

Angeluna, Fort Worth, expensive, 44

Café Madrid, Dallas, moderate, 60

Dove's Nest Waxahachie, moderate, 171–72

EatZi's, Dallas, inexpensive/moderate, 35–36

Goodhues Wood-Fired Grill, McKinney, moderate to expensive, 156

Grape, Dallas, expensive, 49

Green Room, Dallas, expensive, 49

Hennington's Texas Café, Granbury, moderate, 167

Kathleen's Art Café, Dallas, moderate, 66

Rough Creek Lodge, Glen Rose, expensive, 122

New Mexican

Blue Mesa, Fort Worth, moderate, 42, 113–14

Sandwiches

Buffet, Fort Worth, inexpensive, 25

Cupboard Café, Denton, inexpensive, 147

Longhorn Bar and Grill, Mineral Wells, inexpensive, 176

19th Hole Grill, Possum Kingdom Lake, inexpensive, 93

Palace Tea Room, Mineral Wells, inexpensive, 176–77

Seafood

Catfish Plantation, Waxahachie, inexpensive to moderate, 172

Fish, Dallas, expensive, 128

J&J Oyster Bar, Fort Worth, inexpensive, 55

Landry's Seafood House, Dallas, moderate, 83

S&D Oyster Company, Dallas, inexpensive, 65

Southwestern

Cool River Café, Las Colinas, moderate to expensive, 89–90

Michael's Fort Worth, moderate, 68

Reata, Fort Worth, moderate, 20, 42

Star Canyon, Dallas, very expensive, 36

Y.O. Ranch, Dallas, moderate, 11–12

Steaks

Cattleman's Steak House, Fort Worth, moderate to expensive, 135

Del Frisco's Double Eagle Steakhouse, Fort Worth, expensive, 112

H3 Ranch, Fort Worth, moderate, 53

Hoffbrau, Fort Worth, inexpensive to moderate, 40–41, 73

Morton's of Chicago, Dallas, expensive, 128

Sushi

Jinbeh, Las Colinas, moderate, 89

Teppo, Dallas, expensive, 60

Tea

Lady Primrose, Dallas, 12

Adolphus Hotel, Dallas, 13, 64

Traditional American

Bluebonnet Café in the Glen Rose Emporium, inexpensive, 119

Café on the Green, Las Colinas, moderate, 88, 90

Cliffs Restaurant, Possum Kingdom Lake, expensive, 93

Corner Bakery, Grapevine, Plano, inexpensive, 91, 153

Dick's Last Resort, Dallas, moderate, 84

Dixie House, Dallas, inexpensive, 103

Downtown Café, Weatherford, inexpensive, 140

Ginger Brown's, Fort Worth, inexpensive, 110

Jubilee House Restaurant & Club, Athens, moderate, 162

Loft, Grapevine, inexpensive, 91

Mesquite Pit, Weatherford, inexpensive to moderate, 142

Ol' South Pancake House, Fort Worth, inexpensive, 112

Opera House Restaurant, McKinney, inexpensive, 155

Palm, Dallas, expensive, 83

Palomino, Dallas, moderate, 13

Rafters Restaurant on Scenic Point,

Possum Kingdom Lake, inexpensive, 94

Randall's, Fort Worth, moderate, 41

Riscky's Bar-B-Q, Fort Worth, inexpensive, 132

Shotguns, Mineral Wells, moderate, 176

Texican Grill, Denton, moderate, 148–49

Tommy's, Fort Worth, inexpensive, 28

Western Kitchen, Glen Rose, inexpensive, 119

Yorkshire Club, Dallas, moderate, 126

Vietnamese

Phuong, Fort Worth, inexpensive, 60

Miscellaneous

Caddo Mercantile, Caddo, Possum Kingdom Lake, inexpensive, 94

EVENING DIVERSIONS

Cocktail Lounges and Bars

Ancho Chile Bar, Fort Worth, 26

Blue Mesa, Fort Worth, 42, 113–14

Bobby Valentine's, Arlington, 79

8.0, Fort Worth, 20

Flying Saucer Draught Emporium, Fort Worth, 54

Grotto Bar-Caravan of Dreams, Fort Worth, 20, 45

Lobby Bar, Fort Worth, 42

Reata, Fort Worth, 20, 42

Reunion Tower, Dallas, 13

Starck, Dallas, 84

Tarantino's, Dallas, 37

Walt Garrison Rodeo Bar, Dallas, 127

Dancing

Billy Bob's Texas, Fort Worth, 53–54, 136

El Paraiso Latin Club, Fort Worth, 54

Red Jacket, Dallas, 51
White Elephant Saloon, Fort Worth, 53, 136

Movie Theaters

AMC Palace 9, Fort Worth, 22
AMC Sundance 11, Fort Worth, 22
Omni Theater at the Fort Worth Museum of Science and History, 28–29

Music Venues

Blue Cat Blues, Dallas, 50
Caravan of Dreams, Fort Worth, 20, 45, 54
Club Clearview, Dallas, 51
Flying Saucer Draught Emporium, Fort Worth, 54
J&J Blues Bar, Fort Worth, 54–55
Poor David's Pub, Dallas, 105
Pyramid Room in the Fairmont Hotel, Dallas, 128
Rick's Place, Denton, 149
Rubber Gloves Rehearsal Studios, Denton, 149
Sambuca, Dallas, 50
Sardine's, Fort Worth, 55
Sons of Hermann Hall, Dallas, 50
Terilli's, Dallas, 105
Wreck Room, Fort Worth, 55

Performing Arts

Bass Performance Hall, Fort Worth, 41, 44–45
Casa Manana, Fort Worth, 46
Dallas Summer Musicals at Fair Park Music Hall, Dallas, 33, 37–38
Majestic Theater, Dallas, 33, 38
McKinney Avenue Contemporary, Dallas, 35
Meyerson Symphony Center, Dallas, 33, 37

Theater

Arts District Theater, Dallas, 34
Bass Performance Hall, Fort Worth, 41, 44–45
Dallas Theater Center, 34

Caravan of Dreams, Fort Worth, 20, 45, 54
Casa on the Square, Fort Worth, 42
Circle Theater, Fort Worth, 41–42
Jubilee Theatre, Fort Worth, 41
Kalita Humphreys Theater, Dallas, 34
McKinney Avenue Contemporary, Dallas , 35
Opera House, Granbury, 167–68
Stage West, Fort Worth, 45–46
Teatro Dallas, Dallas, 34–35
Theatre Three, Dallas, 34

MUSEUMS AND GALLERIES

African American Museum, Dallas, 14
American Airlines C.R. Smith Museum, Fort Worth, 88–89
Amon Carter Museum, Fort Worth, 25–26, 42
Arlington Museum of Art, 80
Carol Henderson Gallery/ Artenergies, Fort Worth, 67–68
Cattle Raisers Museum, Fort Worth, 137
Cavanaugh Flight Museum, Dallas, 130
Conspiracy Museum, Dallas, 126
Dallas Aquarium, 104
Dallas Museum of Art, 11
Dallas Museum of Natural History, 15
Dallas World Aquarium, 107
David Dike Fine Art, Dallas, 64
Deep Ellum Center for the Arts, Dallas, 51
Edmund Craig Gallery, Fort Worth, 67
Ellis County Museum, Waxahachie, 170–71
Evelyn Siegel Gallery Inc, Fort Worth, 67

Fire Station No. 1, Fort Worth, 17–18

Fort Worth Museum of Science and History , 28

Frontiers of Flight Museum, 129–30

Gallery of Sports Art, Arlington, 79

Gallery Two-O-Nine, Dallas, 65

Gerald Peters Gallery, Dallas, 64

Gowns of the First Ladies of Texas, Denton, 48

Hall of State, Dallas, 14–15

Hangar 10 Flying Museum, Denton, 149–50

Heard Museum and Wildlife Sanctuary, McKinney, 155–56

Heritage Gallery, Weatherford, 141

Ivanffy & Uhler Gallery, Dallas, 69

Kimbell Art Museum, Fort Worth, 24–25, 42

Legends of the Game Baseball Museum, Arlington, 78–79

Log Cabin Village, Fort Worth, 40

Longhorn Gallery, Denton, 147

Meadows Museum of Art, Dallas, 32–33

Modern Art Museum of Fort Worth, 28, 42

Modern at Sundance Square, Fort Worth, 21–22

Mustangs of Las Colinas, 90

National Cowgirl Museum & Hall of Fame, Fort Worth, 19

Noble Planetarium at the Fort Worth Museum of Science and History, 29

Old Jail and Hood County Historical Museum, Granbury, 167

Photographic Archives Lab & Library, Dallas, 69

Rare Book Room and Texana Collections, Denton, 147–48

Science Place in Fair Park and IMAX Theater, Dallas, 104

Sid Richardson Collection of Western Art, Fort Worth, 18

Sims Library, Waxahachie, 172

Sixth Floor: JFK and the Memory of a Nation, Dallas, 125–26

Stockyards Station Gallery, Fort Worth, 133–34

Stockyards Museum, Fort Worth, 134

Thomas Kinkade at the Main Street Gallery, Fort Worth, 18–19

Vintage Flying Museum, Fort Worth, 43

Webb Gallery, Waxahachie, 173

William Campbell Contemporary Art, Fort Worth, 69

William E. Johnson Fine Art, Dallas, 64

SHOPPING

Alley Antique Mall, Athens, 163

Anteks, 66

Antiquarian of Dallas, 64–65

Barnes & Noble Booksellers, Fort Worth, 19

Books on the Square, Granbury, 166

Boudreau Gardens Herb Farm, Mineral Wells, 179

Brazos River Trading Company, Granbury, 166

Cadeaux, Dallas, 66

Courthouse Antiques, Waxahachie, 172

Crate & Barrel, Dallas, 65–66

Dallas Farmers Market, 84–85

Earth Bones, Fort Worth, 21

Earth Harvest Market, Granbury, 167

Evers Hardware, Denton, 146

Famous Water Company, Mineral Wells, 178

Fincher's Western Store, Fort Worth, 134

First Monday Trade Days, Canton, 162–63

First Monday Trade Days, Weatherford, 140

Farmers Market, Weatherford, 143

Garrets, Mineral Wells, 176

General Store, Fort Worth, 135

Glen Rose Emporium, 119

Grapevine Mills, 91

Haltom's Jewelers, Fort Worth, 20

Hanchey Leather Goods, Mineral Wells, 175–76

Justin Discount Boots, Justin, 99

Kabin Fever, Fort Worth, 68

Legacy Trading Company, Fort Worth, 21

Leigh-Boyd, Fort Worth, 68–69

Lovers Lane Antique Market, Dallas, 69

Market, Fort Worth, 68

Miss B's, Weatherford, 140

M. L. Leddy's Boot & Saddlery, Fort Worth, 134–35

Modern at Sundance Square, Fort Worth, 21–22

Neiman Marcus, Dallas, 83

Out West Down South, Fort Worth, 68

Pangburn's, Fort Worth, 19–20

Pier 1 Imports, Fort Worth, 21

Prairie Rose, Fort Worth, 68

Recycled Books, Records and CDs, Denton, 147

Red Elk, Granbury, 167

Remember This Antique Mall, McKinney, 154

Sleeping Lizards, Denton, 146

Strings, Fort Worth, 68

This Old House, Denton, 146

Town Square Antiques, McKinney, 154

Treasure Chest Boutique, Weatherford, 140

Treasures from the Past, McKinney, 154

Wagon Yard Antiques, Granbury, 166

Waxahachie Crafters and Antique Mall, 172

W. D. Woodworks, Mineral Wells, 176

West End Marketplace, Dallas, 12, 83

Flea Markets

380 Flea Market, Denton, 73

Cattle Barn Flea Market, Fort Worth, 72

Trader's Village, Grand Prairie, 71

OUTDOOR ACTIVITIES

Black Beauty Ranch, Athens, 159

Chandor Gardens, Weatherford, 142

Chestnut Square, McKinney, 153–54

Dallas Arboretum and Botanical Garden, 103

Dallas Farmers Market, 84–85

Dallas Horticulture Center, 104

Dallas Nature Center, 107

Dallas on Ice, 82

Dallas Zoo , 105, 106

Dinosaur Valley State Park, Glen Rose, 119–21

5 Bar K Stables, Las Colinas, 91

Fort Worth Botanic Garden , 114–15

Fort Worth Nature Center and Refuge , 111

Fort Worth Zoo , 112–113

Fossil Rim Wildlife Center, Glen Rose, 117–119

Four Seasons Resort and Club at Las Colinas, 87

Granbury Cemetery, 168

Greenwood Cemetery, Weatherford, 140–41

Heard Museum and Wildlife Sanctuary, McKinney, 155–56

Highway 4, Mineral Wells, 177

Holland Lake Park, Weatherford, 143

horse-drawn carriage ride, Fort Worth, 21

Jolabec Riding Stables, McKinney, 157

Lake Mineral Wells State Park , 178–79

Log Cabin Village, Fort Worth, 40

Possum Kingdom Lake, 96

Possum Kingdom State Park, 94–96

Pro Shop; The Cliffs, Possum Kingdom Lake, 93

Rails-to-Trails, Mineral Wells, 179

River Legacy Park and Living Science Center, Arlington, 115

Rochelle's Canoe Rentals, Mineral Wells, 177

Scarborough Faire, Waxahachie, 173

Ship's Store, The Cliffs, Possum Kingdom Lake, 93

Six Flags Hurricane Harbor, Arlington, 80

Six Flags Over Texas, Arlington, 80

Stockyards Station, Fort Worth, 132

Texas Freshwater Fisheries Center, Athens, 160–61

Texas Stadium, Irving, 91

Trinity Park, Fort Worth, 115

visitor information center, Fort Worth, 132

Woodland Park Cemetery, Mineral Wells, 179

Wine Tasting

Grape Escape, Fort Worth, 61

La Buena Vida, Grapevine, 61

Marty's, Dallas, 58

Professional Sports

Ballpark in Arlington, 77–78

Cowtown Coliseum, Fort Worth, 135–36

Dr Pepper StarCenter, Dallas, 82

Lone Star Park at Grand Prairie, 85

Reunion Arena, Dallas, 84

Texas Stadium, Irving, 91

ISTORIC SITES/
UILDINGS

Chaska House, Waxahachie, 170

Crazy Water Hotel and Pavilion, Mineral Wells, 175

Dallas County Historical Plaza, 125

Denton County Courthouse, 145

Denton County Historical Museum, 145

Dowell House Bed & Breakfast, McKinney , 153

Eddleman McFarland House, Fort Worth, 136–37

Elizabeth Boulevard Historical District, Fort Worth, 41

Ellis County Courthouse, Waxahachie, 171

Ellis County Museum, Waxahachie, 170–71

Evers Hardware, Denton , 146

Fair Park, Dallas, 14

Fincher's Western Store, Fort Worth, 134

First Presbyterian Church, Mineral Wells, 177

General Store, Fort Worth, 135

Granbury Cemetery, 168

Greenwood Cemetery, Weatherford, 140–41

John F. Kennedy Memorial, Dallas, 125

John Neely Bryan Cabin, Dallas, 125

Little Chapel-in-the-Woods, Denton, 148

Miss Molly's, Fort Worth, 52–53, 132

M. L. Leddy's Boot & Saddlery, Fort Worth, 134–35

Old City Park, Dallas, 127

Old Jail and Hood County Historical Museum, Granbury, 167

Old Red Courthouse, Dallas, 125

Opera House, Granbury, 167–68

Palace Tea Room Mineral Wells, 176–77

Parker County Courthouse, Weatherford, 139

Sims Library, Waxahachie, 172

Sixth Floor: JFK and the Memory of a Nation, Dallas, 125–26

St. Botolph Inn Bed & Breakfast, Weatherford, 139

Stockyards Hotel, Fort Worth, 53, 132

Swiss Avenue Historic District, Dallas, 128–29

Texas White House, Fort Worth, 23–24

Thistle Hill, Fort Worth, 137

SPECIALTY TOURS

Baker Hotel, Mineral Wells, 176

Chestnut Square, McKinney, 153–54

Dallas Communications Complex, Las Colinas, 88

Dulaney House, McKinney, 154

Eddleman McFarland House, Fort Worth, 136–37

Forest Park Miniature Train, Fort Worth, 113

Fossil Rim Wildlife Center, Glen Rose, 117–19

Heard Museum and Wildlife Sanctuary, McKinney, 155–56

Ship's Store, Possum Kingdom Lake, 93

Studios at Las Colinas, 88

Tarantula Train, Fort Worth, 132–33

Texas Exotic Feline Foundation, Fort Worth, 109–110

Thistle Hill, Fort Worth, 137

Geographic Index

ARLINGTON

Evening Diversions
Bobby Valentine's, 79
Lodging
Arlington Marriott, 77
Courtyard by Marriott, 17, 64, 72, 77
Museums and Galleries
Arlington Museum of Art, 80
Gallery of Sports Art, 79
Legends of the Game Baseball Museum, 78–79
Outdoor Activities
River Legacy Park and Living Science Center, 115
Six Flags Hurricane Harbor, 80
Six Flags Over Texas, 80
Restaurants
Calloway's, 170
Cozymel's, 77
New Main Street Café, 79
Pappadeaux Seafood Kitchen, 79
Sports
Ballpark in Arlington, The, 77–78

ATHENS

Lodging
Oak Meadow Bed & Breakfast, 161–62
Carriage House, The, 161
Outdoor Activities
Black Beauty Ranch, 159

Texas Freshwater Fisheries Center, 160–61
Restaurants
Danny's Smokehouse Bar-B-Q, 160
Garden of Eating, 160
Jubilee House Restaurant & Club, 162
Shopping
Alley Antiques Mall, 163

BEDFORD

Restaurants
Einstein Bros. Bagels, 153
Filipiniana Bakeshop and Cafée, 60–61

CANTON

Shopping
First Monday Trade Days, 162–63

DALLAS

Evening Diversions
Blue Cat Blues, 50
Club Clearview, 51
Dallas Summer Musicals at Fair Park Music Hall, 33, 37–38
Dallas Theater Center, 34
Deep Ellum Center for the Arts, 51
Majestic Theater, 33, 38
McKinney Avenue Contemporary, 35

Meyerson Symphony Center, 33, 37

Pyramid Room in the Fairmont Hotel, 128

Red Jacket, The, 51

Reunion Tower, 13

Sambuca, 50

Sons of Hermann Hall, 50

Starck, 84

Tarantino's, 37

Teatro Dallas, 34–35

Theatre Three, 34

Walt Garrison Rodeo Bar, 127

Historic Buildings

Dallas County Historical Plaza, 125

Fair Park Music Hall, 33, 37

John F. Kennedy Memorial, 125

John Neely Bryan Cabin, 125

Old City Park, 127

Old Red Courthouse, 125

Swiss Avenue Historic District, 128–29

Lodging

Adam's Mark Hotel, 57

Adolphus Hotel, The, 13, 64

Amelia's Place, 48–49

Courtyard on the Trail, 102

Embassy Suites Hotel Dallas Market Center, 82

Fairmont Hotel, 124–25

Hotel St. Germain, 10, 11

Hyatt Regency Dallas, 81–82

La Quinta City Place, 32

Mansion on Turtle Creek, The, 30–31

Melrose Hotel, The, 32

Paramount Hotel, 125

Southern House, 32

Stoneleigh Hotel, 11

Museums and Galleries

African American Museum, 14

Cavanaugh Flight Museum, 130

Conspiracy Museum, 126

Dallas Aquarium, 104

Dallas Museum of Art, 11

Dallas Museum of Natural History, 15

Dallas World Aquarium, 107

David Dike Fine Art, 64

Frontiers of Flight Museum, 129–30

Gallery Two-O-Nine, 65

Gerald Peters Gallery, 64

Hall of State, 14–15

IMAX Theater, 104

Ivanffy & Uhler Gallery, 69

Meadows Museum of Art, 32–33

Photographic Archives Lab & Library, 69

Science Place in Fair Park, The, 104

Sixth Floor: JFK and the Memory of a Nation, The, 125–26

William E. Johnson Fine Art, 64

Outdoor Activities

Dallas Arboretum and Botanical Garden, 103

Dallas Farmers Market, 84–85

Dallas Horticulture Center, 104

Dallas Nature Center, 107

Dallas on Ice, 82

Dallas Zoo, 106

Restaurants

Al Biernat's, 34

Avanti Café, 126

Beau Nash, 14

Beckley Grill, 70

Bistro A, 33

Bombay Cricket Club, 65

Breadwinners, 35

Brownie's, 14

Café Brazil, 105–6

Café Istanbul, 59

Café Izmir, 104–5

Café Madrid, 60

Chuy's, 66
Dick's Last Resort, 84
Dixie House, 103
Dream Café, 37
EatZi's, 35–36
Fish, 128
Gloria's, 58
Grape, The, 49
Green Room, The, 49
Kathleen's Art Café, 66
Lady Primrose, 12
Landry's Seafood House, 83
Las Mananitas, 106–7
Marrakesh, 59
Mecca, 144–45
Mediterraneo, 13
Morton's of Chicago, 128
Nuevo Leon, 49
Palm, The, 83
Palomino, 13
Queen of Sheba, 59
S&D Oyster Company, 65
Sambuca, 50
Sol's Taco Lounge, 49
Star Canyon, 36
Tei Tei Robata Bar, 59
Teppo, 60
Terilli's, 105
Vern's Place, 170
Y. O. Ranch, 11–12
Yorkshire Club, The, 126

Shopping
Anteks, 66
Antiquarian of Dallas, 64–65
Cadeaux, 66
Crate & Barrel, 65–66
Dallas Farmers Market, 84–85
Lovers Lane Antique Market, 69
Neiman Marcus, 83
West End Marketplace, 12, 83

Sports
Dr Pepper StarCenter, 82
Reunion Arena, 84

DENTON
Evening Diversions
Groovy Mule, 99
Rick's Place, 149
Rubber Gloves Rehearsal Studios, 149
Flea Markets
380 Flea Market, 73
Historic Buildings
Denton County Historical Museum, 145
Denton County Courthouse, 145
Evers Hardware, 146
Little Chapel-in-the-Woods, 148
Lodging
Magnolia Inn, 99
Red Bud Inn, 145
Museums and Galleries
Gowns of the First Ladies of Texas, 148
Hangar 10 Flying Museum, 149–50
Longhorn Gallery, 147
Rare Book Room and Texana Collections, 147–48
Restaurants
Cupboard Café, 147
Texican Grill, The, 148–49
Shopping
Evers Hardware, 146
Recycled Books, Records and Cds, 147
Sleeping Lizards, 146
This Old House, 146

EULESS
Evening Diversions
El Paraiso Latin Club, 54

FORT WORTH

Evening Diversions

Ancho Chile Bar, 26
Bass Performance Hall, 41, 44–45
Billy Bob's Texas, 53–54, 136
Blue Mesa, 42, 113–14
Caravan of Dreams, 20, 45, 54
Casa Manana, 46
Casa on the Square, 42
Circle Theater, 41–42
8.0, 20
Grape Escape, The, 61
Grotto Bar-Caravan of Dreams, 20
J&J Blues Bar, 54–55
Jubilee Theatre, 41
Lobby Bar, 42
Reata, 20, 42
Stage West, 45–46
White Elephant Saloon, 53, 136
Wreck Room, The, 55

Flea Markets

Cattle Barn Flea Market, 72

Historic Buildings

Eddleman McFarland House, 136–37
Elizabeth Boulevard Historical District, 41
Fincher's Western Store, 134
General Store, 135
M. L. Leddy's Boot & Saddlery, 134–35
Miss Molly's, 52–53, 132
Stockyards Hotel, 53, 132
Texas White House, 23–24
Thistle Hill, 137

Lodging

Azalea Plantation, 39
Bed & Breakfast at the Ranch, 108–9
Etta's Place, 17
Miss Molly's, 52–53, 132
Radisson Plaza Hotel Fort Worth, 109
Stockyards Hotel, 53, 132
Texas Hotel, 53, 131–32
Texas White House, 53, 131–32
Worthington Hotel, The, 16–17

Movie Theaters

AMC Palace 9, 22
AMC Sundance 11, 22
Omni Theater, 28–29

Museums and Galleries

American Airlines C.R. Smith Museum, 88–89
Amon Carter Museum, 25–26, 42
Carol Henderson Gallery/Artenergies, 67–68
Cattle Raisers Museum, 137
Edmund Craig Gallery, 67
Evelyn Siegel Gallery Inc., 67
Fire Station No. 1, 17–18
Fort Worth Museum of Science and History, 28
Kimbell Art Museum, 24–25, 42
Log Cabin Village, 40
Modern Art Museum of Fort Worth, 28, 42
Modern at Sundance Square, The, 21–22
National Cowgirl Museum & Hall of Fame, The, 19
Noble Planetarium, 29
Sid Richardson Collection of Western Art, 18
Stockyards Museum, The, 134
Stockyards Station Gallery, 133–34
Thomas Kinkade at the Main Street Gallery, 18–19
Vintage Flying Museum, 43
William Campbell Contemporary Art, 69

Outdoor Activities

Fort Worth Botanic Garden, 114–15
Fort Worth Nature Center and Refuge, 111
Fort Worth Zoo, 112–13

horse-drawn carriage rides, 21
Stockyards Station, 132
Trinity Park, 115
Visitor Information Center, 132

Restaurants

Angeluna, 44
Arizola's, 110–11
Back Porch, 27
Blue Mesa, 42, 113–14
Buffet, The, 25
Byblos, 112
Cabo Mix-Mex Grill, 54
Cactus Flower Café, 42, 145
Cattleman's Steak House, 135
Del Frisco's Double Eagle
   Steakhouse, 112
Esperanza's, 136
Ginger Brown's, 110
H3 Ranch, 53
Hedary's, 62
Hoffbrau, 40–41, 73
J&J Oyster Bar, 55
Joe T. Garcia's Mexican Dishes, 135
Jubilee Café, 27, 67
La Familia, 28
La Madeleine, 21, 175
La Playa Maya, 62
Loredo's, 55
Mi Cocina, 19
Michaels, 68
Ol' South Pancake House, 73, 112
Paris Coffee Shop, 70
Railhead Smokehouse, The, 27
Randall's, 41
Razzoo's, 22
Reata, 20, 42
Reflections, 44
Riscky's Bar-B-Q, 132
Saint-Emilion, 26
Tommy's, 28
Uncle Julio's, 43

Shopping

Barnes & Noble Booksellers, 19
Earth Bones, 21
Fincher's Western Store, 134
General Store, 135
Haltom's Jewelers, 20
Kabin Fever, 68
Legacy Trading Company, 21
Leigh-Boyd, 68–69
M.L. Leddy's Boot & Saddlery,
   134–35
Market, The, 68
Modern at Sundance Square, The,
   21–22
Out West Down South, 68
Pier 1 Imports, 21
Prairie Rose, 68
Strings, 68

Specialty Tours

Eddleman McFarland House, 136–37
Forest Park Miniature Train, 113
Tarantula Train, 132–33
Texas Exotic Feline Foundation,
   109–110
Thistle Hill, 137

Sports

Cowtown Coliseum, 135–36

GLEN ROSE

Lodging

Foothills Safari Camp, 122
Hummingbird Lodge, 117
Inn on the River, 117
Lodge at Fossil Rim, 122

Outdoor Activities

Dinosaur Valley State Park, 119–21
Fossil Rim Wildlife Center, 117–19

Restaurants

Bluebonnet Café in the Glen Rose
   Emporium, 119
Rough Creek Lodge, 122

Western Kitchen, 119
Shopping
Glen Rose Emporium, 119
Specialty Tours
Fossil Rim Wildlife Center, 117–19

GRANBURY
Evening Diversions
Opera House, 167–68
Historic Buildings
Old Jail and Hood County
Historical Museum, 167
Opera House, 167–68
Lodging
Arbor House, The, 165
Iron Horse Inn, The, 165
Museums and Galleries
Old Jail and Hood County
Historical Museum, 167
Outdoor Activities
Granbury Cemetery, 168
Restaurants
Coffee Grinder Espresso Bar, 167
Hennington's Texas Café, 167
Niester's, 164–65
Pearl Street Pasta House, 166
Shopping
Books On The Square, 166
Brazos River Trading Company, 166
Earth Harvest Market, 167
Red Elk, The, 167
Wagon Yard Antiques, 166

GRAND PRAIRIE
Flea Markets
Trader's Village, 71
Sports
Lone Star Park at Grand Prairie, 85

GRAPEVINE
Evening Diversions
La Buena Vida, 61
Restaurants
Corner Bakery, 91, 153
Shopping
Grapevine Mills, 91
Specialty Tours
La Buena Vida, 61

HALTOM CITY
Restaurants
Phuong, 60

JUSTIN
Guest/Dude Ranches
Texas Lil's Dude Ranch, 98
Restaurants
Rocking J Café, 97
Shopping
Justin Discount Boots, 99

IRVING–LAS COLINAS
Lodging
Four Seasons Resort And Club at Las
Colinas, 87
Homewood Suites Las Colinas, 87
Museums and Galleries
Mustangs of Las Colinas, The, 90
Outdoor Activities
5 Bar K Stables, 91
Four Seasons Resort And Club at
Las Colinas, 87
Texas Stadium, 91
Restaurants
Café on the Green, 88, 90
Cool River Café, 89–90
Jinbeh, 89

Le Peep, 90
Specialty Tours
Dallas Communications Complex, 88
Studios at Las Colinas, 88
Sports
Texas Stadium, 91

CKINNEY
Historic Buildings
Dowell House Bed & Breakfast, 153
Lodging
Bingham House, The, 153
Dowell House Bed & Breakfast, 153
Museums and Galleries
Heard Museum and Wildlife Sanctuary, The, 155–56
Outdoor Activities
Chestnut Square, 153–54
Heard Museum and Wildlife Sanctuary, The, 155–56
Jolabec Riding Stables, 157
Restaurants
Backstage Coffee Company, 155
Café Juarez, 155
Goodhues Wood-Fired Grill, 156
Opera House Restaurant, 155
Shopping
Remember This Antique Mall, 154
Town Square Antiques, 154
Treasures From the Past, 154
Specialty Tours
Chestnut Square, 153–54
Dulaney House, The, 154
Heard Museum and Wildlife Sanctuary, The, 155–56

INERAL WELLS
Historic Buildings
Crazy Water Hotel and Pavilion, 175
First Presbyterian Church, The, 177
Palace Tea Room, 176–77

Lodging
Silk Stocking Row Bed & Breakfast, 175, 178
Outdoor Activities
Lake Mineral Wells State Park, 178–79
Rails-to-Trails, 179
Rochelle's Canoe Rentals, 177
Woodland Park Cemetery, 179
Restaurants
Baris Pizza & Pasta, 178
Longhorn Bar and Grill, 176
Palace Tea Room, 176–77
Shotguns, 176
Shopping
Famous Water Company, 178
Garrets, 176
Hanchey Leather Goods, 175–76
W. D. Woodworks, 176
Specialty Tours
Baker Hotel, 176

POSSUM KINGDOM LAKE
Lodging
Cliffs, The, 92
Outdoor Activities
Possum Kingdom State Park, 94–96
Pro Shop, 93
Ship's Store, The, 93
Restaurants
Caddo Mercantile, 94
Cliffs Restaurant, The, 93
19th Hole Grill, 93
Rafters Restaurant on Scenic Point, 94
Specialty Tours
Ship's Store, The, 93

WAXAHACHIE
Historic Buildings
Chaska House, The, 170

Ellis County Courthouse, 171
Ellis County Museum, 170–71
Sims Library, 172
Lodging
BonnyNook Inn, 170
Chaska House, The, 170
Museums and Galleries
Ellis County Museum, 170–71
Sims Library, 172
Webb Gallery, 173
Outdoor Activities
Scarborough Faire, 173
Restaurants
Catfish Plantation, 172
Dove's Nest, The, 171–72
Shopping
Courthouse Antiques, 172
Waxahachie Crafters and Antique
    Mall, 172

WEATHERFORD
Historic Buildings
Angel's Nest Bed & Breakfast, 139
Farmers Market, 143

Parker County Courthouse, 139–40
St. Botolph Inn Bed & Breakfast, 139
Lodging
Angel's Nest & Breakfast, 139
St. Botolph Inn Bed & Breakfast, 139
Museums and Galleries
Heritage Gallery, 141
Outdoor Activities
Chandor Gardens, 142
Greenwood Cemetery, 140–41
Holland Lake Park, 143
Restaurants
Downtown Café, 140
Jack's Family Restaurant, 139
Mesquite Pit, 142
Shopping
Farmers Market, 143
First Monday Trade Days, 140
Miss B's, 140
Treasure Chest Boutique, 140

General Index

A

Adam's Mark Hotel, 57
Adolphus Hotel, The, 13, 64
African American Museum, 14
Al Biernat's, 34
Alley Antique Mall, 163
AMC Palace 9, 22
AMC Sundance 11, 22
Amelia's Place, 48–49
American Airlines C.R. Smith Museum, 88–89
Amon Carter Museum, 25–26, 42
Ancho Chile Bar, 26
Angel's Nest & Breakfast, 139
Angeluna, 44
Anteks, 66
Antiquarian of Dallas, 64–65
Arbor House, The, 165
Arizola's, 110–11
Arlington Marriott, 77
Arlington Museum of Art, 80
Arts District Theater, 34
Athens, 158–63
Avanti Café, 126
Azalea Plantation, 39

B

Back Porch, 27
Backstage Coffee Company, 155
Baker Hotel, 176
Ballpark in Arlington, The, 77–78
Baris Pizza & Pasta, 178
Barnes & Noble Booksellers, 19
Bass Performance Hall, 41, 44–45

Beau Nash, 14
Beckley Grill, 70
Bed & Breakfast at the Ranch, 108–9
Billy Bob's Texas, 53–54, 136
Bingham House, 153
Bistro A, 33
Black Beauty Ranch, 159
Blue Cat Blues, 50
Blue Mesa, 42, 113–14
Bluebonnet Café, 119
Bobby Valentine's, 79
Bombay Cricket Club, 65
BonnyNook Inn, 170
Books On The Square, 166
Boudreau Gardens Herb Farm, 179
Brazos River Trading Company, 166
Breadwinners, 35
Bridge, The, 21
Brownie's, 14
Buffet, The, 25
Byblos, 112

C

Cabo Mix-Mex Grill, 54
Cactus Flower Café, 42, 145
Caddo Mercantile, 94
Cadeaux, 66
Café Brazil, 105–6
Café Istanbul, 59
Café Izmir, 104–5
Café Juarez, 155
Café Madrid, 60
Café on the Green, 88, 90
Calloway's, 170
Canton, 162–63

Caravan of Dreams, 20, 45, 54
Carol Henderson Gallery/Artenergies, 67–68
Carriage House, The, 161
Casa Manana, 46
Casa on the Square, 42
Catfish Plantation, 172
Cattle Barn Flea Market, 72
Cattle Raisers Museum, 137
Cattleman's Steak House, 135
Cavanaugh Flight Museum, 130
Chandor Gardens, 142
Chaska House, The, 170
Chestnut Square, 153–54
Chuy's, 66
Circle Theater, 41–42
Cliffs Restaurant, The, 93
Cliffs, The, 92
Club Clearview, 51
Coffee Grinder Espresso Bar, 167
Conspiracy Museum, 126
Cool River Café, 89–90
Corner Bakery, 91, 153
Courthouse Antiques, 172
Courtyard by Marriott, 64, 72, 77
Courtyard on the Trail, 102
Cowtown Coliseum, 135–36
Cozymel's, 77
Crandall Cotton Gin, 159
Crate & Barrel, 65–66
Crazy Water Hotel and Pavilion, 175
Cultural District, 42
Cupboard Café, 147

Dallas Aquarium, 104
Dallas Arboretum and Botanical Garden, 103
Dallas Communications Complex, 88
Dallas County Historical Plaza, 125
Dallas Farmers Market, 84–85
Dallas Horticulture Center, 104
Dallas Museum of Art, 11
Dallas Museum of Natural History, 15
Dallas Nature Center, 107
Dallas on Ice, 82
Dallas Summer Musicals at the Fair Park Music Hall, 33, 37–38
Dallas Theater Center, 34
Dallas World Aquarium, 107
Dallas Zoo, 105, 106
Danny's Smokehouse Bar-B-Q, 160
Dan's Bar, 99
David Dike Fine Art, 64
Deep Ellum Center for the Arts, 51
Del Frisco's Double Eagle Steakhouse, 112
Denton, 144–50
Denton County Courthouse, 145
Denton County Historical Museum, 145
Dick's Last Resort, 84
Dinosaur Valley State Park, 119–21
Dixie House, 103
Dove's Nest, The, 171–72
Dowell House Bed & Breakfast, 153
Downtown Café, 140
Dr Pepper StarCenter, 82
Dream Café, 37
Dulaney House, The, 154

Earth Bones, 21
Earth Harvest Market, 167
EatZi's, 35–36
Eddleman McFarland House, 136–3?
Edmund Craig Gallery, 67
8.0, 20
Einstein Bros. Bagels, 153
El Paraiso Latin Club, 54
Elizabeth Boulevard Historical Distri?
41
Ellis County Courthouse, 171
Ellis County Museum, 170–71
Embassy Suites Hotel Dallas Market Center, 82
Esperanza's, 136
Etta's Place, 17

Evelyn Siegel Gallery Inc., 67
Evers Hardware, 146
ExecuCar Sedan Service, 58

Fair Park, 14
Fair Park Music Hall, 33, 37
Fairmont Hotel, 124–25
Famous Water Company, 178
Farmers Market, 143
Filipiniana Bakeshop and Café, 60–61
Fincher's Western Store, 134
Fire Station No. 1, 17–18
First Limousine Service, 58
First Monday Trade Days, 140, 162–63
First Presbyterian Church, The, 178
Fish, 128
5 Bar K Stables, 91
508 Davis Street, 141
Flying Saucer Draught Emporium, 54
Foothills Safari Camp, 122
Forest Park Miniature Train, 113
Fort Worth Botanic Garden, 114–15
Fort Worth Museum of Science and History, 28
Fort Worth Nature Center and Refuge, 111
Fort Worth Zoo, 112–13
Fossil Rim Wildlife Center, 117–19
Four Seasons Resort and Club at Las Colinas, 87
Frontiers of Flight Museum, 129–30

Gallery of Sports Art, 79
Gallery Two-O-Nine, 65
GameWorks, 91
Garden of Eating, 160
Garrets, 176
General Store, 135
Gerald Peters Gallery, 64
Ginger Brown's, 110
Glen Rose, 116–22

Glen Rose Emporium, 119
Gloria's, 58
Goodhues Wood-Fired Grill, 156
Gowns of the First Ladies of Texas, 148
Granbury, 164–68
Granbury Cemetery, 168
Grape Escape, The, 61
Grape, The, 49
Grapevine Mills, 91
Green Room, The, 49
Greenwood Cemetery, 140–41
Groovy Mule, 99
Gypsy Tea Room, 50–51

H3 Ranch, 53
Half-Price Books, Records and Magazines, 55–56
Hall of State, 14–15
Haltom's Jewelers, 20
Hampton Inn, II
Hanchey Leather Goods, 175–76
Hangar 10 Flying Museum, 149–50
Heard Museum and Wildlife Sanctuary, The, 155–56
Hedary's, 62
Hennington's Texas Café, 167
Heritage Gallery, 141
Highway 4, 177
Hoffbrau, 40–41, 73
Holland Lake Park, 143
Homewood Suites Las Colinas, 87
horse-drawn carriage ride, 21
Hotel St. Germain, 10–11
Hummingbird Lodge, 117
Hyatt Regency Dallas, 81–82

IMAX Theater, 104
Inn on the River, 117
Iron Horse Inn, The, 165
Ivanffy & Uhler Gallery, 69

J

J&J Blues Bar, 54–55
J&J Oyster Bar, 55
Jack's Family Restaurant, 139
Javier's Gourmet Mexicano, 34
Jinbeh, 89
Joe T. Garcia's Mexican Dishes, 135
John F. Kennedy Memorial, 125
John Neely Bryan Cabin, 125
Jolabec Riding Stables, 157
Jubilee Café, 27, 67
Jubilee House Restaurant & Club, 162
Jubilee Theatre, 41
Justin, 99
Justin Discount Boots, 99

K

Kabin Fever, 68
Kalita's Humphreys Theater, 34
Kathleen's Art Café, 66
Kimbell Art Museum, 24–25, 42

L

La Buena Vida, 61
La Familia, 28
La Madeleine, 21, 175
La Playa Maya, 62
La Quinta City Place, 32
Lady Primrose, 12
Lake Mineral Wells State Park, 178–79
Landry's Seafood House, 83
Las Mananitas, 106–7
Le Peep, 90
Legacy Trading Company, 21
Legends of the Game Baseball Museum, 78–79
Leigh-Boyd, 68–69
Little Chapel-in-the-Woods, 148

Lobby Bar, 42
Lodge at Fossil Rim, The, 122
Loft, The, 91
Log Cabin Village, 40
Lone Star Park at Grand Prairie, 185
Longhorn Bar and Grill, 176
Longhorn Gallery, 147
Loredo's, 55
Lovers Lane Antique Market, 69

M

Magnolia Inn Bed & Breakfast, 99
Majestic Theater, The, 33, 38
Mansion on Turtle Creek, The, 30–31
Mariano's, 71
Market, The, 68
Marrakesh, 59
Marty's, 58
McKinney, 152–57
McKinney Avenue Contemporary, 35
Meadows Museum of Art, 32–33
Mecca, 144–45
Mediterraneo, 13
Melrose Hotel, The, 32
Mesquite Pit, 142
Meyerson Symphony Center, 33, 37
Mi Cocina, 19
Michaels, 68
Mineral Wells, 174–79
Miss B's, 140
Miss Molly's, 52–53, 132
M. L. Leddy's Boot & Saddlery, 134–35
Modern Art Museum of Fort Worth, 28, 42
Modern at Sundance Square, The, 21–22
Morton's of Chicago, 128
Mustangs of Las Colinas, The, 90

N

Nancy Lee and Perry R. Bass Performance Hall, 41–45

National Cowgirl Museum & Hall of Fame, The, 19
Neiman Marcus, 83
New Main Street Cafe, 79
Niester's, 164–65
19th Hole Grill, 93
Noble Planetarium, 29
Norma's Cafe, 128
Nuevo Leon, 49–50

Oak Meadow Bed & Breakfast, 161–62
Ol' South Pancake House, 73, 112
Old City Park, 127
Old Jail and Hood County Historical Museum, 167
Old Red Courthouse, 125
Omni Theater, 28–29
Opera House, 167–68
Opera House Restaurant, 155
Out West Down South, 68

Palace Tea Room, 176–77
Palm, The, 83
Palomino, 13
Pangburn's, 19–20
Pappadeaux Seafood Kitchen, 79
Paramount Hotel, 125
Paris Coffee Shop, 70
Parker County Courthouse, 139–40
Pearl Street Pasta House, 166
Photographic Archives Lab & Library, 69
Phuong, 60
Pier 1 Imports, 21
Poor David's Pub, 105
Possum Kingdom State Park, 94–96
Prairie Rose, 68
Pro Shop, 93
Pyramid Room in the Fairmont Hotel, 128

Queen of Sheba, 59

Radisson Plaza Hotel Fort Worth, 109
Rafters Restaurant on Scenic Point, 94
Railhead Smokehouse, The, 27
Rails-to-Trails, 179
Ranchman's Cafe, 98
Randall's, 41
Rare Book Room and Texana Collections, 147–48
Razzoo's, 22
Reata, 20, 42
Recycled Books, Records and CDs, 147
Red Elk, The, 167
Red Jacket, The, 51
Redbud Inn, 145
Reflections, 44
Remember This Antique Mall, 154
Reunion Arena, 84
Reunion Tower, 13
Rick's Place, 149
Riscky's Bar-B-Q, 132
River Legacy Park and Living Science Center, 115
Rochelle's Canoe Rentals, 177
Rocking J Café, 97
Rough Creek Lodge, 122
Rubber Gloves Rehearsal Studios, 149

S&D Oyster Company, 65
St. Botolph Inn Bed & Breakfast, 139
Saint-Emilion, 26
Sambuca, 50
Santa Fe Depot, 138
Sardine's, 55

Scarborough Faire, 173
Science Place in Fair Park, The, 104
Ship's Store, The, 93
Shotguns, 176
Sid Richardson Collection of Western Art, 18
Silk Stocking Row Bed & Breakfast, 175, 178
Sims Library, 172
Six Flags Hurricane Harbor, 80
Six Flags Over Texas, 80
604 South Alamo Street, 141
Sixth Floor: JFK and the Memory of a Nation, The, 125–26
Sleeping Lizards, 146
Sol's Taco Lounge, 49
Sons of Hermann Hall, 50
Southern House, 32
Stage West, 45–46
Star Canyon, 36
Starbucks Café, 45
Starck, 84
Stockyards Hotel, 53, 132
Stockyards Museum, The, 134
Stockyards Station, 132
Stockyards Station Gallery, 133–34
Stoneleigh Hotel, 11
Strings, 68
Studios at Las Colinas, 88
Swiss Avenue Historic District, 128–29

T

Tarantino's, 37
Tarantula Train, 132–33
Teatro Dallas, 34–35
Tei Tei Robata Bar, 59
Teppo, 60
Terilli's, 105
Texas Exotic Feline Foundation, 109–10
Texas Freshwater Fisheries Center, 160–61
Texas Hotel, 53, 131–32

Texas Lil's Dude Ranch, 98
Texas Stadium, 91
Texas White House, 23–24
Texican Grill, The, 148–49
Theatre Three, 34
This Old House, 146
Thistle Hill, 137
Thomas Kinkade at the Main Street Gallery, 18–19
380 Flea Market, 73
Tin Star, 36
Tommy's, 28
Town Square Antiques, 154
Trader's Village, 71
Treasure Chest Boutique, 140
Treasures From the Past, 154
Trinity Park, 115
202 West Oak Street, 141–42

U

Uncle Julio's, 43

V

Vern's Place, 170
Vintage Flying Museum, 43
Visitor Information Center, Stockyards, 132

W

Wagon Yard Antiques, 166
Walt Garrison Rodeo Bar, 127
Waxahachie, 169–73
Waxahachie Crafters and Antique Mall, 172
Weatherford, 138–43
W. D. Woodworks, 176
Webb Gallery, 173
West End Marketplace, 83
Western Kitchen, 119
White Elephant Saloon, 53, 136
William Campbell Contemporary Art, 69

William E. Johnson Fine Art, 64
Woodland Park Cemetery, 179
Worthington Hotel, The, 16–17
Wreck Room, The, 55

XYZ

Y. O. Ranch, 11–12
Yorkshire Club, The, 126

About the Author

A sixth-generation Texan and Fort Worth native, June Naylor Rodrigu has been a writer for the *Fort Worth Star-Telegram* since January 1984, wo ing in sports and news before moving to the travel, lifestyle, food a entertainment sections. Currently she writes about food, dining, and Te travel for the *Star-Telegram*. She is author of *Texas: Off the Beaten Path* a *Quick Escapes from Dallas-Fort Worth*, both published by the Globe Pequ Press.